SHUT OFF

Shut Off

The Canadian Digital Television Transition

GREGORY TAYLOR

McGill-Queen's University Press
Montreal & Kingston • London • Ithaca

ISBN 978-0-7735-4048-4 (cloth)
ISBN 978-0-7735-4049-1 (paper)

Legal deposit second quarter 2013
Bibliothèque nationale du Québec

Printed in Canada on acid-free paper that is 100% ancient forest free (100% post-consumer recycled), processed chlorine free.

This book has been published with the help of a grant from the Canadian Federation for the Humanities and Social Sciences, through the Awards to Scholarly Publications Program, using funds provided by the Social Sciences and Humanities Research Council of Canada.

McGill-Queen's University Press acknowledges the support of the Canada Council for the Arts for our publishing program. We also acknowledge the financial support of the Government of Canada through the Canada Book Fund for our publishing activities.

Library and Archives Canada Cataloguing in Publication

Taylor, Gregory, 1967–
Shut off : the Canadian digital television transition / Gregory Taylor.

Includes bibliographical references and index.
ISBN 978-0-7735-4048-4 (bound).–
ISBN 978-0-7735-4049-1 (pbk.)

1. Digital television – Canada. 2. Digital television – Government policy – Canada. 3. Television broadcasting policy – Canada. 4. Digital communications – Government policy – Canada. I. Title.

HE8700.9.C3T39 2013 621.388'07 C2012-907974-X

This book was typeset by True to Type in 10.5/13 Sabon

To my parents, Gregory and Helen Taylor, for their love and support.

Contents

Acknowledgments

I wish to thank Anuradha Gobin of McGill University for all her help through every stage of this book project. For editorial assistance, friendship, fun, and support, I extend my sincere thanks to Dr Stephen Pender of the University of Windsor. Dr Catherine Middleton, Canada Research Chair in Communication Technologies in the Information Society at Ryerson University, was a great source of support and insight. I especially want to recognize my father Gregory Taylor in Collingwood, Ontario, for his editorial suggestions and encouragement.

I would also like to thank my PhD supervisor, Professor Marc Raboy, as well as Dr Darin Barney and the faculty of McGill University's Department of Art History and Communication Studies. This book would not have been possible without the support of the Fonds québécois de la recherche sur la société et la culture, the GRAND Network of Centres of Excellence: Digital Infrastructures Project, Clémentine Sallée, Bram Abramson, Dickson Davidson and Kirsten Greenleaf for Ottawa accommodation, Ian Morrison and the Friends of Canadian Broadcasting, the *Canadian Journal of Communication*, the Beaverbrook Canadian Foundation, and Media@McGill.

Jonathan Crago at McGill-Queen's University Press provided clear guidance along the way. I greatly appreciate his continued efforts. I would also like to thank the peer reviewers, who provided insightful critiques that strengthened this work.

Finally, I would like to thank the people in the public and private sectors, too numerous to mention here, who generously allowed me time to discuss Canada's digital television transition. Many of the observations and conclusions in this book are derived from the accounts of these primary actors.

Acronyms

ADSL	Asymmetric Digital Subscriber Line
ASO	Analogue shut off
ATSC	Advanced Television Systems Committee
BDU	Broadcast distribution undertaking
CAB	Canadian Association of Broadcasters
CBC	Canadian Broadcasting Corporation
CBSC	Canadian Broadcast Standards Council
CCSA	Canadian Cable Systems Alliance
CCTA	Canadian Cable Television Association
CDTV	Canadian Digital Television
CMR	Communication Monitoring Report
CRTC	Canadian Radio-television and Telecommunications Commission
DAB	Digital audio broadcasting
DMB-T	Digital media broadcasting terrestrial
DSL	Digital subscriber lines
DTV	Digital television
DVB	Digital video broadcasting
FCC	Federal Communications Commission
FFC	Fee for carriage
HD	High definition (television)
HDTV	A Canadian company. Sometimes refers to HD television.
ICT	Information and communications technology
IP	Internet Protocol
ISDB	Integrated Services Digital Broadcasting
ITU	International Telecommunication Union
LPIF	Local Program Improvement Fund

LTSS	Local Television Satellite Solution
NII	National Information Infrastructure
NTSC	National Television System Committee
OFDM	Orthogonal frequency division multiplex
OTA	Over the air
OTT	Over the top
PAL	Phase alternating line
PPV	Pay-per-view
PVR	Personal video recorder
SD	Standard definition (television)
SDTV	Sometimes refers to SD television
SECAM	Séquentiel couleur à mémoire or sequential colour with memory
SFN	Single frequency network
VOD	Video on demand

SHUT OFF

If there is one media business with a chance of completing the perilous journey to the digital future looking as healthy as it did when it set off, it is television.

Economist, 29 April 2010

INTRODUCTION

Please Adjust Your Set

The transition from analogue to digital is the greatest single technological leap in the history of the most powerful medium of the last century. Digitalization alters the experience of television for viewers, distributors, and producers. Digital television is more than exponential channel choice, video on demand (VOD), personal video recorders (PVRS), Internet television, and the increasingly commonplace "wow" factor of high definition (HD), although these are all significant broadcasting developments. It is also an important locus for academic study because it has been the site of a political and economic struggle that directly affects Canadian living rooms.

The switch to digital television has profound consequences for a wide range of Canadian communications. *Shut Off: The Canadian Digital Television Transition* chronicles the development of this game-changing technology and examines the essential normative debate concerning the public service role of television in Canadian society during a period of intensified technological upheaval and within a policy structure largely determined by increased reliance on market forces.

As the analogue era comes to a close, the Canadian broadcasting system as pieced together over the last century is on very shaky footing. Technological, political, and economic developments that run decidedly against the grain of national sovereignty and public access now challenge the national project of providing space for Canadian stories and freely accessible information. Of course, the challenge to national control of mass communications has been a common refrain in media transitions since the arrival of the printing press and is often justly seen as a positive development toward a more open society, but such eras of disruption also provide the opportunity for information to move from public to private control. Digital television in Canada is a potentially disruptive technology that presents enormous regulatory and economic challenges. It has also, for nearly twenty years, been woefully under-reported by all but a few industry journalists and largely ignored by Canadian communication scholars.

The progress of Canada's digital television transition from 1997 to the present reveals much more than a technological modification. It encapsulates much of the prevailing economic orthodoxy and dominant political trends of the last two decades. The Canadian government and the national public media regulator, the Canadian Radio-television and Telecommunications Commission (CRTC), have intervened as little as possible for much of this period and have adhered to the prominent ideology of light-touch regulation, which insists market mechanisms function as the key regulatory tool. Indeed, for more than a decade the Canadian digital television transition was among the most market-driven in the developed world. I argue that the results of this approach have proven a great disappointment for the goal of universal access in Canadian broadcasting and have inhibited the growth of new digital technologies.

The stakes are high for the Canadian broadcasting industry, the government, the CRTC, and the public. This transition sets the stage for further infrastructure development that will be key to Canada's economic vitality and sense of nationhood in the twenty-first century. The interests of governments across the globe are piqued because digital television is also the site of a power struggle concerning an increasingly valuable – yet often taken for granted – national public resource: the electromagnetic spectrum. Though digital broadcasting uses considerably less spectrum than analogue, it must compete with more and more services for access to frequencies. Demand for radio waves increases with every new wireless application, tablet device, and growth in mobile telephony – and all are posed to challenge television broadcasters' comfortable, long-established place on the spectrum.

Spectrum scarcity, notes one American study, "has always been the underlying raison d'être for broadcast regulation."[1] It is also the engine driving the digital television transition. Despite digital television's more limited frequency requirements, the growth of wireless industries over the last decade has meant spectrum availability is more hotly contested than ever before. Frequencies are being reallocated, or re-farmed, worldwide, which results in changes in international, national, and local usage. Standard definition digital transmission's narrower bandwidth requirement (approximately one-sixth that of an analogue channel under the North American digital standard) results in more free space and a reorganized broadcasting spectrum, allowing for the sale of spectrum frequencies via government auction. Such auctions, first held in New Zealand in 1990, have since become the de facto method of spectrum assignment for governments around the globe. Right now, spectrum buyers are usually mobile telephone and Internet providers, but the exploration of new digital spectrum applications is still in its relative infancy.

Countries worldwide are scrambling to position themselves at the forefront of digital television, though their routes vary and remain subject to local prerogatives. Although many countries today face similar dilemmas, few have invested as much time and energy into designing their communications landscape as Canada. From Guglielmo Marconi's first trans-Atlantic radio signal from England to St John's in 1901, to becoming the most cabled country in the world in the 1970s, to launching the first national communications satellite (the Anik A1) in 1972, Canada has had a prominent international role in media development and bringing communications technology to sparsely populated regions.[2] Of course, the main impetus for much of the national media policy development has been the omnipresence of the most powerful broadcasting centre in the world, the United States, less than two hours' drive to the south of most of Canada's urban centres. Nevertheless, Canada's contributions to the evolution of communications infrastructure was matched by leading advances in the politics accompanying the technology.

In the early twentieth century, it became apparent that, if Canada were to have a unique voice in mass communications, it would require extensive market intervention via public broadcasting and regulation, as opposed to the more market-based approach of the United States. Since its inception, Canadian broadcasting has been infused with a sense of nation building. Shortly after the 1932 Radio Broadcasting Act passed, Prime Minister R.B. Bennett remarked to passionate public broadcasting advocate Graham Spry: "It may well be, Graham, that you have saved Canada for the British Commonwealth."[3] Cultural ties to Britain may have waned, but contemporary discourse on Canadian broadcasting still includes the voices of those who see mass media as an essential tool for Canada's sense of nationhood.[4] From the 1920s to the 1980s, the combined elements of geographic expanse, dual official languages (and later multiculturalism), a public/private mixed system, and proximity to US broadcast signals positioned Canada as a global leader in innovative national broadcasting policy.[5] When he evaluated the development of satellite-based communications networks in Europe and the loss of public monopolies in most nations in favour of a mixed system in the 1980s, UK communication scholar Richard Collins wrote that the European experience was becoming "Canadianized."[6] In essence, this meant the Atlantic Ocean no longer sheltered Europe from American radio and television signals, and public broadcasting monopolies had to learn to coexist with the private sector.

The common metaphor for the Canadian communications system is the modern railroad: a technical and economic infrastructure designed to forge east-west bonds against the seemingly stronger north-south attraction.[7] Just as trains faced competition from trucks and airlines not anchored to the soil of any one nation, the communications network must accept and adapt to the new reality of a myriad of digital communications options, including satellites and broadband Internet connections that offer truly global media reception and transmission possibilities.

The diminishing regime of analogue broadcasting technology is characterized by scarce frequencies, distinctive industry sectors, few intermediaries, and linear programming – all of which the regulatory structure reflects. Digitalization takes data such as alphanumeric text, still and moving pictures, sound, and graphics and translates them to zeros and ones or digital bits. This encoded information is easily stored in large volumes and can be transferred on a common carrier. Photos, music, and film take the same form when digitalized, and all may be accessed via new digital television sets. Thus, digital television promises access, not just to traditional broadcasting but also to a wide range of digital media, including the Internet. The idiot box is no more.

Indeed, the digital environment challenges the notion of "broadcasting" itself. Broadcasting by definition is a one-to-many communications structure that is traditionally differentiated from personal one-to-one communications such as the telephone. Raymond Williams describes broadcasting as "a technology of varied messages to a general public."[8] This idea of "mass" information and its inherent powers of persuasion, coupled with the need for spectrum oversight, is the traditional source of legitimizing broadcasting regulation. This has significant legal and regulatory implications in the digital era. Broadcasting is a "push" medium in which content is sent to the receiver, as opposed to a "pull" medium in which the receiver actively seeks out content. The printed press has never been subject to the same level of government oversight because regulators view it as a pull medium. Digitalization blurs these lines. Communication legal scholar Stefaan Verhulst clarifies the push/pull distinction: "In a push environment this appears to be a traditional broadcasting environment in which you basically are the receiver of a programming format and content upon which you don't have that much control except for switching off the television. In a pull environment [on demand services, non-linear services] – in that environment you see a shift to control by the user."[9]

Digital television broadcasting introduces many of the pull services (video on demand, interactivity) into what was previously a more passive medium, but so far these new features serve as a compliment, not a replacement technology, for the push elements of broadcasting. The power and appeal of programming designed for mass audience has not gone away. In this book, I argue there is still a role for government oversight in the digital era, but there is no denying there are more prospects for pulling information than ever before – increasing control now lies in the hands of the viewer. This new paradigm requires a re-examination of the continued role of regulation in broadcasting; however, calls for the removal of regulations developed over decades are decidedly premature.[10]

Recent years have seen some surprising resurgences of so-called traditional media. In Canada in 2007, Rogers, the traditional broadcasting distribution undertaking (BDU), purchased CityTV and established itself as a significant television broadcaster. In 2010, powerful Canadian distribution companies Shaw and Bell offered to purchase Global Television and CTV respectively. That same year, a surprising bidding war erupted over Canwest newspapers as new surveys demonstrated the Internet generation trusts print newspapers (41 per cent) and television (31 per cent) as information sources above social networks (13 per cent) and blogs (8 per cent).[11] In the United Kingdom, the first-ever televised debates for the party leaders were key moments in the historic 2010 national election that resulted in a coalition British government. The *Economist* called this "a triumph for old media" in which newspapers and television played key roles.[12] The *Economist* also dedicated an issue in the spring of 2010 to the television industry and offered a healthy prognosis, calling it "the great survivor" and noting that despite threats from the increasing range of media options, "far from being cowed by new media, TV is colonising it."[13] The magazine offered layers of praise for the future of television and its ability to remain relevant and profitable: "When it comes to mobilising a mass audience, nothing can touch television."[14] Clearly, despite ever-increasing digital possibilities, there is still life in push media.

There is often a clear disengagement between the public's appetite for television programming and its collective willingness to discuss the political and economic structure of the medium itself. In an end-of-year piece, *Globe and Mail* journalist Kate Taylor boldly predicted digital television would be "the single most important cultural issue the country will face in 2006."[15] The continued silence on the issue in the following years once again proves the inherent dangers of New Year's prognostications. The research and interviews I conducted for this book point toward a Canadian public that is largely ill-informed about the transition to digital television. This is not true of only the general population: a *Globe and Mail* editorial in March 2012 incorrectly described the "ending of the rabbit-ears TV era," despite the continued availability of over-the-air (OTA) signals (in HD) in many Canadian cities.[16] While other contemporary issues such as digital copyright and Internet neutrality have seen groundswells of Canadian popular support in recent years, the potential of digital television has not captured attention in the same way.

The public has, by either design or chance, been relegated to the margins of this debate. Deliberations over the future of OTA broadcasting, inter-industry battles over fee for carriage, increasing media convergence, and other essential issues have largely been confined to the rather limited world of the CRTC and a relatively small group of industry critics. The public disconnect from digital television has been a key factor in allowing it to develop in Canada as an almost completely industry-led project.

THE CANADIAN TELEVISION MARKET

As it is in many jurisdictions around the world, the Canadian broadcasting industry is dominated by a few large corporations. Among private conventional broadcasters in English Canada, Bell Canada Enter-

Table 0.1
Canadian television broadcasters, 2007–10

Company	*Viewer Share, Conventional*	*Viewer Share, Discretionary (specialty, VOD)*	*Revenue Share, Private Sector, Conventional*	*Revenue Share, Private Sector, Discretionary (2010)*
		ENGLISH LANGUAGE MARKET		
BCE	17.7–17.5%	15.6–17.7%	47.0%	33.0%
Shaw	11.4–8.6	11.5–12.5	33.0	16.0
Corus	0.3–0.4	9.6–10.4		17.0
CBC	6.9–7.0	1.7–1.3		
Rogers	5.6–4.9	2.8–4.0	14.0	13.0
Astral		5.9–5.8		10.0
		FRENCH LANGUAGE MARKET		
Quebecor	25.6–23.8	4.1–5.8	65.0	
SRC (CBC)	13.9–12.7	3.2–4.0		15.0
Astral		17.4–17.6		48.0
BCE		6.1–6.3		27.0
Remstar (TQS)	8.4–7.5		18.0	

prises (BCE) has a 47 per cent revenue share, Shaw has 33 per cent, and Rogers Broadcasting has 14 per cent. In the French language private conventional sector, Quebecor enjoys a revenue share of 65 per cent and Remstar (V) has 18 per cent.[17] The consolidated nature of Canadian broadcasting allows broadcasters to monetize programming by exhibition across various platforms. The major private broadcasters are subsidiaries of larger BDUs that also own a variety of specialty channels.

Revenues at the Canadian Broadcasting Corporation (CBC) are a mix of advertising and parliamentary appropriations and so do not offer an easy point of comparison with private broadcasters. The national public broadcaster plays an increasingly diminished role in terms of ratings. In 2009/2010, the CBC averaged between 6.3 per cent viewing share in the English broadcasting market, versus the 26.6 per cent share held by private conventional broadcasters; while the Société Radio-Canada (SRC) averaged 12.5 per cent in the francophone broadcasting sector in the same period. Table 0.1 summarizes some key industry data from the CRTC's 2010 and 2011 *Communications Monitoring Report*. Conventional television broadcasters are distributed over the air but are also carried via BDU, while discretionary channels are only available via BDU. Not all Canadian broadcasters are active in all broadcasting sectors.

In the key area of distribution, five large companies lead the market. The "big four" cable operators are Rogers with 2.3 million subscribers, Shaw with 2.3 million, Quebecor Media's Videotron with approximately 1.8 million, and Cogeco with 881,000. Between them, the big four serve 65 per cent of all BDU programming subscribers. Two DTH satellite operators (Bell TV with almost 2 million subscribers and Shaw Direct with over 900,000) serve another 25 per cent of the national television distribution market.[18] Five BDU operators generate 92 per cent of all distribution revenues in Canada.

A great deal is at stake in the emerging world of digital television for the financially robust, domestically protected industry that has grown around the Canadian broadcasting system. Talk of "market" forces in Canadian broadcasting is always misleading: the industry actors involved are sheltered from foreign and in some cases domestic competition (all broadcasters), granted advertising monopolies in certain markets (local television), have at times openly agreed to non-competition understandings (cable companies), and are often recipients of government funding (the production sector). Thus, despite the market rhetoric, the Canadian broadcasting marketplace has traditionally been far more hothouse than jungle.

Even in this protected environment, Canadian broadcasters increasingly face legitimate financial challenges, in particular in the diminishing OTA sector, which provides the traditional advertising-supported broadcasting that is accessible with a simple antenna. In 2008, the engineering firm Spectrum Expert Inc estimated that the total cost to Canadian broadcasters to convert all 738 Canadian full-power television transmitters to DTV on their newly assigned channels would be between $378 and $425 million.[19] This is a substantial investment; however, the revenues of private conventional broadcasters grew from $1.97 billion in 2009 to $2.15 billion in 2010. Overall, the Canadian digital television transition has been characterized by a palpable lack of urgency on behalf of broadcasters, even though a firm deadline of 31 August 2011 for analogue shut off (ASO) became official CRTC regulation in 2007. In a 2008 speech, CRTC chair Konrad von Finckenstein told an audience of broadcasting executives that the date was "carved in stone."[20]

Canadian broadcasters challenged the strength of the CRTC's resolve and succeeded in chipping away at the rock face of the shut-off date. In November 2009 CRTC hearings, CTV, CBC, and Global stated they would not be prepared for digital over-the-air broadcasts by August 2011 and would need until 2013 in some major Canadian markets (see chapter 5). In March 2010, the CRTC declared that delays were unacceptable and the 2011 shut-off date was firm, an announcement that received public support from government officials, including then-Industry Minister Tony Clement. In the summer of 2010, CTV and Global presented the CRTC with surprising initiatives and said they might be able to meet the original deadline. In some cases, industry positions in 2010 completely contradicted statements made less than twelve months previously. This abrupt about-face is one of many indications that industry had been trying to "game" the digital transition to its advantage, as business is wont to do in the give-and-take of broadcasting policy, by avoiding the investment required to successfully complete the digital switchover. With no strong plan in place, Canada has been the site of a largely disjointed and dysfunctional digital television transition.

As the uncertainty surrounding the OTA sector demonstrates, broadcasters and the CRTC found themselves on a collision course over key aspects of the digital television transition. This has happened despite years of a hands-off regulatory approach. In 2008, legal communication scholars Liora Salter and Felix Odartey-Wellington described the CRTC as "about as pro-market as it is possible to be and still exist and be a regulator."[21] This essential conflict between public service obligations of broadcasting and industrial growth in the sector provides much of the incentive for this book. While many countries have made largely successful conversions to digital television, Canada is at a crossroads.

It need not be this way. Digital television did not sneak up on anyone. The technology necessary for digital television was introduced in the early 1990s and the first major Canadian study on the implications of changing from the analogue format, *Canadian Television in the Digital Era*, was filed with the Minister of Canadian Heritage and Industry Canada in October 1997. The technological roots run even deeper. Canada played a lead role in the early development of digital television the 1980s, when Ottawa was the site of a series of international conferences on advanced television services – then still an analogue-based HD technology.

Since those early days, Canada has ceded ground on digital television, while other countries, such as Brazil and Japan, have expanded their influence. Despite Canada's fixed ASO of 31 August 2011, in late 2010 neither the CRTC nor the government had begun a public awareness campaign or earmarked funding to help Canadians purchase converters so older analogue television sets could display digital signals – methods that were incorporated as part of the successful United States transition strategy in 2009.[22] Post-ASO in Canada, there was still no clear agenda for the eventual digital transition for many smaller markets that kept analogue over-the-air signals.

The Canadian OTA digital television transition is not nation-wide as originally planned, but is restricted to twenty-eight major markets. Other areas will remain analogue for an indefinite period or, in many cases, lose their OTA signal altogether. From a strictly administrative perspective, the transition succeeded: channels 52 to 69 were cleared of television broadcasts as planned; however, many regions lost OTA service and the CBC is no longer freely available over the air in rural and small-town Canada. Summer 2011 created a digital divide in Canada's living rooms.

There are several reasons for the lack of public engagement on the issue of digital television in Canada. First and foremost is the fact that over 90 per cent of Canadians receive their television signals via cable or satellite BDUs and therefore noticed little change after the switch, as their distribution services looked after it. The OTA situation is more volatile and has cut off thousands of Canadians from the very over-the-air broadcasting system originally designed to unify them. The digital transition calls into question the traditional Canadian broadcasting normative pillar that Canadian broadcasting is a public good and must be accessible to all citizens. Increased reliance on BDUs moves broadcasting further into the control of private interests. In large areas of Canada, viewers must now subscribe to a BDU to access the tax-supported national public broadcaster.

There were advanced warnings of Canadian television's ill-prepared digital horizon. A damning report on the progress of the Canadian transition by Michael McEwen, a former CBC executive and central figure in Canadian digital television, was submitted to the CRTC in 2006. McEwen pointed out that the successful transitions in other nations had required a stronger place for government and regulators than had been the case in Canada. The CRTC set the analogue shut-off date shortly thereafter but actual progress remained inexplicably slow.

Despite public criticism for almost half a decade, the Canadian government remained disengaged from the project.

Canada, long a leader in broadcasting innovation, lags well behind world leaders such as the United Kingdom and the United States, who are respectively close to or have successfully completed their digital transitions. A 2009 study by the CRTC examined the successful digital conversions in these two countries, and provides a stark contrast to the situation in Canada just over a year before the scheduled ASO. According to the study, success in the United States and the United Kingdom was largely attributable to:

- TV households were made aware of the switchover and understood what was going to happen, when it was going to happen, and how to prepare as the result of an effective communications campaign. (The CRTC stated a campaign was expected, not mandated, by March 2011. The ensuing campaign of public service notices was comparatively weak.)
- The transition authority provided technical support for individual households (nothing of this sort exists in Canada).
- Financial support was made available to the TV households (e.g., subsidizing digital receivers) and the broadcasting industry (the Canadian government continually rejected this proposal and no subsidies were offered).
- Digital terrestrial television (DTT) receivers were available to the market on time (these were available at many electronics retailers in Canada).
- Support for the transition was coordinated with standards set for television manufacturers – the United States mandated digital tuners for all new TV sets (Canada has followed the US lead on this).
- In the United Kingdom, the forum Digital UK was formed and placed in charge of orchestrating the switchover. Digital UK involved all relevant stakeholders including broadcasters, cable and satellite distributors, professional and consumer equipment manufacturers, retailers and installers, and governments and regulators (no such organization exists in Canada).[23]

Both the UK and US governments have been far more active in their respective transitions than has been the case for the Canadian government. After establishing the shut-off date in 2007, the CRTC made an effort to bring some order to the transition, while the Canadian government remained silent.

How disengaged has the Canadian federal government been from the digital television process? Consider this: Greg O'Brien of Cartt.ca, one of the few Canadian journalists to offer continued critical analysis of the digital television transition, published a scathing commentary that included an interview with then-Heritage Minister James Moore on 1 April 2010. Moore went on record as saying: "I know Tony Clement is looking at all the different options [for the transition] ... he will be leading on this and will have something to say on this soon."[24] Only four weeks later, Clement acknowledged he and Moore had clarified who was in charge of the digital television transition file:

> O'BRIEN: Well, my first question is about the confusion on the digital transition and who is actually overseeing the file.
> CLEMENT: It's Heritage.
> O'BRIEN: It is Heritage?
> CLEMENT: We double-checked on it after your commentary and the reasoning behind it is that 100% of the stakeholders are Heritage stakeholders.[25]

Thirteen years after the release of the first comprehensive report of digital television in Canada, four years after the tabling of Michael McEwen's critical study, and seventeen months before the scheduled cessation of analogue signals, the Canadian government finally clarified areas of responsibility between ministries – and that was only after an embarrassing editorial on an industry news website. This example encapsulates the overall government disengagement from the process. In *New Television, Old Politics*, Hernan Galperin labelled such government foot-dragging "conscious inaction."[26]

THE PUBLIC REGULATOR

Communications systems worldwide are going through a period of technical, economic, and political turbulence with national communications regulators in its midst. The primary institution charged with overseeing in the Canadian digital television transition is the CRTC. Regulatory bodies such as the United States' Federal Communications Commission (FCC), the United Kingdom's Office of Communications (Ofcom), and the CRTC have the formidable task of bringing order to a fractured, morphing system. They must protect the public interest and simultaneously create a predictable and vibrant playing field for the private sector. As UK economist Colin Rowat notes, "Regulators have always faced the problem of regulating for a future that does not yet exist, but that future is upon them much more quickly than it has been in the past."[27]

Since 1920, six different authorities have regulated broadcasting in Canada: the Ministry of Marine and Fisheries (1920–32), the Canadian Radio Broadcasting Commission (1932–36), the Canadian Broadcasting Corporation (1936–58), the Board of Broadcast Governors (1958–68), the Canadian Radio-television Commission (1968–76), and the Canadian Radio-television and Telecommunications Commission (1976–present). The CRTC has had the longest run, and presided over massive communications upheavals such as the introduction of cable in the 1970s and satellite distribution in the 1990s. However, the current digital transition offers the greatest challenge yet to the power and adaptability of the federal regulator.

It is safe to say that at no point in its forty-year history has the CRTC been free of public criticism. In a 1995 speech, then-CRTC chair Keith Spicer observed: "Somebody has to be the referee and there are not many standing ovations for the referee."[28] In the last decade, it has become almost fashionable to attack the CRTC. Canadian voices from across the political spectrum have argued, for sometimes-contradictory reasons, that the CRTC is ill suited to the demands of the changing media environment.[29] It is my position in this book that the CRTC is more relevant in the 2010s than it has been since the early 1970s under Chair Pierre Juneau, when it first introduced Canadian content regulations and foreign ownership restrictions.

Communication scholar Monroe Price and political theorist Jürgen Habermas each have invoked the metaphor of "constellations" to describe the new power structure that challenges traditional notions of national sovereignty.[30] Constellations are collections of stars, planets, and systems that combined form an altogether new shape – individual pieces that form a greater whole. They also contain contributions from old fading stars. Are media regulators and broadcasting regulation fading stars that must yield to the demands of greater consumer choice that only the private sector can provide? Is there a role for public input in defining these new constellations of power? Digital television provides a key test case for national communications hierarchies in the early twenty-first century.

Industry officials and communication scholars have used the expression "command and control" to describe the traditional regulatory approach for Canadian television. This implies a top-down process in which powerful regulators dictate the rules of the game. The extent of the CRTC's traditional ability to command and control is debatable. Broadcasting policy formulation has always been a more inclusive process than this expression would have one believe and, as I will show, the early digital transition in Canada can hardly be described as commanding. The normative pillars stated in the policy objectives of the 1991 Broadcasting Act, which the CRTC is legally obligated to uphold, remain and must be central in any broadcasting environment, analogue or digital. Despite some of the rhetoric that accompanies it, digital television is the latest evolution of Canadian communications and not a rupture with the past. The *Aird Report*, the 1929 Royal Commission on Radio Broadcasting's pioneering study, specified the public nature of the airwaves and called for the management of the radio spectrum to be placed under government trusteeship, but it also went much further. The report viewed broadcasting as a public service: "Broadcasting will undoubtedly become a great force in fostering a national spirit and interpreting national citizenship ... we are impelled to the conclusion that these interests can be adequately served only by some form of public ownership, operation and control behind which is the national power and prestige of the whole public of the Dominion of Canada."[31] The 1991 Broadcasting Act echoes this spirit and calls Canadian broadcasting a "public service essential to the maintenance and enhancement of national identity and cultural sovereignty."[32] By this viewpoint, all broadcasters, public and private alike, are obligated to provide a service to Canadian citizens. The difficulty for the CRTC is defining the parameters of this service.

Exactly what constitutes public service or "the public good" is a notoriously slippery concept. A 2004 Canadian government external advisory committee on regulation notes: "Broadly speaking, regulation is meant to serve the public interest. The Committee found that there is no shared definition of the public interest among government departments."[33] UK legal scholar Mike Feintuck defines the public interest this way: "A core meaning [of public interest] could be established in the context of regulation which identifies it closely with the values of equality and citizenship within a democracy."[34] Given the traditional links between media and a robust democracy, this definition is appropriate for broadcasting regulation. The place of democratic institutions in Canadian broadcasting is a contentious issue in the Canadian digital television transition.

The dramatic changes in broadcasting in the last two decades necessitate a reassessment, rather than a dismantling, of current policies, as well as a re-examination of the basis for the role of government in broadcasting. The digital television transition may yet prove the catalyst for this overdue scrutiny. In spring 2010, then-CRTC chair Konrad von Finckenstein called repeatedly for a new broadcasting act, in part to accommodate the changes brought on by the digital transition. The Canadian government, true to its fashion, did not respond.

EVOLUTION, NOT REVOLUTION

To study the digital television transition is to attempt to capture the essence of a creature that is not only moving at a rapid pace, but is shape-shifting as it progresses. I wrote this book largely in 2010 and 2011, and updated it in the post-transition period of spring 2012. There is every reason to expect there will be further changes before the book is released, but this should not change the legitimacy of my points about the transition, nor the lessons I draw from it. In this book, I hope to provoke discussion on a major change to Canadian communications that is thus far frustratingly free of public scrutiny. At its core, this is a book about the place of public policy in the emerging digital world.

This study is the product of dozens of interviews with industry executives, CRTC commissioners and employees, legal experts, electrical engineers who are physically constructing the digital television infrastructure, equipment retailers, academics, and journalists in Canada and abroad. It has involved long hours examining significant CRTC announcements and industry submissions and attending several CRTC public hearings that have proven instrumental in the digital television transition. The research is also based on numerous studies within Canada and other jurisdictions. The digital television transition is a challenging mixture of national and international politics, old and new technology, history, economics, geography, and consumer and marketing studies, and provides a clear contemporary example of the overwhelming power dynamics involved in the effort to access Canadian eyeballs.

Digital television is worthy of greater critical analysis than it has had in Canada until now.[35] Such an immense national project requires public scrutiny for several reasons. This transition restructures all aspects of the television industry, which at least partially explains the slow pace of progress. It also challenges traditional Canadian concerns over national sovereignty of broadcasting. Digital television acts as an Internet conduit in ways analogue predecessors could not, and brings truly national control into question. The successful introduction of the US-based service Netflix to Canada in September 2010 was a clear harbinger of this movement (see chapter 4).

The transition simultaneously challenges many entrenched policies while exemplifying the prevailing political attitude toward the place of regulation in communications over the last twenty years. On a global economic level, the adoption of technical standards that foster new trade in electronic hardware and cultural products are also creating new international bonds. The development of these standards and their impact on international industrial relations is discussed in the first three chapters. Finally, digital television opens the door to many of the new wireless technologies that promise to be essential tools in the future.

In this book, I study the Canadian digital television transition using the approach of critical political economy, a tradition that Canadian communication scholars Harold Innis and Dallas Smythe pioneered and academics such as Robert Babe and Vincent Mosco currently practice. Digital information is not disembodied from the greater material reality of contemporary Canada, and the critical approach to communication explores wider social and economic trends as well as key institutions. Critical political economy also recognizes the central normative elements of broadcasting policy and realizes there is more involved than an exchange of commodities. Feintuck's emphasis on equality and citizenship are key to public service in broadcasting; however, the for-profit private sector in the Canadian television system has been recognized since the *Massey Commission Report* of 1951.[36] The story of digital television in Canada is that of a web of power and influence involving private and public actors at home and abroad. No single sector can be examined in isolation.

It should come as little surprise that the primary foreign influence on the Canadian digital television transition has been the United States. From the selection of a technical standard in the 1990s to the 2011 date for the analogue shut off, Canada has largely followed the US lead. The digital television transition can thus be viewed as the latest incarnation of a merger between the two national communications systems – a process that is well documented in Canadian communication scholarship.[37]

Digital television, with its exponentially increased channel choice from both the United States and from sources worldwide and easy connection to the Internet, challenges the sense of sovereignty established over a century of analogue media. Canadian media currently faces what US communication scholar Robert McChesney dubs a "critical juncture."[38] Does the digital television transition reinforce the idea that Canada is reliant on other more powerful nations for economic and cultural direction, or does it allow for a moment when a distinctly Canadian path may emerge? This juncture is not about interminable debates on Canadian national identity, but about sovereignty, providing access to Canadian stories that do not benefit from the same economies of scale of many foreign productions, and recognizing the inherent democratic role of the mass media, which increasingly includes access to a range of foreign-based media ranging from the BBC to Al-Jazeera.

In May 2010, Industry Canada launched a consultation process on Canada's digital economy – a welcome initiative but one that reinforces the fact that unlike the United States, Australia, and the United Kingdom, as of 2012, Canada lacks a coherent national digital strategy. This has certainly been the case with digital television, which received minimal government guidance. Despite the emphasis on market mechanisms and deregulation in the global communications economy, studies in this field demonstrate that nation states unequivocally still matter. In *New Television, Old Politics*, Galperin concludes: "The case of digital TV reveals that despite the ever increasing internationalization of markets, the development of digital networks on a global scale, and the expanding jurisdiction of intergovernmental bodies, nations remain key instruments to direct the evolution of the media sector ... state authority over media has been more resilient than many have predicted, or preached."[39]

Such a bold assertion of the continued relevance of national authority seems to contradict David Taras' 2001 argument: "There is no doubt that governments and regulators seem to be powerless in the face of huge global conglomerates that want to devour every morsel, every scrap at the media table, that is not yet under their control. Politicians are intimidated by media's capacity to sway public opinion against them and by the collective muscle of media lobby groups to block or influence legislation."[40] Taras may be accurate in his depiction of Canadian government inaction, but the global digital television transition is by no means uniform. Whether or not Canadian politicians were "intimated" is difficult to quantify; however, the international picture for digital television clearly demonstrates a range of national reactions. In this book, I offer clear examples of how governments worldwide have proven anything but powerless and use digital technology to craft new national broadcasting systems.

The digital television transition stands as an early warning system for Canada's digital strategy: will Canada use this moment to establish a system that recognizes the inherent economic and democratic potentials of this new technology, or will a lack of vision and political will render Canada a digital hinterland?

THE STRUCTURE OF THIS BOOK

This book is broken into six chapters. In chapter 1, I examine the development of digital television technology: a saga of brilliant scientific minds, costly failures, and sites of power that extend from basement laboratories to the top levels of the White House. In his 2008 book *The Politics of Media Policy*, UK communication scholar Des Freedman writes that the essential question of "Why digital?" has never been adequately addressed.[41] I attempt to shed some light on the development of digital television technology and its rapid rise to a truly global technological project. Digital television is the product of an intense and expensive struggle between competing industrial nations – a project that has involved a significant level of international corporate and political intrigue. The spoils of this confrontation are immense. The politics of technical standards are a key part of this story. I also examine Canada's prominent yet under-examined role in digital television development. The title of the chapter comes from the 1997 study *Canadian Television in the Digital Era*.

In chapter 2, I trace the surprisingly divergent paths of Canada and the United States. As with all aspects of Canadian broadcasting, comparisons with the United States are inevitable. In the case of digital television, American parallels are necessary as Canada digital television policy has been forthright about its plan to follow the US lead. My primary focus in chapter 2 is the early public policy process for digital television in the two countries. I examine the growth of digital television from the initial studies in Canada and the United States to the tabling of binding regulation. My conclusions, that the US government has been more consistently engaged in the digital television transition, challenge some of the traditional notions of the public place of broadcasting in Canadian society.

In chapter 3, I move beyond North America and situate the Canadian experience within a wider context. The movement to digital broadcasting is now a truly global phenomenon, but is by no means uniform. I illustrate some of the factors at play in the international switch from analogue to digital television. I address issues such as technical standards and how they often reflect greater power dynamics, as well as the role of government. In this chapter, I use case studies of Australia, the United Kingdom, France, China, Brazil, and South Africa to examine digital television adoption strategies in a range of geographies, cultures, and economies.

Delivering signals (via BDUs) is the most profitable part of the Canadian television industry, and in chapter 4, I examine how the emerging digital paradigm affects distribution. In the roughly thirty years since cable was introduced and fifteen years since the arrival of digital satellite receivers, television distribution has altered Canada's media landscape. What were formerly "pipes" are now major access points for most Canadian productions and the distribution industry exercises great control over much of what Canadians watch.

BDU policy in Canada can be a labyrinth, and while it is not always immediately noticeable on the screen, it has enormous implications for the greater television industry. The "fee for carriage" debates, which pitted traditional broadcasters against BDUs, were a debilitating distraction in the Canadian digital television transition; instead of moving forward, many broadcasters focused on acquiring a piece of the lucrative distribution market. The switch to digital distribution promises more changes in how Canadians access television signals:

established distributors can offer new on-demand services, Internet-based broadcasting opens new distribution opportunities and a market niche for upstart companies, and smaller BDUs are less regulated in hopes of inspiring competition in a sector often described as an oligopoly.

In chapter 5, I examine the critical August 2011 analogue shut-off date in Canada and, in particular, the challenges it presented for over-the-air broadcasting. The OTA sector, often depicted as the heart of the transition, has also been the site of the most contentious debates. It is here that the informational shell game common to the Canadian broadcasting policy process is most readily apparent. Some key statements made by broadcasters concerning the feasibility of the OTA transition appear questionable, if not completely contradictory to earlier statements. I also explore the unique and difficult position of the CBC. In the digital era, fundamental questions remain concerning the OTA sector and its continued health and relevance.

In chapter 6, I look at community and civil society activists who have brought unique perspectives to the Canadian digital television from outside the traditional power dynamic of Canadian broadcasting. The case studies range from a community group in Kamloops, British Columbia, that is trying to maintain access to CBC over-the-air signals, to a Toronto graduate student whose web page chronicles the difficulties in trying to get a major Canadian broadcaster to live up to its public obligations.

Canadian digital television offers a rich case study of many of the wider issues that face contemporary structures of broadcasting governance. Television no longer operates independently of other communications sectors. After this expensive and time-consuming process, the digital television transition speaks to the wider direction of Canadian communications policy. In the final chapter of this book, I assess the overall relationship between the digital television transition and Canadian media policy. In addition, I address the question of the digital dividend. In February 2012, Canada still has no comprehensive policy for the upcoming auction of the freed spectrum at the heart of the switch to digital television. Canada's potholed pathway to digital television serves notice that strict adherence to market forces may not allow Canadians the full potentials of new digital technologies.

1

Detours along the Way

A HISTORY OF DIGITAL TELEVISION

Digital television may prove to be an essential mass-broadcasting tool of the twenty-first century, but its development is firmly rooted in the middle decades of the twentieth. Like the development of television itself, which percolated in scientific communities for decades before it became a truly "mass" medium in the 1950s, digital television emerged far more gradually than the recent rush of activity suggests. The application of digital encoding to television signals can be attributed to one individual, but the progress of digital communications and advanced television technology has undergone international development for decades.

There is no specific moment of conception for digital communications, but there are some key moments in the scientific theory behind the technological evolution. In 1948, Claude Shannon of MIT published a seminal essay entitled "A Mathematical Theory of Communication," which provided the mathematical foundation for using digital data in communications. Digital encoding as Shannon proposed uses Pulse Code Modulation (invented by Englishman Alec Reeves in 1937), in which the magnitude of a continuous analogue electronic signal is sampled at uniform time intervals and converted into a series of binary codes that represent changes in the signal. As Shannon theorized: "The fundamental problem of communication is that of reproducing at one point either exactly or approximately a message selected at another point."[1] His hypothesis was ahead of technology and remained largely theoretical until decades later, when the arrival of the transistor in 1947 and the development of the microchip in the late 1950s enabled the processing speeds required to facilitate the flow of digital information.[2]

Shannon built on earlier research at AT&T labs by Swedish-born scientist Harry Nyquist and his work on telegraph capacity. In 1927, Nyquist determined that the number of independent pulses that could travel through a telegraph channel in a given time frame is limited to twice the bandwidth of the channel.[3] Nyquist's work resurfaced in MUSE (multiple sub-Nyquist sampling encoding), the pioneering Japanese high-definition television system developed in the 1970s.

HD television has only gained mass recognition in the last decade, but the ability to create HD images is far older. Like much of the digital television transition, HD technology has bubbled beneath the surface for nearly half a century. As contemporary television consumers are well aware, the contemporary standard for an HD image has at least 720 vertical pixels. In recent years, 1,080 vertical pixels is considered "real" HD, though whether or not the difference is visible on all but larger video screens is debatable. In 1949, France introduced a high-resolution standard at 819 vertical pixels (768i) that was HD even by today's requirements, but it was only available in monochrome. In 1958, the Soviet Union developed a high-resolution television system capable of producing an image composed of 1,125 vertical pixels as a research project for the Russian military, though never deployed it for broadcasting. Both the French and Soviet systems required much more channel bandwidth than the analogue TV systems deployed in North America and Europe.

In 1970, Japanese officials at the NHK Science and Research Laboratories were the first to begin to develop HDTV for a mass audience.[4] Researchers applied HD technology to broadcasting and developed MUSE, which was designed to work with satellite distribution of HD signals. By 1980, Japan was ready to begin demonstrations of the new technology in hopes of further bolstering its already thriving electronics industry.

THE CANADIAN CONNECTION

The history of advanced television in Canada runs deep. The very cameras that are at the heart of the broadcasting of digital images worldwide owe an historical debt to Canadian Willard Boyle (along with colleague George Smith) for his invention of the charge-coupled device in 1969. Instead of using film, this breakthrough technology transformed light patterns into digital information and established the foundation for many forms of modern digital imaging. Boyle and Smith received due recognition for their accomplishment much later in life when they received the 2009 Nobel Prize for Physics. More than a decade after Boyle and Smith made digital images possible, television remained an analogue medium, though one on the cusp of great advancements.

The goal was HD television. While HD had a long history in the scientific community, Canadian media theorist Marshall McLuhan brought the expression into the public lexicon in his seminal 1964 book *Understanding Media: The Extensions of Man*. McLuhan defined HD as "the state of being well-filled with data" and did not restrict its use to describing television.[5] Whether or not HD would have changed McLuhan's categorization of television as a "cool" medium is open to debate, but by the 1980s a much more data-filled television experience was being prepared for a mass audience.

Canada played an influential role in developing and promoting Japan's early analogue-based HD system. Canada hosted a series of three key international conferences on advanced television in the 1980s, which were instrumental in gathering the top researchers in the rapidly expanding field and building momentum for new television technologies. The first colloquium was held in Ottawa in 1982 with one hundred participants. This initial meeting was theoretical in nature and largely limited to proposals for standards; however, later meetings drew larger numbers as the industry realized the potential of this new technology.

As the decade progressed, industry experts increasingly saw the Japanese MUSE system as the de facto international HD standard. American broadcasters supported MUSE as they thought it would secure their claims to spectrum space, which the new and growing cellular phone industries had begun to challenge. By 1987, the Japanese HDTV platform had been successfully demonstrated in Montreal, Ottawa, Toronto, Washington, DC, Los Angeles, New York, and Seattle.

In the late 1980s, advances occurred at a furious pace and countries and corporations scrambled to take positions at the cutting edge. At the Advanced Television Colloquium in Ottawa, Kerns H. Powers of the influential David Sarnoff Research Centre observed in his keynote address: "Now it is 1987 and believe you me the revolution is upon us."[6] Indeed, as I will show in this chapter, explosive development characterized the period between 1987 and the establishment of the new US digital platform in 1995, though much of it had yet to occur by Power's 1987 speech.

The closing address of the same 1987 colloquium was equally forthright in asserting the HD era had now begun. In her closing remarks, Janet A. West-Cyr of the CBC confidently declared of HD television: "We are no longer dealing with a potential medium."[7] It was also at this gathering that cracks began appearing in the Japanese dominance of this new technology. Powers noted the "probable high cost [of MUSE] and that it denies compatibility with the existing population of hundreds of million television receivers throughout the world."[8] These cracks soon grew into irreparable fissures, much to the delight of many of the other nations in attendance in Ottawa in 1987.

Canada also played a lead role in early market research for the economic viability of what would later become digital television. In 1988, the Committee for the North American HDTV Demonstrations to the Public, chaired by K.P. Davies of the CBC and largely composed of Canadian researchers and subjects, presented its *Overview of the Survey Results* to the Federal Communications Commission in Washington. In this study, almost 7,000 members of the public and of interest groups in several North American cities received their first opportunity to view and comment on advanced television. People in Ottawa, Toronto, Montreal, Seattle, and Danbury, Connecticut, most of whom were passers-by in shopping malls, were asked to view one television showing the Japanese MUSE system HD and another television displaying advanced studio-quality broadcasts on the traditional platform. Most respondents were impressed by the HD picture in contrast to its traditional counterpart and most expressed interest in purchasing an HD set. However, as the report observed, "expressed purchase interest diminishes noticeably as prices increase." In other words, HD held appeal, but not so much that people were prepared to pay a hefty premium. This did not bode well for the immediate future, as the few HD televisions available at that time could cost upwards of $10,000. The committee concluded, "It is evident from the foregoing discussion that, although there is considerable demand for advanced television, success in introducing an advanced TV system will be highly dependent on factors such as cost of equipment, availability of program material, and quality of reception."[9]

Canada's pioneering involvement in HDTV in North America went beyond the level of science, engineering, and marketing studies; it also spearheaded production in the field. *Chasing Rainbows*, a CBC and Sony Japan production about the lives of three young people in Montreal in the 1920s, was the first commercial television program in the world to use HDTV technology. The mini-series, starring Canadian actor Paul Gross, was released in 1988 and broadcast in fourteen one-hour episodes in Japan, Europe, the United States, and Canada. It is highly doubtful anyone in Canada outside of a few technical engineers ever saw the show in full HD glory (it was also broadcast in standard analogue format), but it did open international markets, in particular Japan, where the expensive early HD television sets were an item of prestige. Just as equipment manufacturers such as RCA and Westinghouse financed early radio broadcasts in the 1920s, the first HD programming was a thinly veiled attempt to promote new hardware technology. Sony was a major investor in early HD technology.

FROM HD TO DTV

In the late 1980s, there was a strong political imperative in the United States to develop new advanced television technology – a political and industrial movement largely attributable to concerns of a complete Japanese takeover of the worldwide electronics industry. In 1964, American companies accounted for 94 per cent of the colour TV market, but by 1987 that number had dropped to 17 per cent.[10] By the late 1980s, the number of companies in the United States had dwindled to only two television manufacturers, RCA and Zenith, which were increasingly dwarfed by successful Japanese companies such as Sony, Hitachi, and Toshiba. Furthermore, the Japanese had been working on the new HD technology since the late 1970s that threatened to render the entire American television manufacturing industry obsolete. None but a few electronic insiders were aware of the power of this new platform until a Japanese delegation demonstrated their new HD system to a stunned audience in Washington, DC, in January 1987. It was not just the crystal-clear picture and sound that bewildered the crowd; it was the fact that Japan already had HD televisions, cameras, transmitters, and recorders in full production.[11]

In 1987, the United States had barely begun to explore technology that the Japanese were ready to take to market. The reaction in Washington was a mix of awe, fear, and more than a hint of racism. Politicians were shocked to discover such an advanced, well-funded HD system existed in Japan and saw it as a potential threat to American interests beyond the nation's living rooms. During the era of Ronald Reagan and the last days of the Cold War, the US Congress resented that a Japanese company, Toshiba Machine Company (a subsidiary of Toshiba Corporation), had recently sold military technology to the Soviet Union – passions that led several Congressmen to hold a photo-op on the steps of the Capitol building where they pulverized a Toshiba radio with sledgehammers.[12] The Japanese had indeed captured Washington's attention.

Washington requested a second demonstration, which was transmitted via satellite a few days later from the next exhibition site for the Japanese delegation, this time in Ottawa. This signal, beamed from Ottawa to Washington, was the first international HDTV transmission.

The Japanese system, known in the West as MUSE and in Japan as Hi-Vision, had a major shortcoming that American interests were determined to exploit: it was still analogue based and so required enormous amounts of bandwidth – it was only suitable for a satellite transmission platform. MUSE required 27 MHz to transmit its programming, while American and Canadian OTA broadcasters were only allotted 6 MHz of spectrum space per channel. Japanese efforts to adopt the technology to OTA transmission would require an expansion of frequencies for American broadcasters. This prospect led to the early support for MUSE by the US broadcasting industry.

Washington was not as pleased. The United States spearheaded most of the major communications upheavals of the twentieth century and did not wish to concede this development to Japan. By 1989, Europe had also begun to develop an analogue HD platform. The American Electronics Association, a group that represented US electronics manufacturers, lobbied both sides of Congress to support the American industry. Nervous federal politicians quickly offered substantial development funding that the US military – which saw HD as useful for training simulators, weapons displays, navigational devices, and security monitoring systems – expanded. In the late 1980s, HDTV in America gained political momentum. By 1990, according to Hernan Galperin, "a grand total of nine bills had been introduced, and both the House and the Senate held numerous hearings on HDTV."[13]

When the initial Washington funds dwindled by 1990 and some progress but certainly no clear breakthrough on a new system, the United States tried a different approach: an FCC committee, under Commissioner Dick Wiley, announced an international competition to develop an HD system that could be broadcast over the air. The winner of this technological race could receive royalties from all future HD televisions sold in the United States that used the approved platform – a prize considered to be worth potential billions.[14] In 1989, as the industry contestants began to consider their options (and the $175,000 entry fee), the objective was OTA HD analogue broadcasting. At this point, none of the competition was pursuing digital television.

That all changed in 1990. Woo Paik, a San Diego-based engineer for a division of General Instrument who had previously specialized in digital encryption of satellite television signals to avoid piracy, turned his digital knowledge to HDTV signals with some success. Paik's invention, called DigiCipher HDTV, was only a computer simulation, but it was good enough to completely alter the structure of the race for OTA HD and the future of television.

Digital transmission permits the use of information compression and special modulation techniques that can greatly reduce transmission bandwidth requirements; therefore, DigiCipher HDTV opened the door to OTA HD broadcasting without expanding broadcasters' spectrum allocation. The relatively closed world of advanced television systems felt the revolutionary impact of Paik's invention almost immediately.[15] The United States abandoned exploring HDTV systems that were incompatible with the previous NTSC (National Television System Committee) analogue model and began to search for a system that could work within the 6 MHz of spectrum allocated to broadcasters in the United States (and Canada).

In early 1993, the US standards competition dropped MUSE, which had begun the HDTV process more than ten years previously, because of its prohibitively large spectrum requirements. The Japanese, once justifiably confident in the superiority of their HDTV system, watched as DigiCipher HDTV effectively vaporized billions of dollars in research investment. Japan later abandoned MUSE, once a pioneering technology, as its own standard. Europe dumped its emerging standard, MAC (multiplexed analogue components), later the same year after $2 billion in government development research funding. In less than three years, two of the competing international standards conceded to the new American digital platform that, though not yet fully developed, offered superior technology. By late 1993, it was increasingly clear that the future of television would not be analogue. Thus, digital television was born as an unanticipated offshoot in the global race for HD broadcasting.

A television broadcasting system does not consist of only one technology. It requires a series of technical achievements (transmission, compression, reception, sound, and video) working in concert. Paik may have proven digital television was possible but he did not know how to create the full range of technology necessary to make digital HD a reality for the average viewer. By 1993, many of the groups participating in the HDTV competition realized the scope of the project was likely too much for any one organization, and that the potential profits were enough for everyone involved to get very wealthy. With this in mind, Donald Rumsfeld, the General Instrument CEO and a past and future White House advisor, proposed a merger of the top companies involved to expedite the process of creating the new American technical standard.

Rumsfeld, who took over GI in 1990, recognized the futility of these companies working against each other. His contribution in the development of digital television proved pivotal: he proposed an agreement between several major companies that would incorporate their range of specializations. Negotiations between these traditional adversaries were difficult and almost collapsed on numerous occasions, but the desire to gain approval for the first digital television standard proved temptation enough to overcome industrial obstacles. In May 1993, RCA, General Instrument, MIT, Philips, Zenith, and AT&T formed a technological super group (though most companies are US-based, Philips is a European company and, in 1999, founding member Zenith became a subsidiary of the South Korean electronics manufacturer LGE). The new organization called itself the Grand Alliance and combined its branches of expertise to finalize the development of a new digital television standard and win the FCC competition.

The various areas of responsibility fell under different companies' areas of specialization, and there was by no means unanimous consent. AT&T and GI combined their efforts to build the encoder, considered the heart of the system; RCA, under charismatic figure "General" David Sarnoff, built the transport system that organizes the bit stream; Philips built the decoder.[16] The group chose Dolby AC-3 sound as the audio standard.

The various members of the Grand Alliance, driven by the enormous potential profits, brought forth the ATSC (Advanced Television Systems Committee) A/53 digital television transmission platform, which the FCC approved as the American digital television standard in 1995. The same 6 MHz of bandwidth that used to transmit one analogue channel could, using the ATSC standard, transmit one HD program stream, two medium definition program streams, or up to five standard definition (SD) streams, as well as some associated data. The flexibility to create different combinations, known as multiplexing, was a primary benefit of the ATSC standard.[17]

During the early 1990s, Canadians provided input to the ATSC's technical studies through work carried out by the Joint Technical Committee on Advanced Broadcasting. This government and industry consultative group, chaired by G.R. Begley of Industry Canada, conducted a number of studies that compared the performance of the proposed Grand Alliance single-carrier DTV system with the OFDM (orthogonal frequency division multiplex) approach being pursued in Europe, later to be known as DVB-T (digital video broadcasting terrestrial). Canada's studies identified several advantages of the European technology, including much superior mobile reception and the ability to employ single-frequency networks (SFN) to extend service areas and fill coverage holes.[18] Nevertheless, domestic economic interests triumphed in the United States, and in 1995 the FCC adopted a homegrown approach in the form of the ATSC A/53 standard.[19]

Despite the concerns of Canadian engineers, the interests of the legacy industries in Canadian broadcasting prevailed, and Canada soon followed suit. Given the impracticability of employing different DTV transmission standards between Canada and the United States, it came as little surprise that in 1997, the Task Force on the Implementation of Digital Television recommended the adoption of the ATSC A/53 standard for Canadian digital television. Economies of scale for new digital equipment and the reliance of Canadian broadcasters on American productions proved a powerful force. The links between American broadcasting and Canadian reception run deep: in 2009, more than 20 per cent of all television viewing in English Canada was directly from American conventional and specialty broadcasters.[20] To impose a burden of translating to a different standard was a leap of independence Canada (and other NAFTA partner Mexico) was not prepared to take. In addition, many Canadian broadcasters rely on direct simultaneous substitution of American signals (see chapter 4) for large swaths of their prime time schedule – a controversial yet highly profitable practice unique to Canadian broadcasting.[21] The Canadian system was too economically tied to American broadcasting to make a separate technical standard a viable alternative.

Dallas Smythe observed this adherence to American technical protocols in his 1981 book *Dependency Road* when he wrote of Canada's adoption of the NTSC American analogue television standard in the 1950s: "If Canada had seriously intended to protect its culture from total domination by the United States Consciousness Industry, drastic measures would have been employed. Instead of adopting the same technical standards as were used in the United States, Canada would have adopted different and superior standards (French, British or German)."[22] By 1997, there was little chance Canadian broadcasting would reject the American template. Canadian cultural nationalists were generally not part of the dialogue surrounding digital television technical standards. All televisions currently sold in Canada and the United States are equipped to receive the ATSC signal.

The US government continued to put a great deal of political and economic support behind the new technology. Accompanying the ATSC standard in the United States was the ATSC Forum, a lobby group charged with promoting the technology in other countries. *Export America*, a monthly publication of the US Department of Commerce's International Trade Administration, describes its role:

> The ATSC Forum educates broadcasters, manufacturers, and policymakers throughout the world about the benefits of digital television technology, and it advocates adoption of ATSC standards in order to achieve these benefits. The ATSC consists of approximately 140 entities ranging from small firms to large companies, most of which are either US corporations, such as Motorola, Harris, Dolby Laboratories, Microsoft, Sun Microsystems, and Broadcom, or US subsidiaries of foreign companies, such as Zenith, Phillips, Sony, and Panasonic, which employ thousands of Americans. The ATSC Forum seeks to identify and educate smaller companies that could benefit from the adoption of a hemispheric standard, and inform them about opportunities to participate in the forum's events.
>
> The ATSC Forum recently received a partnership grant from the US Department of Commerce through the Market Development Cooperator Program. The goal of the grant is to promote the adoption of the ATSC standard for digital television throughout the Western hemisphere.[23]

As I will detail in chapter 3, despite cooperation from Canada and Mexico, a full hemispheric adoption of the ATSC standard has proven difficult. The power of US lobbying efforts has not sold all countries on the superiority of their ATSC standard. In 2012, there are still regions of the globe weighing their options as to which standard is appropriate for their purposes; however, the benefits of digital television have been largely accepted by governments worldwide. Paik's 1990 discovery has had truly global repercussions.

HOW IS DIGITAL DIFFERENT?

Digital television is not only HD, but also allows for standard-definition programs, audio broadcasts in stereo quality, and multimedia content. There is also the potential for combinations of television, telephone and Internet packaging for services, and increased interactions between users, broadcasters, and content providers. Over-the-air digital signals can offer an HD image that is superior to one offered by cable and satellite, because it does not undergo the same compression in transmission. Canada's transition plan emphasizes HD, unlike the European transition model, which prioritizes a greater choice of standard definition OTA channels on the same amount of spectrum space. The evolution of the European technical standard DVB has allowed for greater compression and the increased ability to deliver HD signals, but that was not the primary impetus for the transition as it was in the United States.

For governments worldwide, much of the benefit in digitalization lies not in the improved sounds and images of digital and HD television but in the vast potential of the digital dividend – the space on the electromagnetic spectrum freed by digital broadcasting's more efficient utilization of the spectrum bands that were side aside for TV use decades ago. The potential income generated by selling vacated TV spectrum via auction is proving irresistible to governments across the globe. Telecommunications carriers, Internet service providers, and public safety services see the spectrum in the 698 to 806 MHz band, which has been vacated by TV on channels 52 to 69 in Canada, as ideal for new wireless services. The expression "beachfront property" often describes these radio waves. A wireless tower that transmits in the 700 MHz band can cover twice the geographic area as one that transmits in the 1,900 MHz band, where many cell phones operate. The sale of freed spectrum space to wireless operators is one obvious benefit and a driving force of the digital television transition.

Mobile telephony was the early instigator behind the demand for new spectrum space; however, other wireless services with the pockets to challenge major telecoms have begun to insist on access to airwaves. Google was an active participant in the 2008 spectrum auction in the United States. Though it did not purchase spectrum, Google is credited with driving up the final price as well as successfully lobbying for open access rules for spectrum.[24] Wireless broadband services are growing worldwide, particularly in places not well served by traditional wired Internet service providers. The explosive growth of the smartphone market, and later tablet computers, has meant that users are no longer satisfied with voice data plans. The growth of new high-speed wireless technology such as Long Term Evolution is seen as a possible solution to the "digital divide" between regions, especially in more rural areas.

Canada does not face the demand for access to new technologies and the challenges posed by the digital television transition alone. When the centres of the global communications industry (Japan, the United States, and the United Kingdom) began the process to digital, other countries felt great pressure to follow suit. Worldwide, governments are largely convinced of the overall benefits of digital broadcasting. Though international power dynamics are a factor, the unique circumstances of each nation and/or region determine the timing and scope of the digital transition. According to Galperin, the key nation-specific factors that determine direction in the digital television transition include:

1 Organization of the state (regime type electoral system, formal rule-making procedures);
2 Normative orientation of media policy; and
3 Legacy of the analogue TV regime.[25]

A brief look at international ASO dates shows Canada largely in the middle of the schedule (see table 1.1). The European Commission set a target date of 2012 for the twenty member states of the EU, allowing until 2015 as the latest date for members.[26]

INTERNATIONAL TECHNICAL STANDARDS

Although they are often well below the radar of all but the most avid electronics enthusiast, the relationships encoded in the technical DNA of communications equipment have strong implications for political,

Table 1.1
International analogue shut-off dates

Country	*Year*
Australia	2010–2012
France	2011
Germany	2010
Mexico	2021
United Kingdom	2012 (rolling shut off complete)
United States	2009
Japan	2011
China	2015
Brazil	2013
Canada	2011

Sources: Garcia Leiva and Starks, "Digital Switchover across the Globe," 787; McEwen, *A Report to the* CRTC *on Digital Transition Strategies in a Number of Different Countries.*

cultural, and economic dynamics among nations worldwide. David Wood of the European Broadcasting Union describes technical standards as "a blueprint to make equipment that will work with a broadcast or other media delivery system, either at the sending or receiving end. It's close to the idea of 'interoperability' ... We like common standards because they open up markets to competition on content, price and features, and bring us closer to the user/consumer's dream of 'maximum choice, maximum quality, minimum cost.'"[27] Technical standards matter for citizens and consumers as they have the power to directly affect entire sections of national economies. There has been a fury of industrial arm-twisting over standards in the last few years because the communications industry knows that once a standard is accepted, it is very difficult to change. The analogue television standards remained in place for over fifty years and spawned great economic growth. Governments and industries worldwide seek maximum return on the research and development investments in digital television.

ANALOGUE STANDARDS

The last such transformative achievement in television technology occurred with the arrival of colour in the 1950s. The NTSC-compatible colour TV standard, adopted in the United States in 1953, was backwards compatible with the existing NTSC monochrome transmission standard. It had a bad habit of changing colour due to phase changes in the colour sub-carrier, and so manufacturers added a hue control to North American TV sets to allow viewers to restore flesh tones. Canada adopted the NTSC standard when it began broadcasting in colour in 1966.

Rather than simply use the American standard, France and Germany used it as a basis to develop their own. Each country developed a system it viewed as superior to the American model, particularly in the areas of colour consistency and transmission range. The French system was known as SECAM (séquentiel couleur à mémoire, or sequential colour with memory) and the German standard was called PAL (phase alternating line). These countries foresaw that developing a unique technical standard would let them benefit from the various electronics manufacturing industries to follow. According to McKnight and Neil of MIT, the French government's aggressive promotion of their SECAM system in the 1960s "resulted in creating an industry that accounted for 0.4% of GDP within a decade."[28]

While regional concerns had an impact, the process was more complex than neighbouring countries adopting the local standard (see table 1.2). The adoption of analogue television standards reflected worldwide power dynamics and the dealmaking and strategies had all the hallmarks of the Cold War era. Language and history influenced the path of the transition in France and the United Kingdom (which adopted PAL), and previous colonial ties proved resilient and were strengthened via communications standards. This allowed not only for the continued trade in cultural goods, but more integrated electronic industries between countries sharing the same standard. In 1987, European manufacturers claimed a 75 per cent share of the European television market.[29]

The United States' newfound post-WWII role as a global military superpower was accompanied by many of its military allies (and in the case of Japan, defeated powers) accepting the NTSC standard. In other countries, choosing a standard was a show of political defiance: Taiwan chose NTSC, while China used PAL, and Yugoslavia asserted its independence rather than follow the lead of the Soviet Union by choosing PAL. Some countries adopted standards following outright bribery: the French gave the Soviets royalty-free access to SECAM in order to open Soviet-dominated markets in Eastern Europe and much of the developing world, none of whom were spared the royalty fee.[30]

Table 1.2
Analogue colour television transmission standards

Standard	*Country of Origin*	*Countries Used*
NTSC (National Television System Committee)	United States	United States, Canada, Mexico, South Korea, Japan, Taiwan, parts of South America
SECAM (Séquentiel couleur à mémoire or sequential colour with memory)	France	France, francophone countries, Russia, Eastern Bloc, Greece, Saudi Arabia
PAL (Phase Alternating Line)	Germany	United Kingdom, the Commonwealth (except Canada and the Caribbean), Brazil, Argentina, India, Germany, non-French African countries, China, Yugoslavia

DIGITAL STANDARDS

Television technology may have undergone a dramatic shift with the arrival of digital, but the desire of nations to use standards to gain a competitive advantage demonstrated a stubborn constancy. Like much of the movement to digital media, early theorists believed digital television might spell an end to the global divides known under the analogue regime. MIT visionary Nicholas Negroponte saw great possibilities in digital:

> We are more accustomed to scaling computer systems up, getting better display, installing enhanced sound, and fully expecting our software to work better, versus not at all. Why isn't TV like that?
>
> It will be. Today we are stuck with three analogue TV standards. In the United States and Japan we use NTSC (which stands for National Television Systems Committee, although Europeans will tell you "Never the Same Colour"). PAL (Phase Alternating Line) dominates Europe and is trailed in France by SECAM (Sequential Couleur avec Memoire) Americans have been known to say it really means "Something Essentially Contrary to America." The rest of the world follows willy-nilly, using one of the three in its

> pure of impure form, with almost as much logic as the national choice for a second language.
>
> Being digital is the option to be independent of confining standards.[31]

As the television transition progressed, the digital utopian hope that the world would embrace a common standard was quickly dashed on the predictable rocks of national economic self-interest (see table 1.3). Computers and televisions may now speak a common digital language, but not all television systems can get along. Wood explains the difference between the common Internet standard and the divided world of television:

> The single system that we have for Internet is the only thing that could work for Internet, because it is a worldwide system. If there were not a worldwide system, in a sense the *raison d'être* for the Internet would disappear. For broadcasting, the system still works with national systems, because the services are usually national. For the Internet, standards are essentially decided by an "alliance" – the Internet Society and its son the Internet Engineering Task Force (IETF). This is a single worldwide body with vast numbers of enthusiastic engineers who decide standards by "running code" – you've got to make a proposal and prove your proposal works. Broadcasting could learn a lot from the IETF. Oh, for there to be a body like that for broadcasting![32]

The business of television technology has always been steeped in nationalist rhetoric, and the digital paradigm has proven no exception. The United States viewed its path to a digital standard as a national priority; at the same time, Europe raced to succeed its aging analogue systems. The timing was right: patents for PAL and SECAM, which had served European economic interests for decades, expired in the 1980s, potentially allowing non-European manufacturers to enter the market. The push by European governments resulted in some expensive stumbles. The failure of the analogue MAC standard in the early 1990s, after billions in government funding, was followed by the more successful DVB (digital video broadcasting) platform.

A guiding principle of the DVB project is that it is "market-driven and its standards are *implementable*."[33] Expensive failures such as MAC

Table 1.3
International digital broadcasting standards

Standard	*Characteristics*	*Adopted By*
ATSC (United States)	-HD priority, weak mobile reception -Has a higher rate of coverage for the same transmitter power than DVB or IDSB*	Canada Mexico South Korea
MAC (defunct)	-Tried to overcome the PAL/SECAM analogue divide in Europe	Australia New Zealand
DVB (Europe)	-MAC was abandoned -Linked technical standards for a range of media -Plan is to have all of Europe on DVB by 2012 -Initially not well-suited to HD terrestrial but new compression technology changing that	Singapore European Union
IDSB (Japan)	-TV sets can handle both satellite and terrestrial reception -Similar to DVB	Brazil
DMB-T (China)	-Keeping up to date with TV receivers for manufacturing industry	China
ISDTV (Brazil)	-Uses the MPEG-4 standard for digital video coding. The adoption of MPEG-4 is a key innovation of ISDTV -Ginga middleware has been designed for application to ISDTV to create a Japanese-Brazilian standard	-Brazil-Japanese hybrid -Being considered by other South American countries

*According to Wayne Stacey, this was the original rationale the ATSC used to justify their choice of a single-carrier DTV standard. However, field experience has now shown that the power levels adopted for ATSC do not always guarantee that analogue service areas can be fully duplicated.

and Japan's MUSE made most, but not all, countries wary of developing a unique digital standard. There is increasing pressure on governments worldwide to adopt one of the international digital television standards already on the market. The Japanese HD project spearheaded the movement to advanced television technology, but the United States had the first market-ready digital platform when it approved the ATSC standard. Since then, other countries have come forward with standards they claim are superior to ATSC or more suitable to the needs of a given nation or region.

The initial DVB group was strictly European when the project began in 1993, but has since opened its membership to a wider constituency. DVB is actually comprised of several platforms working from the same general template: DVB-S (satellite) was the first application launched in 1995 in France; DVB-T (terrestrial OTA) which began in Sweden and the United Kingdom in 1998; DVB-C (cable, claimed by the organization as the most common system for digital cable in the world) was developed in 1994 and has recently been upgraded to the next generation DVB-C2; DVB-H (mobile or handset) is a latest evolution of the standard.[34] The DVB standard has proven very adaptable and many who work in the field see it as superior to ATSC.[35]

The Japanese system, ISDB (Integrated Services Digital Broadcasting), shares many similarities with the DVB standard, especially its interoperability between media devices (satellite, cable, terrestrial, multi-media, and mobile). Unlike the American or European standards, ISDB was designed for mobile reception from the outset.[36] As a Japanese government official noted at a digital television conference in 2005: "Cellular phones with television make it possible for people to view television programs anywhere anytime with stable reception quality, which is a significant marketing tool for TV advertising, considering many people are commuting by train in metropolitan areas. A few companies already released prototypes of cellular phones cum digital television. Broadcasters are planning to begin the TV programming for mobile reception in 2005."[37] Japan also broke technological ground by developing televisions with built-in terrestrial and satellite reception. The country was not an early adapter of terrestrial digital television, and launched its first digital signals in 2003. Mountainous terrain presents certain difficulties for terrestrial broadcasting: many of the smaller cable companies in Japan do not offer a wide range of options, but use their master antennae to receive terrestrial signals that are then distributed by the local cable system.[38] Nevertheless, Japan became the first Asian country to complete its analogue shut off in June 2011.

Like so much of the digital transition, the movement toward standards is in flux and countries may yet choose different standards as the transition progresses. Brazil has brokered a unique agreement with Japan concerning its adoption of the ISDB standard that will have implications for Japanese interests in South America (see chapter 3). After all the digital utopia rhetoric, and despite dramatic improvements in the science of television broadcasting, the desire to gain competitive advantage has resulted in a global divide similar to that under the analogue regime. Though alliances and power structures have changed since the analogue structure was established in the 1950s, standards again divide the world. Any idealistic hope of a global digital standard now seems as dated as talk of an information superhighway. I will explore the various adaptations of international digital television standards in more detail in chapter 3.

For the purposes of the Canadian transition, the obvious country of consequence is the United States. There are clear economic and political reasons behind why Canada would choose to adopt the US standard, especially as the two country's economies further intertwine under NAFTA. Canada's role in the early part of the transition was clearly one of leadership: it hosted international meetings on advanced television, provided North American market analysis necessary to convince the FCC there was a public interest in this technology, and co-produced the first HDTV production. This position at the forefront of new television technologies did not last.

Canada had tried a more independent path when digital radio emerged, with terrible results. Much like digital television, Canada was at the forefront of early studies into digital audio broadcasting (DAB); unlike television, Canada was an early adopter and announced its position before the United States. In 1994, Industry Canada announced the Eureka-147 as the standard for digital broadcasting and allocated 40 MHz of spectrum in the L-band range (1,452 to 1,492 MHz) for new digital radio broadcast services.[39] Experts believed this would offer the highest quality audio broadcasts. However, since that area of the spectrum was set aside for military use in the United States, Canadian consumers and broadcasters were unable to use electrical equipment made for the US market. Economies of scale were not in Canada's favour. The result was a failure for the new broadcasting technology. Initially, a high-end DAB receiver in Canada cost over $2,000, and consumers indicated the increase in audio quality was not worth the expense. There were sixty-two operational DAB radio stations in Canada in 2006; however listenership remained very low.[40] A 2007 study by O'Neill notes: "DAB receivers were still not readily available whether for home, portable, or car use. Industry professionals expressed disillusionment and regarded the years since 1995 as an unproductive, stalled, or even failed period of development."[41] In a policy that would be repeated for digital television, the CRTC's position was that DAB should be an industry-led project. According to O'Neill, the tepid response by industry "underscores the weakness of a laissez-faire or market-driven approach."[42] Canadian digital radio stands as an example of industrial and policy mismanagement that cost broadcasters and offered little in return. In

2009, Industry Canada declared: "The mission for DAB in the band 1452–1492 MHz, as the digital replacement for the analogue FM and AM broadcasting services, has been abandoned."[43]

There was never any serious debate about Canada going its own route in digital television standards. The economic interrelations between Canadian broadcasters on American signals, via cable relays and simultaneous substitution, meant that an independent approach was not economically feasible. Canada has no television manufacturing sector, so there was little incentive to invest in the research and development required to develop a national standard. The early failures of Japan and Europe in the search for a new HDTV standard served as a warning. Smythe's idea of using technical standards as a form of Canadian cultural protectionism will not be realized under digital television.

Despite Canada's embrace of the ATSC standard, the paths taken by Canada and the United States en route to full digitalized television systems are not as uniform as one might expect. Canada's early leadership role underwent a clear change as "advanced television" gave way to digital.

2

Early Policy Development in Canada and the United States

Canada has historically chosen a distinct broadcasting path to suit its values, incorporating industrial and political requirements as a middle economic power with vast geography and two official languages. These concerns have manifested in the web of regulations that promote and fund Canadian content, limit foreign ownership, protect local broadcasting rights, and provide policy and financial support for public and community broadcasting. While digitalization challenges some of these regulatory tools, there is no reason to believe the digital era will bring about regulatory uniformity between nations.

As Quebec scholar Pierre Trudel writes: "The legislative provisions that States adopt are not the result of chance. They reflect the cultural features of various human societies."[1] The unguarded border – an increasingly inaccurate term – between Canada and the United States has always posed the greatest challenge for Canadian broadcasting policy. The two countries share a great deal, but many of their differences are apparent in the histories of their respective broadcasting regulations.

Regulation in American broadcasting, as outlined in Paul Siegel's *Communication Law in America*, is guided by spectrum scarcity, pervasiveness (and implied invasiveness), and the desire to protect children.[2] This model reveals greater social apprehensions concerning privacy, the economic necessities of a well-managed system, and content concerns than exist in Canada.[3] The current guiding legislation for broadcasting in the United States reflects these values. The 1996 Telecommunications Act, the first update to broadcasting legislation since the 1934 Communications Act, commits the United States to flexibility in spectrum management (section 201), outlines the rules of license renewal (sections 203 and 204), and explicitly references violence and obscenity in broadcasting (sections 500 to 562).[4] The role of the government in this approach is to facilitate market interactions and ensure restrictions on content that falls outside traditional social norms.

Given the United States' constitutional emphasis on individual liberties, the legal place of the government in media is a continued point of contention. The seminal modern case was FCC *v. Pacifica* in 1978, which ruled that regulation was justified as broadcasting signals "intrude into the home, are more pervasive, and are more difficult to control than print media."[5] This case was spurred by a New York radio broadcast of comedian George Carlin's "Filthy Words" – a monologue that questions why some words are deemed unfit for broadcasting. In 2004, Janet Jackson's infamous "wardrobe malfunction" at the Superbowl reinforced the idea of offensive images invading the home and resulted in new regulations from the FCC that require increased fines for broadcasting harmful content.

Broadcasting regulation in Canada has a different normative foundation. Protection from harmful content has never been a top priority for Canadian regulators. Legal scholars Liora Salter and Felix Odartey-Wellington observe: "What matters to the CRTC are the options that Canadians have available and, more particularly, whether or not such options include Canadian programs and services ... The CRTC has no wish to educate viewers and no particular agenda for what they should see, except inasmuch as the Canadian broadcasting system contains Canadian programming choices, reflects diversity and is representative of the Canadian population as a whole."[6] Instead, in a clear allusion to the broadcasting power south of the border, the central concern of Canadian policy since broadcasting's infancy has been national sovereignty and control. In his 1932 speech to introduce public radio broadcasting to Canada, Prime Minister R.B. Bennett stated: "First of all, this country must be assured of complete control of broadcasting from Canadian sources, free from foreign interference or influence."[7] Given the limited range of broadcasting signals in 1932, Bennett did not need to explicitly identify the foreign source in question. Six decades later, the guiding Canadian policy enshrined in the 1991 Broadcasting Act continues this theme:

> 3. (1) It is hereby declared as the broadcasting policy for Canada that ...
> (d) the Canadian broadcasting system should
> (i) serve to safeguard, enrich and strengthen the cultural, political, social and economic fabric of Canada,
> (ii) encourage the development of Canadian expression by providing a wide range of programming that reflects Canadian attitudes, opinions, ideas, values and artistic creativity, by displaying Canadian talent in entertainment programming and by offering information and analysis concerning Canada and other countries from a Canadian point of view.[8]

Sovereignty, so important in the Canadian context, has never been of explicit consequence in the American regulatory structure (with the notable exception of foreign ownership restrictions). Being the unquestioned global leader in broadcasting content production and having the population base to amortize programming investment even before hitting the hungry international market, tends to ease the regulatory burden for domestic control.

The United States and Canada, despite numerous parallels, have often taken different paths vis-à-vis the place of the state in broadcasting policy. The digital television transition offers an occasion to reassess each country's approaches to regulation. These positions are not what some Canadians, who have traditionally accepted a stronger place for government, would expect: in the United States the government has been decidedly hands-on with digital television, whereas in Canada the private realm has proceeded with little political or public intervention.

THE DIGITAL TELEVISION TRANSITION IN THE UNITED STATES

In 1997, Vice President Al Gore championed the change from analogue to digital television as "the greatest transformation in television's history ... one that is truly bigger than the shift from black and white to color ... It's like the difference between a one-man band and a symphony."[9] By 1997, this technological symphony had been tuning up for some time. In the 1980s, the United States, threatened by Japan's MUSE system, pursued its own alternative. In the early 1990s, after a fiercely competitive development program, the United States surpassed MUSE and Europe's MAC high-definition technology by successfully digitalizing the signal and making it suitable for terrestrial broadcasting (the ATSC standard). By the mid-1990s, the digital television transition was a concern at the highest levels of government in the United States.

In 1993, President Bill Clinton signed the Omnibus Reconciliation Act of 1993, which gave the FCC the right to sell spectrum. The 1996 Telecommunications Act was the pioneering legislative framework for the digital transition and put the industrial and political process irreversibly in motion. The act included a new section entitled Broadcast Spectrum Flexibility (section 336) that outlined the use of new "advanced television services" and set the stage for spectrum auctions a decade later. From the outset, broadcasters lobbied Congress to maintain the full 6 MHz of spectrum they had enjoyed under the analogue model. There was no political will to use the transition to introduce new competition to the television sector. As Galperin observes: "Congress managed to protect a convenient arrangement with local broadcasters from a wave of market reforms and technological innovations that directly challenged the justification for such arrangement."[10] US broadcasters kept their 6 MHz. The 1996 act doubled the spectrum space allotted to most broadcasters for the duration of the digital transition but mandated that previously held analogue spectrum space eventually "be surrendered to the Commission for reallocation or reassignment (or both) pursuant to Commission regulation."[11] By 1996, the digital television transition was a fait accompli in America.

Clinton established the Advisory Committee on the Public Interest Obligations of Digital Television Broadcasters, or PIAC (Public Interest Advisory Committee), on 11 March 1997. He charged PIAC with determining how public interest objectives would best be served in the television environment created by the 1996 act, which legislated an ASO date of 2006. Specifically, the president requested that the advisory committee advise Gore on the public interest obligations of digital television broadcasters. The committee was comprised of twenty-five members, including representatives of industry, public broadcasting, academics, native groups, and children's television advocates, among others. PIAC tabled its report, *Charting the Digital Broadcasting Future*, on 18 December 1998.

The 160-page report was forthright in its assertion that public interest objectives and the role of government regulation were still applicable in the digital environment: "It is important to help affirmatively shape the new digital television era, in concert with market forces and the technology itself, by recommending appropriate legal obligations and marketplace rules."[12] A key point is the desire to "affirmatively" structure the digital era using FCC policy tools "in concert with," but not simply allowing for, a marketplace solution. The authors emphatically endorsed the position that "people are citizens as well as consumers."[13] The report echoed a position taken in the landmark *Red Lion Broadcasting v.* FCC *US Supreme Court* decision of 1969, which upheld the constitutionality of the public interest standard in American broadcasting: "It is the right of the viewers and listeners, not the right of the broadcasters, which is paramount."[14]

The committee urged the FCC to use the extra programming potential of digital television to improve the quality of political discourse in the United States, including a controversial recommendation that politicians should be allowed five minutes of free air time each night in the thirty days leading up to an election.[15] As American communications scholar Philip Napoli notes, the report "represented an important starting point for a meaningful examination and reassessment of how broadcast television could better contribute to American political and cultural life."[16] The impact of the report resonated in Washington corridors of power and sparked a reassessment of broadcasters' public contributions. It also prompted an FCC inquiry on digital broadcasters' public interest obligations.[17] However, the FCC never released a report in response to this notice of inquiry.[18] According to Napoli, much of this public interest movement was undercut by the change from a Democrat-controlled White House to the Republican administration of George W. Bush and his selection of Michael Powell as FCC chair in 2001.[19] The emphasis switched to more practical, industrial issues such as building televisions with digital receivers and reaching ASO deadlines, and less on normative debates concerning the public interest and the digital transition.

Advocacy groups, such as the Benton Foundation, Public Interest, Public Airwaves Coalition, Common Cause, and Freepress, maintained political pressure on the FCC to respond to public interest concerns and won some concessions. In particular, the FCC required digital broadcasters to provide programming for children and offer parents information about which programs are appropriate for young viewers.[20] These measures were not controversial – the paucity of quality television programming for children in the United States is a popular political issue that dates back to the Kennedy era and is unlikely to face opposition from either party in Congress.[21]

However, despite this regulatory olive branch, the outcry for public interest in American broadcasting never fully subsided, and indeed intensified as civil society groups continued pressure. In 2005, the Benton Foundation, a public interest advocacy group funded by the Ford Foundation, published the *Citizen's Guide to the Public Interest Obligations of Digital Television Broadcasters*, which observed "as new technology innovations unlock new potential, policymakers must not loose [*sic*] sight of the goal on the horizon – ensuring that America's media choices serve the public's growing and very real needs."[22] The report listed dozens of civil society groups involved with the digital broadcasting policy struggle and urged broad public involvement.

There was also debate within the FCC itself. In response to the inaction of the regulator, the FCC's Consumer Advisory Committee released a statement in November 2005 to chastise the lack of progress:

> Consumers deserve to know how broadcasters will serve their day-to-day television needs – healthy programming for children, healthy programming for our democracy, healthy programming for our communities, and as much information about the TV that comes into our living rooms as the food that comes into our kitchens.
>
> The transition to digital television offers profound opportunity to improve television broadcasters' service to the public by enhancing the diversity of viewpoints, promoting civic participation, expanding local and community programming, and increasing children's programming.[23]

In the US political debate, the digital transition issue also found surprisingly strong public interest advocates from within the Republican Party. In the late 1990s, Republican senator and presidential candidate Bob Dole fought, and ultimately lost, the political battle to make broadcasters pay for their use of the public spectrum.[24] In 2005, another future Republican presidential candidate, Senator John McCain, took up the cause of digital television and was blunt in his assessment of the transition at that point: "The transition to digital television has been a grave disappointment for American consumers and nothing short of a spectrum heist, for an indefinite period of time, by television broadcasters."[25] McCain also championed the advisory committee's 1998 request for free air time to candidates and lobbied for a digital transition date of 2007, not 2009 (after the original 2006 date was extended).

McCain and other American politicians believed the digital transition was vital for public safety. The issue of radio spectrum usage became a matter of national security following the release of the *9/11 Commission Report*. The report notes the poor communications between emergency response units in the wake of the terrorist attacks and believes the increasingly congested US spectrum space was partially to blame. The commission explicitly recommended: "Congress should support pending legislation which provides for the expedited and increased assignment of radio spectrum for public safety purposes."[26] The digital transition, according to McCain and the 9/11 Commission, is not only a matter of home entertainment and information, but is a necessary step to freeing up spectrum capacity for emergency response units.

President Barack Obama continued to use national security as a key rationale for the digital television transition when he encouraged Americans to prepare for the digital transition in June 2009: "The transition to digital will free up airwaves for broadband and enhanced emergency communications for our police officers, firefighters, and other first responders."[27] Though issues of public safety are not traditionally part of the discourse and literature surrounding public interest in broadcasting, it is nevertheless a matter still decidedly in the public realm and not confined to the more private interests of industry.

Despite the outcry from the Washington power elite and civil society groups, many remained unsatisfied with the level of public interest objectives achieved in the US digital television transition. Political action has not matched the rhetoric. In 2007, FCC Commissioner Jonathan Adelstein noted this policy disconnect: "In order to maximize the benefits to the American people, the Commission needs to determine DTV broadcasters' public interest obligations. This proceeding has been pending since 1999, and the Commission has failed to produce final rules."[28]

Regardless of its shortcomings, the American experience has nevertheless produced some impressive results. The United States, despite a six-month delay, achieved its goal of a complete analogue shut off in June 2009. Given the size and scope of its transition, this is an enormous accomplishment. While other nations have used gradual roll-out strategies or a focus on major urban centres, the United States (with some low-power broadcasting exceptions) completed a nationwide shut off.

The US government played a central role in the transition, including in the costly decision in 2005 to set aside nearly $1 billion for a coupon program to help Americans purchase digital converters for older analogue television sets.[29] In early 2009, Congress made changes to the 2005 Digital Television Transition and Public Safety Act and approved an extra $20 million for a public education campaign.[30] To ensure the broadcasters did not dawdle in vacating their frequencies, the United States held a spectrum auction on 24 January 2008 for the rights to operate in the coveted 700 MHz frequency band. OTA television broadcasters had little choice but to convert to digital as the spectrum was sold out from under them.

The FCC has taken additional aggressive action to open the door to further spectrum development post-transition. The 2008 FCC decision to allow public use of white space, the unused spectrum space between channels designed to accommodate the frequency spillover common to the less precise analogue system, is a major victory for new technologies and citizens and a stinging rebuke for established broadcasting interests, which fought to maintain control of the spectrum. White space may yet prove to be a major avenue for public communications in the twenty-first century.

The United States successfully completed its digital television transition and now concerns itself with issues of national spectrum usage by way of the digital dividend. Such developments are in their relative infancy in Canada, where the federal government has provided little leadership. The main priority of the Canadian digital television transition has been to protect legacy industries, rather than to explore new possibilities.

THE EARLY DIGITAL TELEVISION TRANSITION IN CANADA

By 1997, with the American digital roll-out underway, Canada faced the prospect of following suit or falling behind. Since the earliest days of radio, Britain and the United States have been the systems against which Canada measures itself. Canada's unique mix of public and private elements within the broadcasting system is a hybrid of these two approaches. When Canada followed the recommendation of the 1997

Digital Task Force and chose American-developed ATSC as its technical standard while the United Kingdom joined the European DVB standard, the United States became the primary point of comparison for the Canadian digital television transition. The United States made it clear that it expected Canada to rid itself of signals in the 700 MHz spectrum on channels 52 to 69, as these were to be free of broadcasting signals in the United States post-transition and could potentially cause interference problems if still used for Canadian broadcasting near the US border.

While in the United States, politicians and civil society groups are still vigorously engaged in the public interest battle, in Canada, such a debate has never really begun. Despite the geographic, economic, technical, and cultural similarities between the two nations, Canada's digital television switchover has taken a decidedly different trajectory from the United States, one that belies its traditional approach to the inherent public nature of broadcasting.

Simply put, Canadian digital television policy has been far more market-centred than its American counterpart. After more than a decade of this approach, it has become clear that faith placed in the forces of the media marketplace to guide the transition was misplaced. Market leadership has proven inadequate to the task at hand. In a study prepared for the CRTC in 2006, Michel McEwen, a former CBC executive and leading figure in the digital transition, critiqued the Canadian policy plan: "Government has, to date, shown no inclination to make any change in its policy of a market driven approach. This in the context of the mounting evidence of successful European, Asian, and American transition strategies, which have specific milestones, firm ASO targets, and legislation to back the plans up."[31]

This regulator and government disconnect from public interest objectives in the digital television transition began early in the process. In 1995, the Canadian government created a task force virtually in tandem with the American advisory committee established by President Clinton, though its structure, mission, and conclusions were decidedly different. The Canadian committee did not have the same high-level launch, nor did it share the mandate to re-evaluate the role of broadcasting as an essential public good. In 1995, the Canadian government charged the Task Force on the Implementation of Digital Television with proposing a roll-out plan for digital television in Canada. The initial technical parameters for the Canadian digital television system were recommended by Advanced Broadcasting Systems of Canada (ABSOC), a government and industry group that tabled a report in 1993 that called for, among other things, adoption of the MPEG-2 compression standard and the American audio standard. The CRTC did not specifically recommend full implementation of the ABSOC criteria, but in 1994 it did "wis[h] to state its support for the 16 December 1993 ABSOC resolution concerning digital TV."[32]

The task force was chaired by McEwen and consisted entirely of industry representatives. The brief report (forty-seven pages including appendices), *Canadian Television in the Digital Era*, filed with the Minister of Canadian Heritage and Industry Canada in October 1997, was largely technical in nature. Among the seventeen recommendations was a request for a time lag so that Canadian broadcasters would be twelve to eighteen months behind the American switchover – a strategy designed to benefit industry in terms of the price of new hardware and a chance to learn from the mistakes of their American colleagues. As the report understates, "We can reasonably expect bumps and detours along the way."[33]

The period of transition between the American and Canadian ASO was not the only aspect of the plan designed to benefit the task force's industry-based membership. While the early American report sought to "shape" the digital era "in concert with market forces," the Canadian task force made it clear that its focus was "the continuing financial health of Canadian television broadcasting system."[34] Such has been the Canadian approach to the digital transition since: the transition is more about maintaining a consumer base for legacy industries than exploring the possibilities afforded by new technology.

Early elements of the Canadian digital transition were influenced by deficit-slashing federal budgets in the mid-1900s. The federal Liberal government's 1996 budget plan announced its intention to take steps "to permit auctioning of the radio spectrum, where appropriate, in the future."[35] The priority for the Canadian government was creating new sources of revenue, not enhancing the national broadcasting system.

On the recommendation of the task force, a group formed to offer further advice and monitor progress as the Canadian digital switch progressed. Canadian DTV Inc (CDTV) existed from 1999 to 2006 and, once again, was comprised entirely of industry representatives and chaired by McEwen. He notes: "Industry was in control of virtually all elements of the [digital television] transition, including the important element of timing."[36] This position was echoed in an interview with

Robert Scarth, the CBC's director of regulatory affairs, who observed that CDTV had "no government leadership" and there was "never a public forum."[37]

True to its market-centred policy, the CRTC largely allowed industry to chart its own course through the early stages of the digital transition. In its 2000 public notice *Establishment of an Industry Working Group to Examine the Digital Distribution of Existing Pay and Specialty Services*, the CRTC asked industry to develop proposals to govern the migration of existing pay and specialty services from analogue to digital distribution.[38] Like the early task force, industry interests dominated the working group, which included members of the Canadian Cable Television Association (CCTA), the Canadian Cable Systems Alliance (CCSA, a group that represents small cable companies), the Canadian Association of Broadcasters (CAB), and the Specialty and Premium Television Association (later amalgamated with the CAB).

A single PIAC representative was included to, in the CRTC's words, "ensure that the views of consumers were taken into account."[39] However, according to the report appendix, Andrew Reddick of the PIAC only attended one of the eight working group meetings in the fall of 2000.[40] Though they managed to issue a report (*The Distribution of Existing Analogue Pay and Specialty Services on a Digital Basis*), differences between industrial interests plagued the group. At the time, the *Wire Report* described the conclusions of the working group:

> Programmers and distributors at odds on how to roll out digital TV across Canada. There is little industry consensus between distributors and programmers on how to convert to digital television, according to a new report prepared for the CRTC by an industry task force studying the issue.
>
> "We really didn't agree on much. Whatever was agreed on, were small items," says David Saxe, who represented the Canadian Cable System Alliance on the working group ...
>
> There is agreement on one point – that the conversion to digital will be neither smooth nor quick.[41]

Despite the ominous press and obvious difficulties with the approach, the CRTC called on the Digital Migration Group yet again in 2001 "to consider the resolution of outstanding migration issues as they pertain to the larger cable systems."[42] The reconvened working group did not result in any further consensus, and it adjourned indefinitely in March 2003.[43]

In 2001, the CRTC issued the following position statement: "The Commission also considers that a voluntary model, i.e., one that would develop at a pace set by the marketplace rather than mandated, is the most appropriate approach for the Canadian broadcasting system."[44] With this one sentence, the CRTC set the Canadian broadcasting system on a very different policy course from that of most industrialized nations, one that primarily emphasized industry overcoming the inherent divisions within the various facets of the broadcasting sector. Canada affirmed that it would protect established television broadcasting interests and trust market mechanisms to guide the transition. This remained the fundamental guiding principle for the Canadian process until roughly the announcement of the analogue shut-off date in 2007. With the keys to the transition turned over to industry, Canada effectively entered a period of digital television stagnation between 2001 and 2007.

Given that digital television evolved from HD, not the other way around as is commonly thought, it should come as little surprise that Canada has strongly encouraged the spread of HD signals. The CRTC has emphasized the expansion of the high definition format because it is well suited to the ATSC standard and places Canada in a stronger international position in the global media marketplace where HD programming is in demand. This position contrasts the many European systems that have paid less early attention to HD and much more to multiple free over-the-air standard definition digital channels.[45]

From the very beginning of the digital transition, the United States has seen HD as the prime consumer benefit of over-the-air digital transmission. The US government, the FCC, and the industry have cited HD as the "gold standard" for over-the-air digital service.[46] It has also been the prime mover in the brisk sales of new televisions over the last decade. In 2006, hardware manufacturer LG Electronics called on the CRTC to set a stronger regulatory plan and a firm digital transition completion date at a time when broadcasters demonstrated little enthusiasm for the digital project.[47] HD was viewed as a necessary investment for content producers. For Canadian programs to have a chance to gain access to, and be competitive in, the American market, programming will have to be produced in HD. In the early years of the transition, the CRTC was clear that all-HD was the goal for Canadian broadcasting: "The transition will be complete when all viewers in

Canada can receive high definition programming ... low definition services would be phased out and all services would be produced and distributed in high definition."[48]

From 2001 to 2008, Canadian policy included strict milestones for HD broadcasting, but dropped them in 2008 when the CRTC determined that market demand was enough to encourage HD development.[49] Broadcasters had vigorously lobbied the regulator to ease the previous HD benchmarks and won substantial concessions.[50] It would not be the only time the Canadian transition saw regulatory capitulations (see chapters 4 and 5).

Thus, in HD, the CRTC backtracked in the one area in which it tried to provide clear transition milestones. The stifling industry inertia in the digital television transition, coupled with the regulatory reliance on market forces and a seemingly disinterested government, meant little progress was made during the early Canadian transition. By December 2008, 28 of the 738 analogue OTA transmitters in Canada had been equipped with digital transmitters.[51] In 2007, the CRTC felt it had little choice but to become more engaged and set a clear analogue shut-off date.

CONCLUSION

The United States addressed the issue of public interest in digital broadcasting at the executive and legislative branches of government, as well as within the federal regulator itself; Canada has used obscure task forces and industry groups of which few citizens are aware and a plan designed, first and foremost, to protect industry interests.

Marc Raboy once noted of Canadian communications policy: "No major change to the system can be instituted, or even seriously contemplated, without public consultation."[52] This has not been the case in the Canadian digital television transition. Various hearings at the federal regulator are indeed open for public submissions; however, these hearings address various specific elements of the digital transition, not the overall direction. The meetings are also inconvenient and prohibitively expensive for those from outside Ottawa who may wish to participate. It was not until 2012 that the CRTC established a fund to cover expenses of citizens who wished to participate in public hearings.[53] The public was rarely consulted during the formative first years of the process, and so digital television in Canada has never really undergone rigorous democratic scrutiny.

Table 2.1
Task Force on the Implementation of Digital Television

Group	*Industry Representatives (including CBC)*	*Non-industry Representatives*
Main Task Force Members (including resource people)	14	3: Canadian Heritage, Industry Canada, and Association of Tele-Education in Canada (+ 3 observers)
Working Group 1: Policies and Regulations	16	2: Canadian Heritage, Industry Canada + CRTC (observer)
Working Group 2: Economics and Consumer Services and Product Implementation	18	1: CRTC Observer
Working Group 3: Digital Television Technology	13	1: Industry Canada
Working Group 4: Production Considerations	10	1: Association of Tele-Education in Canada

This democratic disconnect follows an unfortunate contemporary pattern observed by Darin Barney in his book *Communication Technology*. Barney writes that the paramount concern for information and communications technology (ICT) development in Canada has been "characterized by a consistent overrepresentation of powerful private actors with vested interest in this policy area, and only token representation of public interest groups and other constituencies."[54] He notes that 62 per cent of the 1994 Information Highway Advisory Council's members were representatives of the private sector. That same figure for the main groups of the initial task force on the Implementation of Digital Television is roughly 80 per cent, and higher when one factors in the various working groups (see table 2.1).[55]

The initial primary indicators for the Canadian digital television system revealed a strong pro-industry position with little interest for the greater democratic potentials of the new technology. The neoliberal orthodoxy of open markets and light government, so prevalent in the last twenty years, dominated the Canadian process. Given that Canada's traditionally more leftist media culture has accepted a role for the government, and the stronger place of the public broadcaster within the greater broadcasting system since the 1920s, it is surprising that when it comes to the contemporary essential question of public interest obligations in digital television, the debate within the United States has been far more robust.

The American public has clearly benefitted from being engaged in this political debate. The US government offered subsidies to ensure no citizens were excluded from the digital television transition for financial reasons. The US plan allowed for a subsidy for citizens in the form of coupons for digital tuners, set at $40 per coupon, two coupons per household if required. The US Congress set aside $1.4 billion accordingly. The Canadian government continually rejected such a subsidy.

The engagement of civil society groups that accompanied the early development of digital television in the United States continues in the Obama administration. A post-transition issue concerns the public use of white space – the small, unused portions of the spectrum in between licensed channels that could be used for public wireless Internet, among other initiatives. In 2008, the FCC unanimously approved white space in the 300 and 400 MHz range for unlicensed use, rejecting the pleas of traditional broadcasters.[56] The FCC studied the issue for six years before passing judgement that allows for public exploration of what the *Economist* calls "Wi-Fi on steroids."[57]

Such innovative thinking on matters of the public interest is possible because a significant amount of the population, including elected officials, has been part of the digital debate since the 1990s. The American civil society infrastructure is already in place. Digital television's history coincided with unprecedented development in US civil society groups that focused on media policy issues. Between 1998 and 2008, the Ford Foundation directed over $20 million to the media democracy movement, which included groups like the Benton Foundation.[58] Canada has no such well-funded groups.[59] As I outline in more detail in chapter 6, in recent years, a few organizations in Canada have enjoyed some voice in digital television policy but they do not have nearly the financial resources, staff, nor media exposure of similar organizations in the United States.

Given the current power dynamic in digital television policy, which places incumbent industrial interests at the forefront, it is highly doubtful that Canadian policy will pursue an option such as expanding multiplexing or unregulated use of white space when powerful broadcasters are united in opposition. Under the Canadian regime, there is no market-based incentive to examine the new possibilities afforded by digital television, and plenty of entrenched legacy industries that logically seek to protect their investments. The digital television policy process suffered from a dearth of voices, which has left opportunities of the technology unexplored.

3

The Global Transition

There is no one-size-fits-all solution to broadcasting regulation in the digital era. Just as the United States and Canada have had different approaches in their digital television transitions, so have nations around the world. Though countries face many similar problems, their reactions will, and should, depend on certain national priorities. Digital television has become an international phenomenon, but not all nations are in a hurry to be pioneers in the field. Japan (MUSE) and Europe's (MAC) expensive failed efforts to develop early technical standards, coupled with the transition difficulties in countries such as Canada and Australia, have legitimized the "wait and see" approach for much of the rest of the world and made many nations wary of the first-mover advantage.

International pressures, in particular the intense lobbying efforts to adopt one of the current international standards, are formidable factors as countries move toward digital television broadcasting, but in the end, national governments make the final decision. In his 2007 book, *Switching to Digital Television*, UK scholar Michael Starks claims later adopters have the advantage of learning from other transitions, but must accommodate local requirements: "Differences in market conditions and in political and social factors will no doubt remain critically important and each nation will therefore need to plan its own itinerary accordingly. Blindly following the driver in front will not work."[1] On the other side of the globe, Australian communication scholar Jock Givens echoes the significance of the local experience when he observes in *Turning off the Television*: "Broadcasting, as always, [is] different things in different places."[2]

There are essentially two reasons for the continuing relevance of the nation-state in the digital television transition. First, the regulatory tradition developed in the analogue era when it was much easier to see broadcasting as a localized activity – radio and television transmitters could be regulated within a general geographical area more easily than satellites and the Internet. For much of the world over the last century, the rise of broadcasting coincided with the rise of the modern nation-state. The policy structures reflected local concerns, even despite the rise of cable and satellite, which greatly expanded transmission zones. While the new digital system will call for a substantial shift, there is no need to completely rewrite all regulatory traditions. A legacy effect is at work: much of the established analogue national media policy will be grandfathered into the digital age. The scaffolding is already in place; the task for regulators is to determine proper adjustments.

The second reason lies in the strong link between broadcasting and democracy. Simply put, the nation state is the recognized political entity with the democratic legitimacy to speak on behalf of citizens.[3] Even efforts such as the European Union's 1989 Television without Frontiers directive, a supranational agreement designed to facilitate the free flow of broadcasting signals between European member states, included the following caveat: "It is consequently necessary and sufficient that all broadcasts comply with the law of Member State from which they emanate."[4]

In an era where broadcasting is increasingly global in scope, the tie to the nation-state remains significant, for no democratic regulatory global body exists. There have been attempts to democratize international communications. More globalized efforts in communications regulation, such as the New World Information and Communication Order that began in the 1970s and sought to address media imbalances on an international level, had little lasting impact.[5] International trade agreements and bodies such as the International Telecommunication Union (ITU) play a key role in contemporary communications policy, but none are accountable to citizens in the same way as national governments.

Within the Canadian confederation, there have been debates around the centrality of the federal government in Canadian broadcasting in the last century. In 1929, the *Aird Report* originally called for more provincial autonomy, but in 1932, the British Privy Council ruled that broadcasting was under federal jurisdiction. Broadcasting in Canada has remained in the federal domain ever since. For any nation state to be seen as legitimate, it must be engaged in a dialogue with its own people. For the last century, this exchange has largely been carried out via broadcasting.

NATIONAL CASE STUDIES

I explore the examples of the United Kingdom, Australia, France, China, Brazil, and South Africa in this chapter because they present unique approaches to the transition from a wide range of political-economic cultures and disparate geographical regions of the globe. Some of these countries are established communications powers, while others are developing a unique and increasingly influential voice. While certain countries seek to expand the impact of local imperatives on the national system, others use the arrival of digital to further entrench power and control in the central government. Aside from clear national industrial and political dynamics, internal factors such as existing cable and satellite penetration and external factors such as traditional trading partners and regional economic agreements also determine the direction of each country.

The adoption of a new digital television standard reflects the shifts in international power regimes and trading regions over the last fifty years. There are significant changes from the analogue colour television standards that proved so durable in the post-WWII era. Old alliances crumble, while countries with a new position of strength demand a piece of the lucrative royalty market; others insist that a royalty-free approach is more in keeping with the zeitgeist of the Internet age. While many governments have committed to a standard, others have not, and the digital television policy remains fluid in many regions. Behind closed doors, government and industry lobbyists from Japan, Europe, and the United States continue to try to persuade officials that their respective standards are best. Governments may officially introduce plans, but there remains room for change – a point that international lobbyists continually exploit. As the Canadian digital television transition demonstrates, just because a government declares a completion date does not mean it will unfold according to plan.

The countries in this chapter indicate the range of options for nations as they move toward an all-digital broadcasting system. They also offer a glimpse into the powerful economic and political forces at work as current digital standards are promoted in various countries. This chapter is a survey of the varying approaches to digital television around the globe.

The United Kingdom

After a difficult early start that saw the development of the expensive and never-implemented MAC advanced television platform, the United Kingdom experienced a few further stumbles along the digital path but eventually organized an ambitious and successful digital transition plan. Following a decade that saw broadcasting start-ups quickly perish or merge for survival, the current digital roll-out for the United Kingdom is organized and on schedule. After charging out of the blocks in the 1980s, the country has settled into a structured plan that involves government, public service, and industrial interests. Above all, the UK system has benefitted from steadfast government support. In his 2006 report to the CRTC, Michael McEwen notes that in the United Kingdom, "political will seems to be in place to see analogue switch off through to successful completion, making delays less likely to be tolerated."[6] Therein lies a prerequisite for successful national transitions: political will is paramount.

In the early years of its transition, the United Kingdom saw digital as a possible way to address the problem of media ownership concentration – an issue many countries face. In 1990, the government-approved British Satellite Broadcasting (BSB) launched with much fanfare; however, Rupert Murdoch's Sky satellite service (broadcasting in the older PAL analogue standard) had launched thirteen months earlier and already had a strong foothold in the market. Sky was not based in the United Kingdom, but could not be excluded from broadcasting in it under the EU's Television without Frontiers directive, which allows free signals between EU members. UK companies were subject to national cross-ownership laws that did not apply to Sky, which was legally under Luxembourg ownership.[7] Despite the market potential, it became quickly apparent that neither company stood to make a healthy profit. As of 1990, more than 85 per cent of UK households still watched analogue terrestrial services. Cable also developed very slowly in the United Kingdom, and in 1990, less than one million homes (out of approximately 23 million) subscribed to television via cable.[8] That same year, Sky and BSB merged in a 50:50 deal and formed BSkyB.

In 1992, BSkyB purchased the right to broadcast live coverage of

Premier League football – a deal that, according to Michael Starks, "laid the foundations of BSkyB's financial fortune."[9] BSkyB's early success most threatened traditional terrestrial channels ITV and BBC. In an effort to curb the dominance of one satellite provider, UK authorities looked to digital terrestrial as a possible solution to BSkyB control of British television.

UK digital television commenced in 1998 with the launch of Independent Television's ONDigital, a pay digital terrestrial transmission service that garnered few subscribers and ceased transmission in 2002. While this start to the terrestrial digital era in the United Kingdom was disastrous, the next effort was more successful. Freeview launched at the end of 2002 and offered free OTA services via digital multiplexes, providing thirty TV channels in standard definition. Freeview grew rapidly and by the end of 2008 served approximately 14 million households, compared to 8.8 million subscribers for BSkyB, and Virgin Media's cable TV base of 4.8 million customers.[10] In the summer of 2007, Ofcom estimated that 80 per cent of UK households making their first steps into the digital TV world did so via Freeview.[11]

Freeview is owned and run by its five shareholders – the BBC, BSkyB, Channel 4, ITV, and Arqiva – and provides free-to-air digital TV channels, radio stations, and interactive services through an aerial.[12] After 2009, digital terrestrial TV networks in the United Kingdom include the potential for HD transmissions without the need to allocate extra spectrum as a result of new MPEG-4 compression technology. Perhaps most importantly, the digital transition introduced increased competition into the UK television sector. As Galperin observes: "The British strategy has been the aggressive promotion of market competition ... whereas in the United States the transition was molded to the existing industry structure, in the United Kingdom it was designed to challenge it."[13]

The UK government realized a transition of this magnitude required a central governing body. In 2005, it charged the industry group Digital UK with overseeing the transition, including the promotion and education campaigns about the analogue shut off. Digital UK is an independent not-for-profit group owned by the United Kingdom's public service broadcasters (BBC, ITV, Channel 4, five, and S4C) and commercial multiplex operators SDN and Arqiva.[14] It formed at the request of the government and Ofcom, but is independent from both. Among its responsibilities, Digital UK managed the highly successful digital transition marketing campaign, which included a children's

Fig. 3.1 Digital UK mascot Digit Al. Courtesy of Digital UK, 2012

education promotion that featured "switchover robot" Digit Al – an instantly recognizable mascot for the sweeping project (see fig. 3.1).

The 2009 Digital Britain Report assessed the overall impact of the switch to digital television in the United Kingdom, and the results are largely positive. The report warns that despite much success, "Terrestrial TV distribution on the other hand still provides a huge challenge (and opportunity) for Government, Ofcom and the industry to accomplish the Digital TV switchover."[16] The terrestrial service in the digital transition was planned as a roll-out that would move across Great Britain over a four-year period. This approach contrasts the US and Canadian plans that call for a complete national shut off on a specified date. This enormous undertaking involves switching off more than one thousand UK analogue transmitters and increasing the power of the digital transmitters already set up for the Freeview service. The first closure of an analogue signal happened in the small town of Whitehaven in the northwest of England in 2007. In April 2012, London switched off its analogue signal after seventy-five years of service; an event that affected an estimated 12 million television sets.[17] London was digital as it hosted the 2012 Olympics. The entire

Table 3.1
UK digital television transition schedule

Region	*Year*
Border	2007–08
Granada	2009
West Country	2009
Wales	2009–10
Channel Islands	2010
West, STV North	2010
STV (Central Scotland)	2011
Central, Anglia, Yorkshire	2011
London, Meridian, Tyne Tees, Ulster	2012

Source: Department for Culture, Media, and Sport and Department for Business Enterprise and Regulatory Reform, *Digital Britain*, 86.

UK transition is scheduled for completion by the end of 2012 (see table 3.1).

The UK plan also includes an initiative called the Digital Switchover Help Scheme, set up by the BBC and the UK government to assist eligible people – those who are over age seventy-five, are disabled, have lived in a care home for six months or more, or are registered as blind or partially sighted – in making the switch on one of their TV sets. People who receive the service must pay £40, though it is free for eligible people who receive income support.[18] The scheme sends a technician to set up the digital receiver in the home and offer further help via phone and online consultation. According to the help scheme website, over seven million people in the United Kingdom are eligible for the service.[19]

As McEwen notes in his 2006 report to the CRTC, "a feature of the [UK] plan is public communication."[20] After setting clear deadlines, the government established a group to oversee the process and created programs to inform and support all citizens. In London, digital television roadshows explaining the switch took place throughout the city in 2012 to help people understand how the change would affect their household. This emphasis on public communication has paid dividends. After overcoming a few early problems, the UK transition is a model of cooperation between government, regulator, and industry, and of a very effective public awareness campaign.

Australia

With widely dispersed population centres, vast expanses of under-populated territory, prominent public broadcaster (the Australian Broadcasting Corporation, or ABC), and historic appetite for American popular culture, Australia provides a worthy point of comparison for Canada. Australia was an early convert to the digital television transition but, like many countries, experienced some problems along the way.

Australia launched terrestrial digital signals in January 2001 and made digital television available in all major urban centres that same year. The initial transition plan, tabled by the Department of Communications, Information Technology, and the Arts in 2000, called for DTV to be put in motion across the rest of the country by 2011. Analogue signals would be shut off completely in major centres by the end of 2008. The plan outlined details of the shift, which included a peace offering to incumbent broadcasters by declaring a moratorium on new commercial television licenses until the end of 2006.[21] Much like those in Canada, Australian private broadcasters were initially reluctant to make the investment required for a successful transition. In an effort to appease commercial broadcasters' concerns, the plan also limited the use of multichannel offerings by public broadcasters – a tool many private broadcasters saw as a potential form of increased competition.

Australia has a very strong OTA penetration. Cable was only introduced in 1994, and only approximately 30 per cent of households subscribed to cable or satellite in 2006.[22] The early plan was to introduce HD programming into the system by requiring that OTA broadcasters transmit 1,040 hours of HD programming per year, which would in turn create demand for digital HD receivers. Australia chose to adopt the European DVB standard – the only country to choose the DVB-T standard requiring HDTV from the outset.[23]

Despite its availability, Australians were initially slow to switch to digital reception. By 2006, only 20 per cent of Australian households had adopted digital television.[24] This slow growth prompted a government reassessment of the ambitious transition plan that same year. The revised timetable for the digital switchover was announced by Stephen Conroy, the minister for broadband, communications, and the digital economy, on 19 October 2008 and determined the switch from analogue to digital would take place between 2010 and 2013 in a phased approach that would start with the Victorian Region in early

Fig. 3.2 Australia's "Get Ready for Digital TV" mascot Digital Freddy. Courtesy of Digital Switchover Taskforce, 2012

2010 and finish in Western Australia in 2013. The plan would start with small country markets with digital-only stations and hence high take-up (such as Mildura and Tasmania), and would end with the major cities in 2013.

After this scheduling shift, there were clear signs of a successful Australian digital transition. The fourth quarter *2011 Digital Tracker Report*, a government survey of over 10,000 households, found that roughly 95 per cent of respondents were aware of the digital transition and over 82 per cent had already converted to receiving digital signals.[25] The survey found similar positive data for attitude, intention, understanding, and satisfaction of the digital switchover to date. Australia has been very attentive to both the physical roll-out of hardware, and also to the public awareness and knowledge necessary for a successful transition.

There are similarities between the Australian and UK transitions, and with good reason. Andy Townend is the executive director of the Digital Switchover Taskforce, which coordinates and oversees Australia's transition to digital television. Townend was previously the chief operating officer of Digital UK. The taskforce was set up within the Australian Federal Department of Broadband, Communications and the Digital Economy in much the same way that Digital UK was structured as an independent body. The results have been similarly impressive. Australia even has an animated digital television mascot, Digital Freddy, who looks suspiciously like the UK's Digit Al (see fig. 3.2).[26]

In a unique initiative, the Australian government licenses retail employees who pass a government assessment test on digital transition knowledge. These approved "Digital Advisors" wear a badge displaying the government's Get Ready for Digital TV logo, and can inform customers about when the switchover will happen in a local area as well as the range of equipment options available.[27] This is part of a greater quality assurance scheme that gives the government stamp of approval for equipment manufacturers and installation specialists. Approved businesses are also endorsed on the government's "Are You Ready for Digital TV?" website to let citizens know the businesses meet industry standards.

After a shaky launch, the Australian system seems on course for a successful transition to digital television. The country demonstrates attention to detail in all phases of the transition. From the overall infrastructure to a committed roll-out schedule to carefully monitoring public understanding to the retail experience, Australia has invested a great deal of energy in its transition, and the investment has paid off.

France

France is "a success story in digital TV."[28] Few, if any, countries exploited digital television's convergence with the Internet and telecommunications as early and successfully as France. As did all of Europe, France adopted the DVB standard, but has emphasized an integrated communications package more strongly than many other European countries. The French transition took full advantage of multiple distribution systems and relied on a combination of terrestrial, cable, satellite, and a unique French triple play involving Internet, telephone, and digital television. Subscribers receive the triple play offers as Asymmetric Digital Subscriber Line (ADSL) services, which enables faster data transmission over existing copper phone lines. France leveraged the full digitization of its telephone infrastructure, starting in 1975 and was fully digital in the 1980s, which created one of the most advanced telecommunications networks in the world.[29]

For a monthly fee of approximately €30, French subscribers can receive a basic set of TV channels, broadband cable Internet, and unlimited phone calls. The capacity of the French system received a substantial boost in 2004 when ADSL2+ technology increased the speed of the Internet connection from 8 megabits per second to 20 Mb/s.[30] New MPEG-4 compression technology allows for growing HD distribution, which was not required in the original SD-based French transition. The early success of IPTV (Internet Protocol television) is a distinctive feature of the French market: IPTV subscribers increased by more than 2 million in 2008 alone, while IPTV was still in its infancy in North America.[31] France became a world leader in this growing distribution technology. IPTV operators such as France Telecom-Orange, ADSL pioneer Free, and SFR-Neuf Cegetel quickly made IPTV more popular than cable.

France's digital terrestrial TNT (télévision numérique terrestre) service began at the end of March 2005 and the coverage rate reached 88 per cent of the population in July 2009.[32] Digital terrestrial in France offers eighteen free channels, including the four public broadcasting services. For the first time, analogue terrestrial signals were switched off in some locations in 2009, and the complete national transition finished in November 2011.

As with many successful national transition plans, France had an organization designed to raise public awareness. Tous au numerique! (All digital!) was a public information campaign run by le Groupement d'Intérêt Public France Télé Numérique (French Digital Television Public Interest Group) to inform and assist French viewers.[33] The government body that oversaw the French transition was the Comité stratégique pour le numérique (CSN), which included several high-ranking government officials and was chaired by the prime minister. Three key principles for transition guided the committee:

- All French viewers, especially those most in need, will be given the necessary assistance to achieve the digital switchover.
- The spectrum freed by the transition will be used wisely in conjunction with European neighbours.

- All French citizens will benefit from the services (HD, digital radio, mobile television, and wireless) facilitated by the digital transition.[34]

In December 2008, the CSN updated the plan for France to include:

- Funding to allow people unable to access terrestrial digital television after the November 2011 ASO to acquire the necessary satellite equipment.
- A plan for a collective antennae in government-run housing projects so all residents can access digital terrestrial television.
- A plan for residents of island areas that are not part of the digital roll-out strategy.

In 2009, the French prime minister called on the government to make €277 million available for the transition process.[35]

The French approach is noteworthy for its multiple distribution strategy, strong emphasis on accessibility and public interest objectives, high-ranking government involvement, and pioneering work in combining telephone, Internet, and digital television delivery.

China

As it is in many areas of communications, China is finding its own path to digital television. China strives to create a balance between increasing the flow of information and maintaining state control over access to certain material. Given China's place as the world's largest manufacturer of television sets, it should be no surprise that the country has also developed its own technical standard for OTA digital television, known as DMB-T (digital media broadcasting terrestrial, or more formally GB20600-2006. GB stands for *guo biao*, "national standard" in Mandarin). China finalized this standard in 2006 and began transmission with the Beijing Olympics. DMB-T reduces the need to buy foreign products or pay royalties to foreign patents. By waiting and studying other international standards, China believes it may have developed the most comprehensive digital television standard yet.[36]

Control of information remains a unique characteristic of the Chinese market. China banned ownership of DTH satellite dishes in 1993, though it makes exceptions for hotels and foreign compounds. Cable became the most prevalent BDU in the country (140 million households) largely due to the ease of control it allows over foreign transmissions.[37] However, cable still only accounts for 30 per cent of television reception – 70 per cent of households rely on OTA television.[38] As they do in much of the world, the increasing differences between urban and rural areas challenge China's digital television structure. Rural China overwhelmingly relies on freely accessible OTA broadcasts. While the ASO in the major cities began in 2005, the date for completing the transition in the more sparsely populated western region is set for 2015.[39]

DMB-T's late arrival may have worked to China's advantage by improving previous international standards. The signal for DMB-T is strong enough for mobile television reception on a high-speed train going 200 kilometres per hour.[40] According to Raj Karamchedu, whose Fremont, California-based company Legend Silicon Corp developed the standard in conjunction with Tsinghua University in Beijing, the Chinese standard is better equipped to handle changes in weather and physical obstructions in transmission because it is able to rearrange the transmitter signal before transmission in anticipation of the atmospheric effects.[41]

In late December 2008, China's State Administration of Radio, Film, and Television announced that China would invest ¥2.5 billion (USD $366 million) to build a national digital TV network based on the new DMB-T standard. In 2010, Laos allegedly became the first country outside of China to adopt DMB-T.[42] This remains unconfirmed in 2012. When compared to the United States, Europe, and Japan, China has not demonstrated significant interest in promoting its standard on the global marketplace.

Brazil

There is an aspiring communications power growing in South America and it is using the digital television transition to announce its presence on the world stage. Brazil is a clear case of what can happen when a growing economy, coupled with strong government guidance, seizes initiative in a period of intensified technological transition. Under President Luiz Inácio Lula da Silva, Brazil flexed some of its emerging economic muscle to develop a digital standard based on, yet unique from, the Japanese ISDB model. The resulting Sistema Brasilerio de Televisao Digital Terrestre (SBTD-T) has the potential to become the de facto digital television standard for all of South America.

This newest addition to the small list of digital broadcasting standards borrows heavily from Japanese technology, but adds some distinct touches. Though Brazil initially planned to create a completely new technical standard, the costs of such a venture proved overwhelming.[43] Instead, it added specific standards for video encoding and a Brazilian-developed middleware to ISDB. This will ensure that Brazil will reap some of the financial rewards and further its own industrial interests by manufacturing the required middleware. SBTD-T is a truly national Brazilian venture: a total of 105 institutions, including industry, universities, research centres, and broadcasting companies, participated in the project.[44]

The new system remains true to Brazil's commitment to open source technology. Brazil chose the Japanese standard and plans to add locally developed components, which Japan and other countries using ISDB could eventually incorporate into their systems.[45] After examining the international standards, Brazil decided the ATSC emphasis on HD was not nearly as significant as the access to mobile devices offered by Japan. In a manoeuvre that echoed France allowing the Soviet Union free access to its analogue standard fifty years earlier, Japan exempted Brazil from royalty payments and offered funding for the transition from the PAL analogue system to SBTD-T.

The United States recognized the importance of the Brazilian transition within the greater sphere of South America and lobbied hard for Brazil to adopt the American-made ATSC standard. In April 2006, E. Anthony Wayne, the US assistant secretary for the Bureau of Economic and Business Affairs, spoke to the Commercial Association of Sao Paulo, Brazil:

> I'd like to briefly discuss Brazil's vibrant telecommunications industry. I understand that President Lula is going to announce the selection of the Brazilian digital TV standard soon.
>
> Of the several options on the table, we believe the ATSC standard ... offers the best combination of economic, social, and technical advantages. It has been adopted by the US, Canada, Mexico and South Korea. These countries that have adopted the ATSC standards are seeing a rapid increase in the sales of high definition television products. Brazil's adoption of the ATSC standard will ensure a hemispheric standard, creating a market of 800 million people for DTV products and services.

> The US no longer manufactures television sets. This positions Brazil to supply high definition television sets, converter boxes, and transmission equipment throughout the Hemisphere. Brazil's potential role as a leading supplier will help create high-paying, highly skilled jobs and significant economic development.
>
> The US Overseas Private Investment Corporation has set aside $150 million for US companies to invest in information technology development projects in Brazil. And US companies have already expressed their intention of making significant investments in ATSC-related manufacturing in Brazil.
>
> ATSC's open development process ensures Brazil a significant role in the evolution of the standard. Evolving ATSC standards present great opportunities for Brazilian-US and Brazilian-South Korean collaboration and partnership.[46]

The extensive lobbying efforts of the US were unsuccessful. In June 2006, President da Silva signed a decree to officially define the Brazilian transition period from analogue to digital television and establish SBTD as the standard. Digital OTA signals started in Sao Paulo in 2007 and the roll-out is scheduled to continue across the country through 2013.

The Brazilian market is the biggest in South America, and the Brazilian Ministry of Communications has promoted the new Brazilian standard throughout the continent. As of June 2010, Chile, Argentina, Peru, Paraguay, Ecuador, Venezuela, and Costa Rica have adopted this unique Brazilian-Japanese hybrid.[47] Brazil's influence in this sector seems destined to expand in the coming years.

South Africa

South Africa plays a pivotal role in the culture and economy of the southern region of the African continent and the ambiguity of its digital future. While in the bulk of this chapter I have emphasized the role of national governments in determining the progress of digital television for their respective citizens, there is little doubt that the decisions made in South Africa will have strong implications for many African nations. The country is also noteworthy because it was the scene of an intense international lobbying effort in 2010.

Great uncertainty surrounds the future of digital television in South Africa. In 2006, South Africa and other countries in the Southern African Development Community agreed to implement the European standard for terrestrial television, DVB-T, as they switched from analogue to digital terrestrial broadcasts. The South African government publicly committed to launching digital signals across the country by November 2011 and to allowing both analogue and digital signals until 2015.[48] The ASO date of 2015 was part of an agreement signed with African, Middle Eastern, and European representatives at the ITU in 2006.[49] Other regional governments in the area are following South Africa's lead.

In May 2010, the *Financial Mail* of South Africa reported that the government might reverse its agreement with the ITU to adopt DVB-T.[50] Despite the fact that such a decision could set the transition back years, the government reportedly considered other standards, including Japan's integrated services digital broadcasting (ISDB-T) standard. According to the *Financial Mail*, Gerhard Petrick of the Southern African Digital Broadcasting Association believes "that the department of communications has bought into the sales talk of Japanese and Brazilian lobbyists."[51] On 6 May 2010, the official website for the DVB standard posted that "the government is suddenly reviewing its 2006 decision to adopt DVB-T as its national digital terrestrial television standard. In 2006 South Africa signed the [ITU] agreement, confirming the decision to use DVB-T. Now, however, this decision doesn't seem so clear."[52]

The communications industry in South Africa was not pleased at the prospect of changing standards this late in the process. While the World Cup played out in soccer stadiums around the country in 2010, a bitter technological and political battle unfolded. All this was happening as the Brazilian president, Lula da Silva, travelled to South Africa in the summer of 2010 on an official visit. Brazil has industrial interests in digital television and could stand to benefit from a South African move away from DVB-T. Da Silva's visit added further uncertainty to an already volatile situation.

At a 24 January 2012 press conference, the South African minister of communications, Dina Pule, revealed that the public launch date of digital terrestrial television in South Africa would be pushed back from the previously announced April 2012. In the spring of 2012 there was still no official technical standard for the South African system.

CONCLUSION: THE INTERNATIONAL DIGITAL TELEVISION TRANSITION

In a 2009 study in the journal *Media, Culture and Society*, María Trinidad García Leiva and Michael Starks examine the regional patterns of the global digital switchover and conclude there is no global set of standards. However, they note there are a number of consistent factors at play for each country, including characteristics of the analogue TV system, size of the domestic TV market, and sources of imported TV receivers and programs.[53]

The selection of a technical standard is a key stage of the transition and is influenced by national priorities (structure of the analogue platform, mobile TV considerations, traditional sources of programs and equipment, patent royalty costs, etc.) and strong international and regional forces. As the Brazil case demonstrates, more powerful national economies have more room to manoeuvre in these deals – a luxury that may not be afforded to the developing world. It also seems as though another regional power, South Africa, is shopping among suitors for the best deal in technical standards.

After a decade of powerful international lobbying, significant elements of the global switchover remain uncertain. The emergence of new standards in Brazil and China has changed the international landscape of digital television. Galperin notes of the early American aspirations to international dominance in digital television: "Having developed the world's first digital TV system is a rather Pyrrhic victory for a nation without substantial interests in TV set manufacturing and that has been largely unable to capitalize on such technological leadership."[54] In 2009, the ATSC Forum, the lobbying arm of the US digital television standard, announced it was disbanding. This announcement came on the same day that Chile announced it had chosen to use ISDB-T despite twelve years of American lobbying on behalf of ATSC.[55] Far from establishing a new cultural and industrial empire via digital television, the United States has proven vulnerable to more adaptable technology from other countries.

US and European standards may have been the first to go to market, but the ISDB-T system has gained momentum in recent years. In the end, Chile decided that the ATSC reliance on MPEG-2 technology is inferior to ISDB's incorporation of MPEG-4, and ISDB is superior for mobile reception. The ability to access OTA television signals with smartphones is seen as a key selling feature in many regions where the economics are not as tied to cable and satellite distribution. Other undecided countries around the world are watching closely. As of 2012, many Asian countries, including India, have not made official decisions regarding digital television standards.

The success of a country's transition depends on a number of variables including market size; the balance between cable, satellite, and terrestrial; a set period of analogue/digital simulcasting; market size; and maturity. The transition can be made easier when OTA signals are not the dominant mode of reception, since it is easier to switch cable.[56] To judge by much of these criteria, Canada should have been in a position for a relatively smooth digital television transition; yet 2011 saw much of the country's over-the-air market remain analogue, and that the CBC will likely never complete the switch as planned. Why is Canada in this position despite years of preparation, studies, and reports? Karen Wirsig, communications coordinator for the Canadian Media Guild, a group that has consistently voiced concerns over the transition in recent years, stated in an interview that she believes Canada's transition is "as weak as we've seen anywhere in the world."[57]

Almost all the other countries examined in this chapter have a much more involved government presence. In the United Kingdom (Digital UK and the Help Scheme), France (Tous au Numerique), Australia (Digital Ready), and Brazil (Sistema Brasileiro de TV Digital), governments have set up organizations to take the lead in the national transition strategy. In Canada, the technical organization CDTV disbanded in 2006 due to lack of government support and was not replaced as the ASO loomed near. Canada's ATSC standard looks less and less like the best technology possible (it cannot currently run with MPEG-4 and is poorly suited to mobile reception, though an ATSC 2.0 was announced in 2012), but given the interconnectedness of the economies and cultures, there is very little chance it (or Mexico) would try an alternative. In her 1979 book *The Politics of International Standards*, Rhonda Crane refers to standards as a "non-tariff device for promoting an industry."[58] In the NAFTA era, where North America is increasingly treated as one tariff-free market, it should come as little surprise that Canadian digital television will move forward with ATSC.

The rest of the world is not so determined. For some countries, HD is an expensive and largely unnecessary luxury that may eventually come with new compression technology after all. These countries are more concerned with accessibility in remote regions and the ability to incorporate television with expanding wireless and Internet access. In many ways, countries with expanding economies, as opposed to those with entrenched incumbent interests, have more opportunity to explore the potential of digital television.

The limited global success of ATSC indicates changing global economic power dynamics. The Cold War era, as reflected in the distribution of analogue television standards, is clearly no more. Traditional trading partners and geographic regions (North America, Europe, and South America) have solidified their industrial connections through digital television standards, while new and expanding economies like China and Brazil have seized this moment to expand their spheres of economic influence. A survey of the worldwide switch from analogue signals demonstrates the range of options facing individual countries. Digital television is a global technological upheaval; however, from selecting standards to constructing appropriate transition models, national governments remain essential in charting the course for the future of digital broadcasting.

4

Broadcasting Distribution Undertakings

Penetration of cable and satellite distribution is a key precondition in determining the direction of a nation's overall strategy in the transition from analogue to digital television. During the Canadian transition, the development of policy and regulations for distributors has been a primary site of industry debate. In 2010, broadcasting distribution undertakings' (BDUs – cable, satellite, and IPTV in Canada) income accounted for the majority (52 per cent) of all Canadian broadcasting revenue; television accounted for 38 per cent and radio accounted for 10 per cent.[1] The power of cable, and later direct-to-home (DTH) satellite, providers has grown for decades and the digital transition has the potential to consolidate their hold or introduce new distribution methods that could potentially destabilize the overall power structure of Canadian television.

Over 90 per cent of Canadians subscribed to a BDU service in 2010, and so it is not hyperbole to say the future of Canadian broadcasting hangs in the balance. Consumers have shown a strong appetite for the steady increase in channels provided by television distributors and are long past the 500-channel universe. As the CRTC noted in 2008, "The variety of domestic services available to Canadian viewers is greater than that of any other country except the US."[2]

The detailed rules surrounding BDUs are quintessentially Canadian. They determine the opportunity for exposure for many Canadian productions through CanCon obligations; set parameters for funding Canadian productions via BDU contributions to the Canadian Media Fund and Local Programming Improvement Fund; limit foreign ownership (an increasingly contested area); determine which international channels are allowed; and encourage new developments and smaller operations by not subjecting them to the same regulatory obligations as larger distribution systems. In short, BDU regulations offer a window into the greater Canadian broadcasting system.

Despite the technologically neutral language of the 1991 Broadcasting Act, policy and regulations in this field regularly need revision and the CRTC has tried valiantly to stay on top of the rapid evolution.[3] The CRTC released its first policy statement on cable television in 1971 (Canadian Broadcasting "A Single System" – Policy Statement on Cable Television), which attempted to reign in the divisive potential of cable distribution on sovereignty over the greater Canadian system by introducing policies such as substitution of local channels and commercials on distant cable signals.[4] In November 1975, the CRTC released the first formal cable television regulations (Regulations Respecting Broadcasting Receiving Undertakings), which codified much of the 1971 policy announcement.[5] Those regulations were in turn replaced by the Cable Television Regulations, 1986, which, in 1998, was repealed and replaced by the Broadcasting Distribution Regulations (the BDU regulations), since satellite distribution now challenged cable. In 2008, the CRTC made further changes with the new policy document, Regulatory Frameworks for Broadcasting Distribution Undertakings and Discretionary Programming Services (CRTC 2008-100), though the essential elements of the regulations remained intact.

The traditional BDU regulatory structure, which was based on the analogue model and had operated in various forms since the 1970s, is doomed to fail in the digital era. The structure focuses on territories and time slots – the very things challenged in a digital environment. The BDU sector is continually in flux and the options digital makes possible will further challenge current regulatory structures before this book is released.[6] While the overall digital effect on BDUs is still developing, certain patterns have emerged. The still-powerful position of legacy distribution industries is due to a combination of entrenched audience habits, new customer services, and a concerted effort to keep new technologies from disrupting the status quo.

Most broadcasters and program creators in Canada live or die by their access to cable and satellite distribution. Given the dominance of a relatively few players in this area and its central position for other sectors within Canadian broadcasting, increased regulatory reliance on market forces for BDUs is a precarious proposition for the greater system, yet has been the consistent CRTC approach even before basic cable rates were deregulated by the CRTC in 2003.[7] Despite this continued faith in the market's invisible hand, any sense of competitive economic forces at work in this sector is a bit of a stretch. Broadcasting distribution in Canada is a limited economy that incumbents fiercely defend. BDUS occasionally flaunt their clout within the system – they are conscious of their position of power. There are cases of non-competition agreements between companies in certain Canadian regions that mock a genuine free market.[8] The introduction of DTH and, more recently, Internet Protocol television (IPTV) has allowed for some increase in competition, but television distribution in Canada is still largely an oligopoly.

The single language of digitally encoded information greatly increases the possibilities for transmission, and so it is not being determinist to observe that the digital transition is instigating sweeping changes in the broadcasting distribution industry. Cable and, more recently, satellite dominated for decades but now face competition from upstart IPTV, new over-the-top (OTT) services such as Netflix, Apple TV, Google TV, and mobile video on smartphones and tablets. For the foreseeable future, the enormous expansion in choice that digital television affords is largely restricted to Canadians with cable and satellite access, though there has been some regional growth in IPTV. Unlike the UK digital transition plan, the Canadian plan has not emphasized the opportunity digital allows for new entrants in the system. Internet and mobile television applications are intriguing, but have yet to make a dramatic impact in the market.

The regulations for Canadian BDUS are complex and wide ranging; therefore, in this chapter I will focus on the industry changes brought about by the digital transition and some of the BDU regulations and policies that affect the overall viability of the digital television project in Canada.[9] In order to assess the role of BDUS in the greater digital transition, it is necessary to look at the various sectors individually. The challenges facing this branch of the system are by no means uniform. The technical, political, and financial obstacles that face an incumbent power like Rogers are different from those that face a young IPTV distributor serving one small community. Like much of the Canadian broadcasting system, any sense of one cohesive industry is misleading. As I demonstrate in this chapter, the track record of BDUS in the policy-making process leaves little doubt of the clear divisions within this Canadian business.

The growth of this sector over the last two decades has meant profound changes for the greater Canadian system: traditional OTA broadcasting is no longer dominant; revenue comes more from subscriptions than advertising; broadcasters offer a far greater number of channels; broadcasters are much less inclined to invest in transmission equipment for OTA signals; and local broadcasting struggles to stay afloat. Television broadcasters are now far less profitable than the distribution sector built around carrying their signals. As David Taras and Marc Raboy note, in Canada, subscriptions surpassed advertising as the primary basis for financing television services in 1991; the same developments did not occur in the United States and Britain until 2003.[10] This power imbalance has led to some tense standoffs at the CRTC.

THE PUBLIC SKIRMISH

Many Canadians were introduced to the battlefield tactics of broadcasting distribution in the summer of 2009 when the broadcasters and distributors took their lengthy fee-for-carriage (FFC) fight into the public arena with a series of expensive and misleading television advertisements. The FFC debate is not specifically a product of the digital transition, but it does demonstrate the increasing power BDUS wield in the Canadian system. The ensuing rift between BDUS and traditional broadcasters hindered Canada's progression to digital.

At issue was whether BDUS should pay local OTA broadcasters for their signals, as is the case with most channels on cable or satellite. The arrangement has long been that local OTA broadcasters do not receive fee-for-carriage from BDUS because they receive other perks, such as exclusive rights to local advertising, guaranteed carriage on basic cable packages, and the made-in-Canada simultaneous advertising substitution, in which BDUS are required to substitute local advertising when Canadian broadcasters carry a show at the same time as an American station. For example, a viewer watching *House* on Fox out of Buffalo, NY, on Toronto cable will see ads from the local Global affiliate that runs the program at the same time. The thirty-year-old policy reinforces the local programming rights of the broadcaster,[11] and provides extra revenue for OTA broadcasters to compensate for their greater transmission expenses and lack of access to FFC afforded to specialty channels. This simulcasting was far more feasible under the earlier analogue regime when OTA audiences were large, schedules were rigid, and areas of reception, even on cable, were relatively local.

In recent years, OTA broadcasters have repeatedly asked the CRTC to force BDUs to pay local broadcasters for their signals. The CRTC refused this request on two occasions (2007 and 2008), but the battle did not cease.

The significance of the FFC dispute in the Canadian digital television transition cannot be overstated. The series of arguments over OTA broadcaster's right to access BDU subscription fees was instrumental in shaping Canada's current climate of uncertainty in the digital OTA sector. The seemingly interminable squabbles over FFC shifted focus from the required task of converting the sector to digital. In an interview, Michel Arpin, former CRTC vice chair of broadcasting, notes, "Every time the issue [OTA conversion] was brought up, formally and informally, fee-for-carriage was the mantra. 'With fee-for-carriage we'll do it' [switch to digital]. It was a threat to the commission."[12] This prolonged policy drama unfolded in public hearings before the CRTC and in Canada's living rooms. Despite two previous rejections by the CRTC, the fight started again in 2009 – this time with some success for the broadcasters.

In 2009, OTA broadcasters, led by CTV, launched the first salvo of the public relations drive with their "Local TV Matters" campaign. Commercials, often run during local newscasts, claimed the fabric of local broadcasting was at risk if local broadcasters did not receive reimbursement from the BDUs that carried their signals. These ads asked Canadians to notify the government and the CRTC about this injustice. In one memorable 2009 spot, broadcasters enlisted the services of Canadian songwriter Dave Carroll to perform "The Cable Song." Carroll was a minor celebrity at the time for writing a song that became an online hit in protest of United Airlines called "United Breaks Guitars." "The Cable Song" included lines such as "cable company cash cows getting milk for free," and called on the regulator, "come on CRTC, it's show time," while suit-wearing cable executives tried to disguise themselves as cows in order to get free milk. The three-minute ad ran the span of an entire commercial break. It did not contextualize the greater broadcasting system, but was an emotional appeal to a sense of community, as the local farmers (i.e., broadcasters) tried to protect their milk from the cable barons.

The cable companies countered in 2009 with their "Stop the TV Tax" campaign, which used the dreaded "T" word to describe fee-for-carriage. Many of these ads incorporated an ambush technique in which the announcer asked seemingly oblivious passers-by on the street what they thought of a tax on their cable bills. Not surprisingly, citizens expressed anger at the thought. Of course, FFC is not a "tax" at all, but a potential extra expense for BDUs, which they said they would pass to consumers. The advertisements were ripe for parody and received just that when the CBC show the *Rick Mercer Report* offered its version of the overwrought debate. In this spoof, some passers-by were reduced to tears at the thought of a higher cable bill and another asked, "Why couldn't I have been born during biblical times when the worst thing that could happen would be a visit from the angel of death?"[13]

Both campaigns were disingenuous and did little to further critical debate about the place of broadcasting. In the spring of 2010, the CRTC ruled broadcasters, excluding the CBC, could negotiate for fees from BDUs (there was no guarantee, but BDUs objected nonetheless) and potentially withhold their signals. Anticipating legal challenges, the CRTC sent the decision to the Federal Court of Appeal for review.[14] In March 2011, the Federal Court of Appeal ruled FFC should be allowed, which triggered an appeal by TV distributors Cogeco Cable Inc, Rogers Communications Inc, Telus Communications Co, and Shaw Communications Inc to the Supreme Court of Canada. Hearings at the country's highest court began in April 2012.

The argument seems moot in many ways, given the recent consolidation of the Canadian broadcasting industry. Since Shaw purchased Canwest in 2010 and Bell purchased CTV (for the second time – Bell also purchased CTV in 2000 but later sold its interest) that same year, BDUs and conventional broadcasters have been different pieces of the same vertically integrated company. Since 2007, the FFC debates have raged on while the development of digital infrastructure in Canada was left waiting. The years spent in pursuit of cable dollars were devastating for the necessary development of digital OTA distribution infrastructure in Canada.

PRODUCT OR SERVICE?

Legal dramas, satire, and propaganda aside: cable, DTH satellite, and multipoint distribution systems (MDS, found in a few multi-dwelling buildings) are essential, highly profitable elements of Canadian broadcasting and their future is of great consequence to the wider system. Despite a trend of deregulation in the field for more than a decade, there remains little actual competition. Certainly, Canada is no longer subject to the cable monopolies of the pre-DTH era, but large-scale distribution remains a rather exclusive club.

The BDU industry in Canada is run by "the big five," a handful of large, financially robust companies: Bell, Shaw (cable and satellite), Rogers, Quebecor, and Cogeco. The top four cable BDUS and the two DTH providers captured 92 per cent of all BDU subscribers in 2010. The many smaller BDUS serve only 8 per cent of subscribers.[15] The CRTC has traditionally differentiated regulations between class one (those with over 6,000 subscribers), class two (between 2,000 and 6,000 subscribers), and class three (fewer than 2,000 subscribers) BDUS. Each class has different must-carry obligations. In 2008, the CRTC reacted to the changing distribution marketplace and determined that after the digital transition in 2011 there will only be two categories, with some license exemptions made for terrestrial BDUS (cable, MDS, and IPTV) that have less than 20,000 subscribers.[16]

The sector is strong. Revenue growth has remained consistent, even during recent threats of a global recession. The compound annual growth rate for the BDU sector of the Canadian broadcasting system grew by 8.8 per cent between 2006 and 2010.[17] In 2010, the average BDU subscriber paid $59.73 a month and BDU profits accounted for more than half of the total $15.7 billion made in the Canadian broadcasting system, including television and radio.[18] Fortunes are made and lost in the regulations surrounding BDUS.

The CRTC has taken a deregulatory position on BDUS, which has helped fuel years of strong growth in the sector.[19] Since 2001, BDUS have been permitted to own programming services, leading to potential conflicts with competing broadcasters. In 2000, in a break with tradition, the CRTC allowed BDUS to own category two digital channels and, in 2001, permitted BDUS to own discretionary analogue channels.[20] As a result, BDU companies are no longer just pipes, but are increasingly content providers as well. Shaw's bid for the Canwest television network in the spring of 2010, followed by Bell's offer to purchase CTVglobemedia a few months later, and its offer of $3.4 billion for Astral Media in 2012, are just the most recent high-profile examples of a broadcast purchasing spree by Canadian BDUS. In 1987, the CRTC approved the sale of Télé-Métropole, Quebec's most profitable privately owned station (flagship of the TVA network), to cable powerhouse Videotron. In 2001, Quebecor purchased Videotron for $5 billion. Another major cable company dove into television broadcasting when Rogers bought five Chum/CityTV stations across Canada in 2007.

All these acquisitions have a great impact for Canadians, both as media consumers and as citizens who require information. The widespread adoption of BDU services by the Canadian public has placed these distribution companies in the role of television gatekeepers for many citizens. Since BDUs are now often broadcasters as well, there is legitimate concern that carriage arrangements may favour other vertically integrated BDU properties. As such, there is a strong correlation between BDUs and the public interest element within the Canadian broadcasting system; hence the necessity of regulatory oversight. Communication lawyer Bram Abramson describes the place of regulation in this sector: "BDUs are regulated, among other reasons, to ensure that they do not take advantage of their position as access providers in a way that prefers the content they themselves own (to the detriment of their content competitors) and to ensure that programming created by Canadians can make it to the air notwithstanding the substantial cost advantage enjoyed by US programming."[21]

The success of BDUs has made them not only a consumer product, but also a necessary part of the broadcasting system, subject to legislative authority beyond the federal regulator. The CRTC is obligated to enforce the 1991 Broadcasting Act, which mandates that distribution undertakings:

> Should give priority to the carriage of Canadian programming services and, in particular, to the carriage of local Canadian stations,
>
> should provide efficient delivery of programming at affordable rates, using the most effective technologies available at reasonable cost,
>
> should, where programming services are supplied to them by broadcasting undertakings pursuant to contractual arrangements, provide reasonable terms for the carriage, packaging and retailing of those programming services, and may, where the Commission considers it appropriate, originate programming, including local programming, on such terms as are conducive to the achievement of the objectives of the broadcasting policy set out in this subsection, and in particular provide access for underserved linguistic and cultural minority communities.[22]

The legislative emphasis is on Canadian and in particular local services, but the act still grants the CRTC a great deal of leeway in how these policy objectives are achieved.

MUST-CARRY OBLIGATIONS

One of the key policy tools the CRTC has at its disposal is to impose must-carry obligations on BDUS. The digital environment's greater opportunities for choice requires some regulatory reinforcement so that channels continue to receive the coveted must-carry status. In 2006, the CRTC's Digital Migration Framework established that all BDUS must continue to carry services that are deemed to be in the greater public interest (TVA, APTN, CPAC, and VoicePrint – known as 9(1)(h) services, referencing the corresponding paragraph of the Broadcasting Act) in their basic service offerings, whether their system is analogue, digital, or a hybrid.[23] BDUS must offer the Accessible Channel, Météomédia/the Weather Network, CBC Newsworld (in French-language markets), Le Réseau de l'information (RDI; in English-language markets), and Avis de recherche (by BDUS that serve Quebec subscribers) on digital basic service. Section 3 of the act deems 9(1)(h) services beneficial to its greater policy goals, and it is here that the role of BDUS as essential conduits between citizens is most apparent.

The majority of the must-carry rules make certain Canadian viewers can access Canadian productions. In this sense, the BDU regulations serve both cultural and industrial interests. In the hearings that followed the 2004 *Call for Comments on a Proposed Framework for the Licensing and Distribution of High Definition Pay and Specialty Services* (CRTC 2004-58), Canadian BDUS, represented by the CCTA, submitted that the commission's application of traditional must-carry rules for digital HD signals failed to address the realities of the market, and was therefore "inappropriate for a number of reasons."[24] BDUS requested complete discretion over which HD channels they carry. Shaw proposed that there be no carriage obligations imposed on BDUS with respect to the distribution of HD services, either during or after the transition to digital distribution. Rather, the company considered that consumer demand and the capacity of each cable system should determine whether a BDU distributes a particular HD service.[25] This approach would place broadcasters at the whim of the BDUS, and they in turn protested this position. The CRTC ruled against the BDUS and maintained certain must-carry obligations under digital distribution.

BDU regulations are in constant need of revision and the CRTC used the opportunity provided by the 2008 Western Canadian Cable license renewal (not viewed as a major hearing) to clarify the must-carry obligations of cable BDUS across the whole country:

> Accordingly, the Commission will amend the BDU Regulations so as to require terrestrial BDUS to distribute the following priority services on the basic service (the order of services establishes priority for simultaneous substitution purposes, where applicable).
>
> locally owned and operated English- and French-language CBC television stations broadcasting in the market served;
>
> the educational television programming service, the operation of which is the responsibility of an educational authority designated by the province in which the licensed area of the undertaking is located (provincial educational programming service);
>
> all other local television stations;
>
> regional stations owned and operated by the CBC, if no local CBC stations are already carried;
>
> all other regional stations, other than those regional stations affiliated with local of the same network already carried;
>
> at least one owned and operated or affiliate CBC English-language television station and one owned and operated or affiliate CBC French-language television station, if not already carried;
>
> and services mandated for distribution on the basic service pursuant to an order under section 9(1)(h) of the Act.[26]

Thus, cable BDUS must still serve local bases. Since BDUS are legally broadcasters, they are subject to public service obligations as determined by CRTC policy.

The digital transition emphasizes the cable operators, as DTH satellite transmissions have always been a digital service (the twelve-foot-wide reception dishes that sprung up in the 1980s were analogue), though DTH too poses regulatory challenges for HD and transmission capacity. The must-carry obligations of DTH are different from those imposed on cable. Given that the satellite footprint is national, it is not feasible for DTH providers to carry every local channel across the country.[27] As a compromise, the CRTC requires distribution, on the basic service within each province, of a selection of provincially based local television stations, including educational services. Specifically, DTH undertakings are required to distribute one television station per province, where such a station exists, from each of the major broadcast ownership groups: CBC English, CBC French, Canwest, CTV, Rogers, TQS, and TVA.[28]

There are two regulatory approaches based in the analogue era and unique to BDUs: preponderance and tiers. The idea of preponderance ensured that the services BDUs offered would carry a majority of Canadian channels. Tiers referred to the various packages consumers might purchase from a BDU. For example, the Broadcasting Distribution Regulations state that the first tier channels must include all 9(1)(h) services, the CBC in French and English, the provincial education television stations, all local stations, and regional or extra-regional stations where a local station is not available.[29]

There was also a discretionary tier where BDUs had the power to determine carriage requirements and packaging, but had to offer the approved channels to subscribers. Tiers ensure BDUs not only include certain Canadian channels in their services but also give them preferred access. BDUs are not allowed to offer subscribers packages that do not include Canadians channels. This system traditionally provided some support for specialty services, as it ensured they received the benefits of packaging with other services.[30] BDUs argued against maintaining tiers in the digital era to allow them greater flexibility in what they offer consumers.

A tiered system is more difficult to maintain when choice becomes more abundant and viewers select individual programs in a digital environment. It runs counter to the "what I want, when I want" ethos that pervades across digital media. The CRTC recognized that obligations on BDUs are more challenging in a digital system and in 2007 moved toward removing some tier and packaging obligations: "It is the Commission's view that program packaging should be a matter left more to negotiations between programmers and distributors. Accordingly, the Commission proposes to eliminate most of the distribution and linkage rules."[31] Complicated tier requirements are simplified in the digital era, but BDUs must still support Canadian broadcasters. In the 2006 Digital Migration Framework, the CRTC established a more straightforward arrangement in which BDUs must offer analogue and category one digital services in a package before they offer them on a stand-alone basis.[32]

This shift in the approach to packaging requirements poses distinct challenges in Quebec. Astral Broadcasting notes in its 2006 submission to the CRTC that the risks of the digital transition are even more pronounced for French-language services. Specifically, Astral points out that the French-language market is significantly smaller, that one BDU (Quebecor) controls a large proportion of the services' subscriber revenue, and that the number of French-language services is too small to permit the creation of large and attractive digital packages. Accordingly, Astral recommended that the CRTC maintain the existing analogue tiers in a digital environment. In response, in the digital migration framework, the CRTC announced that cable BDUs operating in French-language markets must offer digital subscribers a package that includes all of the French-language specialty services approved prior to the 2000 digital licensing framework.[33] In 2008, the CRTC decided to include the three existing digital French-language category one services (Mystère, Argent, and Réseau Info Sport) in the mandatory Quebec French-language package.[34]

Must-carry obligations remain a point of contention; however, the 1991 Broadcasting Act clearly stipulates that BDUs must give Canadian broadcasters priority.[35] This fundamental regulation often runs contrary to viewer demand for foreign-produced (often American) programming, but such has always been the struggle of Canadian broadcasting. Canadian content policies are often economically unsound. The digital era amplifies this dilemma by placing more control in the hands of the viewer. The CRTC cannot force Canadians to watch domestically produced programs, but it can and does ensure the domestic broadcasting services that air them have access to distribution. The BDU industry has proven continually profitable despite regulatory burdens such as the must-carry obligations. The growth and historical development of these powerful BDUs in Canada followed different trajectories, and the effect of the digital transition will not be uniform across all platforms.

CABLE

Pirate media is nothing new to Canadian broadcasting. In the last two decades, the concern over satellite pirates who access American signals not licensed for Canada has followed a tradition that can trace its roots back to ham radio operators of the 1920s and gained notoriety with the cable television pirates of the 1960s.[36] Early Canadian cable television operators were media smugglers who created large reception antennae and retransmitted local Canadian and American television broadcasts via a cable, for a fee, often to places over-the-air broadcasts would not reach. The early demand for cable often came from rural areas that could not receive traditional OTA broadcasts, but that fell under the licensed territory for authorized broadcasters with exclusive legal rights to the market. Even though households could not receive the OTA signal, the cable operations were breaking the law by offering their distribution service. In a statement eerily similar to the satellite piracy debates of the last decade, Richard Schultz writes that cable in the 1960s "threatened the most fundamental ideas and policies of the traditional broadcasting regulatory regime through its ability to deliver American television signals directly to Canadian viewers."[37] By the 1970s, under inaugural CRTC Chair Pierre Juneau, this cable transmission process was legalized, regulated, and begun to form a profitable section of the broadcasting system. As digital media legal scholar Lawrence Lessig observes: "Last generation's pirates join this generation's country club."[38]

Cable television may have come of age in the analogue era, but it recognizes the growth potential offered by digital. Aside from the increased channel selection allowed by digital compression, digital cable offers a wide selection of on-demand services. Most of these terrestrial BDUs can offer package deals that often include phone and Internet. In 2009, almost 60 per cent of all Canadian cable subscribers received digital cable.[39] Unlike over-the-air television, there is no fixed transition date by which cable will go completely digital. The 2003 *Regulatory Framework for the Distribution of Digital Television Signals* established that once 85 per cent of a cable BDU's subscribers are served digitally, the BDU may apply to be relieved of the obligation to distribute analogue signals.[40] In the 2006 Digital Migration Framework, the CRTC added that the ASO for cable would be 85 per cent digital subscribers or 1 January 2013, whichever occurs first.[41]

The terminology and rules surrounding cable distribution and the services provided can seem impenetrable for all but the most dedicated follower of Canadian broadcasting policy.[42] To appreciate the changes under digital distribution, one must first understand the analogue precedent. Below are a few of the concepts required to navigate these waters.

Analogue Specialty Services: These were the first specialty services initially authorized between 1984 and 1999, before the arrival of digital distribution. There are forty-nine of these channels, which include well-established national brands such as the Sports Network (TSN), Bravo, MuchMusic, and le Réseau du Sports (RDS).[43] They enjoy must-offer status on all BDUs and have proven extremely profitable over two decades. In 2011, TSN had a profit before interest and taxes (PBIT) of 28.4 per cent; Bravo had 29.1 per cent; MuchMusic had 29.3 per cent, and RDS had 35.2 per cent.[44]

Category One Digital: These more recent services, available only in digital format, were first licensed in 2000 after a competitive application process that involved a public hearing. They received mandatory access on BDUs and enjoy niche protection (recognizing the Canadian market may be unable to support multiple offerings of the same genre). There were eighteen category one digital channels in Canada in 2010, including Bio, Argent, the Independent Film Channel, and Fashion Television.

Category Two Digital: If there is truly a sector of the Canadian broadcasting system where the term "free market" can be used with some degree of accuracy, it is with the category two channels established by the CRTC in 2000. This is Canadian broadcasting's Wild West.

BDUs were under no obligation to distribute category two digital channels and there was no limit to approved channels of the same genre. After receiving CRTC approval, the broadcaster had to negotiate its own carriage agreement with a BDU. Many received approval but could not find a distributor and thus were never available to Canadians. In 2010, eighty-six category two digital channels reached distribution agreements, including ethnic broadcasters (Abu Dhabi TV, Tamil Vision), adult channels (Hustler TV, Penthouse), and sports teams (Leafs TV, Raptors NBA TV, the NHL Network). There were dozens of approved category two channels Canadians have never heard of because they never received carriage from a BDU and so have not launched (such little-known offerings include Afroglobal Television, Equestrian Planet, Senior's Life, Women's Sport HD, and many more). All of the channels that had not launched were given a fixed time period in which to find distribution or they were not granted a broadcasting license. Since they are relatively inexpensive to create, some broadcasters continued to create category two's in the hopes that one or two would become profitable.

The effectiveness of the category one/two approach is debatable. In *The CRTC and Broadcasting Regulation in Canada*, Salter and Odartey-Wellington describe this licensing style as "an ingenious solution to adding ever more digital specialty services";[45] whereas in a 2008 interview, Astral Media CEO and former CRTC chair André Bureau was less upbeat in his assessment: "The category two [strategy] didn't produce the anticipated results. From the 600 licenses, only a few have made it, and that's because they're owned by major companies. They have synergies and program acquisition strategies for multiple channels."[46] Bureau believes the lack of genre protection for category two meant too many channels in too small a market. The system favoured incumbents – for smaller broadcasters it was not worth the start up costs. Montreal-based Astral Media has enjoyed financial success with specialty and pay channels like Canal D, Canal Vie, and the Movie Network. In March 2012, Bell Canada agreed to buy Astral Media Inc for $3.38 billion.

Category A and Category B: After establishing precise channel categorizations over the last decade, the CRTC is now prepared to shift again in the digital era. As of 31 August 2011, the previous analogue specialty, category one and category two digital divisions ceased to apply. They are now simplified as categories A and B: category A receives must-carry status and category B resembles the regulation-free marketplace of the previous digital category two.

The channels that previously enjoyed must-carry status maintain that position in the digital era, though they are subject to regular review. There is also a competitive process to allow for a limited amount of new category A channels. The channel provider is obliged to provide evidence to the CRTC that the channel contributes to a series of criteria that relate to the value the channel brings to Canadians, thus "justifying its exceptional status."[47] Again, each BDU's unique position as a service as well as product comes into consideration.

In 2010, the CRTC announced it would not accept applications for new category A services before October 2011.[48] In a well-publicized case in the summer of 2010, Videotron tried to jump the queue and applied for a category A license to launch the Sun TV all-news channel in January 2011. Within weeks of the high-profile announcement, led by former Conservative communications advisor Kory Teneycke, the CRTC rejected proposal. The regulator noted that Sun TV would certainly be considered immediately for a less-lucrative category two license, but that it would not consider further must-carry proposals before the fall of 2011.[49] In November 2010, Sun TV was approved as a category two service.

Pay- and Video-on-Demand Services: BDUs eagerly welcomed video on demand and the increased potential for pay-per-view allowed by digital distribution. The first calls for a pay television license in Canada go back to the 1980s and the eventual launch of Viewer's Choice and

Super Channel in analogue format in 1990 and 1991 respectively.[50] These were premium linear services (they follow a fixed schedule) that could be ordered as an extra on a consumer's cable package. Such services are among the most profitable sectors of the distribution industry. In 2010, there were sixteen pay television channels available in Canada, including the Movie Channel and Family Channel. These services proved lucrative and posted annual PBIT numbers between 29.6 per cent and 26.8 per cent from 2006 to 2008 before dropping to a still-respectable 11.9 per cent in 2009.[51]

Pay-per-view and video on demand differ from pay channels in that the viewer chooses PPV and VOD by the program from a limited menu of options, rather than paying for an entire channel. PPV is a holdover from the analogue era, now in digital form, and is usually a movie, concert, or sporting event (boxing and ultimate fighting are popular PPV offerings). The Pay Television Regulations, 1990, define a PPV program as "a scheduled program that is provided by a license for distribution by a distribution undertaking on a pay-per-view basis."[52] Most large BDUs offer a PPV service and the adoption rate has grown from 6 per cent in 2006 to 15 per cent in 2010 in English Canada, and 7 per cent to 17 per cent in French Canada in the same period.[53] Recent PBIT numbers for PPV range from 14.2 per cent in 2007 to 12.5 per cent in 2009.[54] In 2010, thirteen licensed PPV services operated in Canada. The interactive nature of digital broadcasting is most pronounced in VOD, where the viewer chooses among a variety of options available from central digital providers within the BDU. There is no fixed schedule to VOD.

The development of video on demand and pay-per-view also challenges the traditional structure of the Canadian regulatory system. The historic CanCon approach, which requires a minimum amount of Canadian programming, is not nearly as effective in an "on demand" television environment in which the viewer controls the schedule. In 2000, the CRTC, as it has done with other emerging technologies such as mobile television and the Internet, placed regulations on these new players in the system that were decidedly light. By condition of license, the CRTC requires that a minimum of 5 per cent of English-language feature films, 8 per cent of French-language feature films, and 20 per cent of other programming made available by VOD and PPV undertakings be Canadian. VOD and PPV undertakings must also contribute 5 per cent of gross revenues to a Canadian program production fund.[55] The Regulatory Framework for Video on Demand also stipulates that 25 per cent of the titles promoted on the VOD "barker channel" each month are Canadian.[56] The Pay Television Regulations prohibited these channels from carrying advertising, though in 2010 the CRTC allowed VOD providers "to advertise in programming only if it is acquired directly from licensed Canadian broadcasters."[57]

Part of the rationale behind the relatively lax regulation in this sector is that a healthy cable industry keeps viewers within the Canadians system at a time when so much material is available on the Internet with the click of a mouse.

DTH SATELLITE

DTH providers are subject to less extensive carriage requirements than cable licensees. There are only two licensed services, Shaw and BellTV, so there is less need for intricate categorization between providers. By the rules set out in part four of the Broadcasting Distribution Regulations, DTH providers must carry all pay and specialty channels (excluding category two channels, which are open to negotiation) and at least one English and one French PPV service.[58]

Direct-to-home satellite caused a regulatory uproar when it arrived in the early 1990s. The new pizza-sized satellite dishes, which could pick up American broadcasts directly and economically, were called "tombstones for the CRTC" by former CRTC chair John Meisel.[59] It was not possible to contain the American satellite footprint and Canadians took advantage of the enormous range of American programming via illegal satellite dishes and opting out of the Canadian system altogether.

Like its cable predecessor, satellite shook the foundation of the Canadian broadcasting system. Commenting on the promise and threat of the new DTH services, Richard Schultz writes, "DTH promised to challenge fundamentally both the traditional ideas or rationale for regulating broadcasting in Canada and the current beneficiaries of that regulation: broadcasters, cable companies and, not insignificantly, the CRTC itself."[60]

The birth of DTH satellite broadcasting in Canada was rife with political intrigue. In 1993, the CRTC recognized the impracticality of strictly protectionist measures and began to encourage the growth of DTH services. To entice industry, the CRTC exempted Canadian DTH service providers from licensing and detailed regulation. This meant a Canadian DTH provider that met certain criteria could bypass the lengthy and costly public licensing procedure. In order to qualify, the DTH provider had to use Canadian satellite facilities, offer a preponderance of Canadian channels, not originate programming, and offer only foreign programming services authorized by the CRTC. In August 1994, the CRTC announced that only one applicant had met the criteria, and granted Bell-owned ExpressVu an exemption license. The sole competitor, Power DirecTV, was ruled ineligible because it planned to use American as well as Canadian satellites.

The political furor that followed this decision "was unlike anything that had previously been experienced in Canadian communications regulation."[61] The media and the government criticized the CRTC for its strict rules of exemption and the creation of a non-competitive market. The CRTC claimed that it could eventually license other providers but they would have to go through the public licensing process. The government appointed a panel to review the CRTC decision and the panel came back with a dramatic recommendation: that the Cabinet order the CRTC to license all qualified DTH applicants. The authority for the government to issue a directive to the CRTC had only recently been written into the 1991 Broadcasting Act and had never been used.[62]

In the end, the government issued the order and Canada entered a new era in the power relationship between the sitting government and the broadcast regulator. While the government asserted authority over the CRTC, it was the CRTC that established the parameters of regulation over DTH services. The licenses were still subject to the promotion of Canadian content and certain must-carry obligations, as had been the CRTC policy for cable companies.

The nationally broadcast signals of DTH services present unique regulatory challenges, and the CRTC requires a certain diligence. This division between the broadcasters and DTH providers was brought to the fore during a license renewal hearing for Star Choice satellite distribution in 2004. Shaw, Star Choice's parent company, has been a source of discord within the industry as the digital transition progresses. In the hearing, the CAB alleged that Star Choice took HD signals it received from several different television stations and programming services and compiled them into as many as five omnibus HD channels. In essence, the broadcasters charged that Star Choice was rearranging their broadcasts to suit its spectrum space, making Star Choice de facto programmers and not broadcasting distributors.[63] This, the broadcasters argued, was a violation of the Broadcasting Distribution Regulations. In its determination, the CRTC reminded Star Choice that:

> Section 7 of the Regulations prohibits a licencee from altering or deleting a programming service in a licenced area in the course of its distribution except as required or authorized under a condition of its licence or the Regulations. Canadian programming undertakings and authorized foreign services providing HD programming are distinct services and, like standard definition television services, must be distributed in their entirety on dedicated channels, unless otherwise authorized by the Commission.[64]

The CRTC gave Star Choice its license renewal along with a warning that it not overstep its regulatory boundaries. The message was clear: BDUs in Canada are distributors, not programmers. Shaw and Star Choice were again the source of industry dissent in 2008. This case had to do with simultaneous substitution, a policy that has come under scrutiny by digitalization as scheduling becomes less fixed.

At a license hearing for Western Canada cable companies, the CAB once again launched a complaint against Shaw companies, claiming it had consistently failed to carry out simultaneous substitution on behalf of local stations when broadcasting the distant Canadian signals that are distributed in local markets by DTH satellite signals. The problem was in essence: does the BDU have an obligation to protect the programming rights of the local stations through simultaneous substitution, even if the signal originates from another part of Canada and not the United States as originally intended? The CRTC ruled in favour of the broadcasters' local rights and ordered: "Shaw is required to immediately conform to its regulatory obligations with respect to simultaneous substitution."[65]

Direct-to-home satellite providers are Canada's early warning signal of some of the problems created by digital television: time schedules and geographic divides are no longer a firm basis for regulation. The growth of cable and satellite also demonstrate that the Canadian broadcasting system has historically adapted to accommodate new and potentially disruptive distribution technologies.

SMALL CABLE COMPANIES: PUNCHING ABOVE THEIR WEIGHT

The numerous small cable companies that serve the less than 10 per cent of Canada's BDU subscribers that do not use the big four cable companies or the two licensed DTH satellite providers have played a significant role in the digital transition. This sector includes some larger companies, such as Eastlink in the Maritimes and Access in the Western Canada, but the majority serve between 2,000 and 5,000 customers.[66] They are collectively represented by the Canadian Cable Systems Alliance (CCSA) and have proven to be a surprisingly strong combined force in Canadian digital television policy. In the past, small companies were involved in cable distribution, but over the last decade they have become increasingly involved in ISP service and more recently new Internet Protocol-based television distribution.

The CRTC supported smaller BDUS by easing their regulatory obligations with generally few objections from the major providers. The smaller distributors face obstacles that place them at a decided disadvantage against the larger operators. For instance, small BDUS frequently have a modest customer base spread out over a wide territory, which requires a large investment in cable for a fairly insubstantial rate of return; whereas large BDUS prevail in urban centres where the population is more densely packed and there are obvious economies of scale benefits. Small companies rely on a major satellite service to provide the programming signal to the head of their cable distribution system – an added expense the big companies do not face. Some of the smaller BDUS are community-run cooperatives that do not have the same freedom to raise rates any time they choose. Smaller systems also often have difficulties negotiating wholesale programming fees comparable to those available to larger systems. Many smaller systems have less capacity than larger services, and may find it difficult to offer service packages that can compete with those offered by their competitors.[67] Despite these challenges, given that many small companies function in areas that are not served by OTA broadcasters, their continued operation is an important link for their communities (DTH is available but is strictly a national signal) and a necessary component for a truly inclusive Canadian broadcasting system.

The CRTC has successively relaxed the rules about some of the conditions of license for small cable systems as the digital transition has progressed. In 2001, the CRTC issued the first of these orders and exempted BDUs that serve fewer than 2,000 subscribers from many of the obligations of the Broadcasting Distribution Act.[68] In 2004, the CRTC issued a second exemption order, for BDUs that serve between 2,000 and 6,000 subscribers – though these BDUs were still obligated to carry 9(1)(h) services.[69] As noted above, in 2009 the CRTC issued a general exemption order for all BDUs that serve less than 20,000 subscribers. Small cable operators are also exempt from contributing to the Canadian Media Fund, and instead may direct this money to community channels and community programming. Larger BDUs must contribute 5 per cent of their gross revenue to the fund.

BDUs often negotiate wholesale rates for programming that reflect the size of their subscription bases. For example, a BDU that has 250,000 subscribers would negotiate a lower per channel price with the programmer than a BDU that has only 5,000 subscribers. The CRTC has made it clear that small cable companies will have access to programming at rates comparable to those charged to large BDUs. In 2001, the CRTC stated it expects programmers "to give their consent to small systems for the distribution of previously uncarried analogue services on digital tiers at effective per-subscriber rates that are substantially similar to those offered to their larger competitors (DTH or the incumbent cable company, as the case may be)."[70] In this unique policy approach, small BDUs must still apply for consent, but the CRTC expects the request to be merely a formality.

Even with this support from the broadcasting regulator, Chris Edwards, the vice president of corporate and regulatory affairs for the CCSA, thinks the digital transition presents a "watershed moment" for small cable operators in Canada. He is concerned many will not be able to finance the necessary changes and will simply decide to cease service.[71] While most major BDUs simulcast analogue and digital signals during a transition period, small BDUs cannot accommodate dual signals as easily and will be forced to abruptly cease the analogue signal.[72] The set-top digital converter box that larger BDUs provide for customers are also a substantial investment for smaller companies.

Nevertheless, small cable companies have begun to show signs of new vitality. Edwards observes that the CCSA receives requests for new membership every week and that new technology may ease the digital transition for small operators. One such technology is "switched digital video," a process that allows the cable provider to shut off the flow of channels the viewer uses infrequently, but resume them in less than a second if the viewer selects the channel. In doing so, the distributor frees up bandwidth that would be usually dedicated to a constant stream of that broadcaster's signal. Switched digital video follows similar technology to video on demand and is only be available in a digital environment. This technology has enormous implications for the carrying capacity of cable, allowing smaller BDUs to offer a wider range of channels.

While the digital transition remains a formidable hurdle for many small communications providers in Canada, there is every reason to believe such providers will remain as a key component of the greater system. In an article on Cartt.ca, Greg O'Brien observes:

> Those independents also have to deal with the same regulatory and legislative change, negotiate contracts with programmers and others, and keep on top of the latest tech trends and new business opportunities, too. Which is the reason why the Canadian Cable Systems Alliance exists and thrives. Working collectively, the CCSA members, all independent communications companies, help themselves (with the assistance of the crack CCSA staff) navigate the turbulent waters of the global media, entertainment and communications ocean. Pooling resources like this makes them far more able to punch above their weight and compete with the big guys.[73]

New digital technologies are a financial burden, but also increase the service options for many independent providers. The regulations surrounding these "new media" (an increasingly dated term, now in use for over a decade) have proven a policy challenge for the CRTC.

NEW MEDIA: IPTV AND MOBILE BROADCASTING

For years, the Internet and mobile television have been potential successors to, or at least strong competitors for, traditional cable and satellite BDU service. More television services are available over IPTV, but they have thus been slow to garner the audience, and the ensuing steady monthly profits, of cable and satellite in Canada. The legacy industries have often successfully resisted the intrusion of new services in the market. It is not that Canadians are averse to watching video on the Internet (Canadians watch more video online than people in any country); however, amateur video (e.g., YouTube) remains almost twice as popular as professionally produced video.[74] In 2010, over 40 per cent of Canadians had watched an entire thirty- or sixty-minute television program online, but well under 10 per cent paid for it.[75] In an effort to encourage industrial growth and development, the CRTC has maintained a generally deregulatory approach toward these new digital distribution undertakings. Despite this light-touch regulation and some bold ventures by powerful Internet brands, digital delivery of content in Canada is still largely a work in progress.

In a 2008 report prepared for the CRTC, Columbia University professor Eli Noam observes:

> The agents of change today are three related technological developments that rapidly transform media:
>
> 1 The broadbanding of networks, in which an increasingly powerful transmission infrastructure creates platforms for the individualized production, distribution, and consumption of media content such as video. The most formidable such platform is the Internet.
>
> 2 Wireless ubiquity, which creates a wide geographic reach for two-way communications through cellular networks of increasing power, and enables the transmission of media content such as video.
>
> 3 Digital convergence, which removes many of the technical barriers that separated the various media activities, companies, industries, and regulations.
>
> Together, these forces transform the media landscape. They also raise the question of the role of government.[76]

Noam suggests that this transformed landscape constitutes TV's third generation. After the initial generations of limited TV (few broadcasters), and multichannel TV (cable and satellite), the medium is now emerging as individualized TV. This process is most pronounced in new media. For television distribution in Canada, the new conduits opened by digitalization include the Internet and mobile telephony. Wireless and broadband are altering the shape of Canadian television; however, in 2012, the legacy broadcasting distribution industries have maintained their positions of power.

One of the first shots across the bow of the established broadcasting industries came from Internet television upstart ICraveTV in 1999. Launched by broadcaster and former CRTC policy analyst Bill Craig, this Richmond Hill, Ontario-based operation used an antenna to pick up analogue OTA signals in the Toronto area and digitalized and distributed them over the Internet using RealPlayer streaming technology. To make money, the site sold banner advertising beside its viewing panel. It distributed six television signals based in the United States and ten based in the Toronto area.[77] Craig claimed ICraveTV was an OTA signal distribution service just like cable, and since the CRTC had ruled that Canada would not regulate the Internet in its 1999 New Media decision, Craig did not believe he was in violation of the law.[78] Reaction from established media companies was swift and forceful. Canadian broadcasters, as well as major American media companies such as Disney, Time Warner, CBS, Fox, the NFL, and the NBA, sought legal action to prevent their product from being viewed over what they saw as an inferior distribution method. Though Craig asserted that he designed his service for the Canadian market, ICraveTV is a rare case where major American companies were concerned about the disruptive impact of a Canadian media service. ICraveTV users were asked to provide a Canadian postal code but US companies knew Americans could type in any Canadian postal code and access the service.

ICraveTV was an important case in digital television broadcasting. Canadian communication law professor Hudson Janisch expresses strong support for the company:

> Overall, rather than fulminating about theft and unleashing litigation lawyers to defend the status quo, what needs to be done is to follow a well-established policy route with respect to the Internet as a new transmission technology. This balances the public interest in the development of new options and the private interest of those whose creative energies have produced the programming to be carried.
>
> In my view this would be a win-win solution in which the broadcasters further extend their reach and are compensated with any copyright royalties to which they are entitled, and Internet entrepreneurs test the effectiveness of a new transmission technology.

> Above all, established players should not be allowed to exercise complete control over the evolution and use of new information technology. The future belongs not to the past, but to the future.[79]

Despite Janisch's support, the enormous power of established broadcasting forces brought the upstart website to heel rather quickly. A Pennsylvania court ruled against ICraveTV, which chose to close shop in 2000 rather than face further legal action.[80]

Like cable before it, major Canadian distribution companies have adopted the combination of television and the Internet, albeit in a more genteel form than ICraveTV. For Canadian broadcasters, the Internet is now a significant conduit for licensed programming that appears on company websites such as cbc.ca, ctv.ca, and globaltv.com. These streaming portals became more prevalent in 2007 and 2008; however, according to the CBC's submission to the CRTC's 2011 fact-finding exercise on over-the-top television, there is still no accurate way to determine online audiences.[81] This uncertainty is one of the justifications the CRTC has cited in its continued avoidance of regulation in this burgeoning market.

The impact of Internet technology on the BDU sector is clearer and offers an opportunity for traditional telephone providers to enter the business of television distribution. IPTV video distribution is not the public Internet but uses Internet Protocol technology (information packets) to transfer data. It involves a set-top box that connects a television to the BDU's network and is generally a walled garden in which a service provider offers a finite number of channels, not a connection to the general Internet. Until the recent growth of fibre distribution, digital subscriber lines (DSL) distributed programming through twisted copper telephone lines using IP technology.[82]

Bell first received a license to operate regional terrestrial BDUs in Ontario and Quebec in 2004 using a DSL delivery system, though the company did not widely offer it and growth remained relatively flat. Canada played a pioneering role in HD IPTV over DSL in North America in 2006 when the Crown corporation SaskTel announced that its prairie subscribers would have access to Max HD, an IP-based service that could provide up to twenty-seven HD channels. Max HD had an initial cost of $59 per month for a bundle that included high-speed Internet.[83]

The problem encountered by DSL is that copper wires have difficulty achieving the bandwidth required to offer the range of channels that established BDU methods such as cable and satellite provide. In 2009, 2.7 per cent of television BDU subscribers in Canada used DSL – a 41 per cent growth over the previous year, but still not a major force in Canadian distribution.[84] Given the proliferation of broadband and the rapid expansion of fibre networks the future of Internet-based television in Canada is via fibre, not copper telephone lines.[85] In 2010, the nineteen IPTV service providers in Canada reached 22 per cent of households.[86]

IPTV has further blurred the lines between telecom and broadcasting providers. Just as cable operators such as Rogers began to offer home phone service in 2005, the digital content allows telecoms to offer television. Traditional telecom operators realize they must compete with the package deals offered by major BDUS and use IPTV as a way in to expand their services. Telecom operators have historically enjoyed more freedom from regulatory oversight than their Canadian broadcasting counterparts.[87] In 2009, traditional phone services Bell Aliant, Bell Canada, MTS Allstream, SaskTel, and Telus were licensed as class one BDUS to provide service using IPTV technology.[88] The phone providers are now broadcasting distributors. The CRTC can regulate the operations of telephone companies over private IP networks within the BDU licensing framework, but has not yet seen a reason to: many IPTV services are new and, in 2011, accounted for only 4 per cent of the BDU market share.[89]

IPTV is possible over DSL but is more likely to flourish in the higher speeds offered by cable and fibre connections. IPTV has been available for roughly five years but has proven to be a tough sell in the world of broadcasting distribution; however, some well-situated companies are betting that will soon change. A 2012 report from Ottawa-based Boon Dog's Canadian Digital TV Market Monitor research series predicts IPTV's share of the digital TV market will grow to about 17 per cent by the end of 2014, at the expense of both satellite and cable.[90]

Within their territories, IPTV providers generally report progress in their deployments. For example, MTS Allstream in Manitoba reports that its revenues from IPTV services increased by $11.4 million, or 19.3 per cent, in 2011 when compared to 2010.[91] In 2010, Bell announced plans to increase its IPTV (Fibe) roll-out in Montreal, Toronto, and Quebec City.[92] The IPTV service coincides with Bell's expansion of its fibre network that will have much more bandwidth than DSL services (with the exception of some new buildings, Fibe's "last mile" into the home remains DSL). IPTV providers offer packages in much the same way as cable and satellite companies, with a digital video recording device and access to PPV also included. There is not as much variety as a viewer can receive over cable or satellite, but the more expensive IPTV packages still offer over 140 channels.

Bell waited years to roll out IPTV, choosing to use the adoption rate of AT&T IPTV service in the United States as an indicator of public demand. Bell decided to expand its IPTV services in Canada only after AT&T added one million new American subscribers in 2008.[93] Another major Canadian telephone provider, Telus, also launched its Optik IPTV service in 2010. These initiatives are still too recent to get a sense of their popularity (the CRTC has released limited data) but the development of fibre infrastructure vastly improves IPTV's service. Major Canadian players, such as Bell and Telus, have moved cautiously into this field. IPTV is expanding in Canada but has not yet attracted a large number of providers. However, there are signs of new growth. One new IPTV service is the Montreal-based ColbaNet, which offers a triple play IPTV, Internet, and telephone package in the Montreal area. In the spring of 2012, ColbaNet applied to the CRTC to expand its service and become a national provider; however IPTV requires great investment and the incumbents have a head start.

Over-the-top (OTT) Internet television, which streams online (as opposed to IPTV, which uses walled-garden IP technology) has also experienced some growth and has made some major Canadian broadcasters nervous. There are early indications that OTT television may be a disruptive new technology. Netflix's Canadian launch in 2010 is the most successful effort to monetize Internet video. In just over a year, with few or no first run movies or original programs, Netflix attracted over one million subscribers in Canada. The growth of such new OTT services has contributed to an industry concern that consumers might cancel their BDU services en masse. This predicted exodus from the established distributors, or "cord cutting," has yet to materialize in a significant way in Canada but remains a point of apprehension for the industry.[94]

The foreign owned and operated Netflix caused such concern among established Canadian broadcasters that it was the catalyst for a CRTC fact-finding exercise on online and mobile programming services in the spring of 2011 to determine if these new services violated the Broadcasting Act. The results were inconclusive.[95] In its finding, the CRTC observed: "Significant change is underway in the communications sphere ... However, the evidence does not demonstrate that the presence of OTT providers in Canada and greater consumption of OTT content is having a negative impact on the ability of the system to achieve the policy objectives of the Broadcasting Act or that there are structural impediments to a competitive response by licensed undertakings to the activities of OTT providers."[96] The CRTC decided to allow the market to evolve, and to pursue another OTT hearing at an unspecified later date. This hearing technically encompassed all online distributers, but it was essentially about Netflix since few others have managed to make much of a market impact.

There are no guarantees for these new services. In the spring of 2010, the *Globe and Mail* observed: "Web television has been a minefield for the world's most creative and deep-pocketed companies."[97] Even Apple has seen lukewarm-at-best demand for its Apple TV system despite years of availability and a trusted (if not lionized) brand. The company launched Apple TV in 2007, the same year as the iPhone, but to a much weaker response. Apple TV is a walled garden – it is designed for screening movies and television programs purchased on iTunes exclusively. Apple CEO Tim Cook has described it as "a hobby" for the company.[98] Like many hobbies, it has not been particularly lucrative. Apple relaunched the service in 2010 and claimed sales of 2.8 million units in the 2011 fiscal year – respectable, although nowhere near the sales of the iPhone or iPad.[99]

Despite Apple's early stumbles in the Internet TV market, Google entered the Internet television ring in the fall of 2010. Google announced that Google TV would let users simultaneously navigate television programs, online video, and Web sites on the living room television.[100] Google TV is an amalgamation of three things: TV, DVR, and the Internet. According to the spring 2010 launch announcement, Sony agreed to produce a full line of television sets and a Bluray player integrated with Google TV, and Logitech would produce a companion set-top box to enable users to access the platform. Unlike the walled-garden interface of IPTV services, Google TV is an aggregator that allows for interaction with a range of services over the public Internet.

As of 2012, Google TV is still unavailable in Canada. Like Apple TV, the Google product had disappointing early sales despite the support of a powerful Internet brand. The key sticking point for the growth of Google TV is the common digital debate over license rights. Large broadcasters such as ABC, NBC, CBS, and Fox, and US streaming site Hulu blocked Google TV's access to their online content. This lack of content dealt a serious blow to Google TV's prospects. According to an industry analyst in 2011: "Really, I think right now that Google TV is kind of dead in the water."[101]

The other significant digital distribution system to fall under the regulatory label of new media is mobile television accessed on mobile phones and tablets. There are two potential manifestations of mobile television: a walled garden currently offered by some Canadian wireless services; and the reception of OTA television signals via mobile device, currently unavailable in Canada. Like IPTV and OTT services, the early sales numbers for this new technology were not overwhelming but have seen some growth since the explosion in smartphone sales. The CRTC 2011 *Communications Monitoring Report* shows a jump in adoption rates to 9 per cent in English Canada from 5 per cent in 2010. In French Canada, the number is a 4 per cent, though that is double the 2010 figure. These are not overwhelming statistics when broadband over mobile is available to 96 per cent of the Canadian population.[102] Mobile television differs from general broadband access to online video like YouTube; instead, it is for services where the phone service has obtained the broadcaster's permission (in vertically integrated Canadian media these are often now one and the same) to retransmit its signal.[103] In the form currently available in Canada, the user selects from a set menu of items in a video-on-demand structure. In 2012, Bell offers its Mobile TV service at a rate of $5 a month for ten hours of service.[104]

Early mobile television service received regulatory support in 2007, when the CRTC exempted mobile television broadcasting services from licensing obligations. They meant they do not have to follow the same Canadian content obligations as other larger BDUS and can organize programming as they wish. The CRTC did stipulate that a mobile television provider must receive permission from the programmer for its signal and the provider must be eligible for a Canadian broadcasting license (in other words, be Canadian owned).[105] Contrary to the beliefs of some cyber-libertarians, it was not that the CRTC had no choice in the matter.[106] As Bram Abramson observed in February 2009, mobile television falls "squarely under Canada's Broadcasting Act" and therefore under the authority of the CRTC.[107]

In October 2009, the CRTC revoked the 2007 exemption order for mobile television and placed it under a general new media exemption.[108] The CRTC sought to clarify what it meant by a "new media broadcasting undertaking" in the Canadian system. It stated: "The proposed amendment, in effect, blends the existing definitions of 'new media broadcasting undertaking' and 'mobile television' broadcasting undertaking."[109] It is still too early to determine the implications of this decision for mobile television in Canada. It is however, a clear example of the "policy on the fly" approach forced on the CRTC by the quickly evolving new media sector.

There are still many significant technical details to iron out in Canada's approach to free over-the-air mobile television, despite the fact that the service is already common in many parts of the world. In a 2010 *New York Times* article, Kevin J. O'Brien observes:

> Free, on-the-go viewing is common just about everywhere except the United States and Europe, where operator resistance and a maze of conflicting technical standards and program licensing hurdles have kept the technology out of the global mainstream ... In the United States and Europe, where operators tend to control what technology goes into handsets, a major hurdle to free-to-air broadcasting is, ironically, that it is free. That offers no incentive to operators focused on raising revenue per customer.[110]

Though not named in the piece, Canada's system has followed the American example. European (DVB-H) and Japanese (ISDB-TMM, or integrated services digital broadcasting via terrestrial mobile multimedia) technical standards have so far proven more adaptable to mobile use. The ATSC digital television standard is often accused of not being suitable for mobile broadcasting. It should then come as little surprise that when Rogers initially sought to upgrade its mobile television service in its cellular phones in 2007, it announced it would likely based the improvements on the European digital video broadcasting handheld (DVB-H) technology.[111] As of 2012, DVB-H technology has not gained a foothold in the Canadian market. Mobile television using ATSC, known as ATSC Mobile DTV, ATSC M/H, or just MDTV is in the test phase in Canada. In 2009, Industry Canada's Communications Research Centre announced plans for a three-year test period for OTA DTV mobile broadcasting over ATSC in the Ottawa area.[112] Given the rise in smartphone use and tablet sales over the last several years, it is hard to believe this would not be a popular service; however, Canadian media companies have yet to see the economic potential. In 2012, most Canadians do not realize that over-the-air television on mobile devices is a reality in much of the world. Like much of the new media examined in this chapter, the place of mobile television in the Canadian system is evolving and no one has a clear idea of the position it will take among the more established distribution systems.

CONCLUSION

In his 2008 report prepared for the CRTC, Eli Noam writes: "Given the growth rates for IPTV and mobile TV in other highly developed countries, the new types of TV should move beyond the early buzz stage and become economic and media factors within five years, probably less."[113] Some in the industry are not so certain. At the 2008 National Association of Broadcasters conference in Las Vegas, a key afternoon session asked: Why are new media opportunities taking so long?[114] Greg O'Brien of Cartt.ca put this question to several industry representatives at the conference and came up with the following conclusion: "So far, when it comes right down to it, there's nowhere near enough money in new platforms to pay for content the way there is on television."[115] The legacy industries remain the most lucrative.

That may remain the case in 2012, but the next-generation infrastructure for the IPTV and mobile sector, which can truly challenge the dominance of cable and satellite, is only now being established. In the United States, the Recovery Act of 2009 appropriated $7.2 billion to expand broadband access to unserved and underserved communities. In Canada, as part of the Economic Action Plan, the government gave $225 million to Industry Canada over three years to develop and implement a strategy to extend broadband coverage to as many unserved and underserved households as possible, beginning in 2009 and 2010.[116] IPTV is a far more attractive proposition when using newer high-speed infrastructure. In the private sector, Canadian providers Bell and Telus announced their new fibre lines in 2010. On the wireless new media side, new mobile television applications are growing in the closed, walled-garden approach, while mobile access to OTA signals is still in the test stage.

In other words, the backbone of the new system is still under development, and its impact on the established television distribution power dynamic remains to be seen. If successful, new distributions methods may cause a profound shift in the Canadian broadcasting system; however, many of the ownership groups involved, with some exceptions such as Netflix and Apple, are the legacy players of the analogue era.

From a public interest perspective, the key issue at stake in BDU regulations is the matter of public access, Canadian content, and diversity of opinion. The vast majority of Canadians receive their signals via BDU, which makes the industry a powerful gatekeeper as well as a necessary platform for Canadian productions. It is clear that the commanding market position of BDUs has worked to the detriment of the OTA sector. The incentive to invest in fibre and mobile applications has not been echoed in the development of conventional OTA signals.

The CRTC is has not yet organized a clear long-term plan and, in such a rapidly fluctuating environment with little or no government guidance, it is hard to fault it. Market-led CRTC BDU policy has had a positive impact for many Canadian consumers. Corporations are eager to tap into the potential new revenue streams digital distribution offer and have made large investments. There is little regulatory "stick" required to offer these new services in major markets. Where the CRTC must remain vigilant is enforcing the expressed policy of the Broadcasting Act that BDUs allow space for Canadian programmers.

In a world of fibre connections and mobile broadband, the essential objective of Canadian broadcasting involves allowing room for Canadian stories to be told, just as it did in 1929.

5

Over-the-Air Broadcasting

I would like to make the CRTC's position very clear. Over-the-air transmission has always been the cornerstone of our broadcasting system. We expect that OTA will move to digital and will continue to play that key role. It is here to stay.

CRTC Chair Konrad von Finckenstein, 19 June 2008, speech to the 2008 Broadcasting Invitational Summit, Cambridge, ON

No area of the Canadian broadcasting system has received as much rhetorical support from the CRTC as the over-the-air (OTA) broadcasting sector. Conventional Canadian broadcasters are included in BDU packages (they currently receive no subscription fees) but they are also assigned radio frequencies to broadcast their signals free of charge to anyone with a television and antenna. Accolades such as "cornerstone of the Canadian broadcasting system," "window on the world," and "essential part of a successful broadcasting system" are commonplace.[1] However, despite all the praise, efforts to strengthen this foundational sector have proven elusive. The OTA sector, which the ATSC digital standard was originally designed to enhance, has been a casualty of the Canadian digital television transition. Given that BDUs provide more than 90 per cent of Canadians with television signals, and that watching television over the Internet is becoming more prevalent among younger viewers, the place of conventional OTA broadcasting within the greater television system is considerably diminished. The profitability of OTA broadcasting has dropped in the last decade and in 2009, for the first time, Canadian conventional broadcasters' revenue shrunk by 7.9 per cent over the year before.[2] This drop was partly due to the wider political economy, as advertising expenditures diminished considerably during this period of near economic collapse, particularly for traditional big spenders such as car manufacturers.[3] This drop proved temporary and revenues of conventional broadcasters rebounded to 9.9 per cent in 2010; however, as the 31 August 2011 shut-off date approached, there was little enthusiasm for infrastructure investment in the OTA sector.[4]

The Canadian OTA sector as an industry has developed such that the best economic results are achieved by purchasing US programming to fill the maximum permitted regulatory quota and broadcasting it during the most valuable time slots simultaneously with its American counterpart.[5] Simulcasting had implications for the selection of digital standards, as the current Canadian system requires smooth interoperability with the US signals. Broadcasters generally seek Canadian programming that complements the American programming in order to fulfill regulatory requirements and lose as little money as possible. In the current Canadian system, Canadian broadcasters promote, market, and sell top US shows to maximize audiences and revenue and create as much lift in audience numbers as possible for required Canadian fare.[6]

The falling fortune of the OTA sector is attributable to the soaring number of specialty channels offered over the last fifteen years. In 1998, there were thirty-seven specialty channels available in Canada; by 2008, there were 150. These new offerings steadfastly eroded the conventional viewer base as more channels competed for the same eyeballs. Fragmentation is particularly apparent in the English Canadian market, as the CRTC noted in 2010: "From 1998 to 2008, the overall viewing share of private OTA and CBC stations in English Canada decreased by 17.7%, from 46.6% to 29.3%. Conversely, over the same period, the overall share of viewing to pay and specialty services increased 23.2%, from 14.7% to 37.9%."[7] Conventional broadcasters also access audiences through mandatory BDU carriage, but their place of prominence in the television system has continued to slip throughout the digital transition.

The place of traditional, free (though advertising-supported is a more accurate description), rabbit-ear-antenna-received television is the most contentious issue of the changes brought about by Canada's digital television transition. After viewing the steadily declining audience share of OTA, broadcasters have been reluctant to make the costly investments required to maintain analogue levels of coverage. The invisible hand of the marketplace, charged with the overall task of guiding the pace and direction of Canada's digital transition, has remained decidedly idle in the OTA sector. The result is a shifting policy foundation, broadcasters that exercise continued gamesmanship, and a population that is justifiably confused or outright unaware about the future of OTA television. The future of OTA television in Canada remains a question mark.

The uncertainty surrounding the OTA sector is not restricted to the public. In 2009, less than two years before the ASO, the CRTC asked a group of industry experts to draft a report on the progress of digital television in Canada. They could reach no conclusions on the OTA sector: "In light of the recent public statements by both public and private broadcasters and the public regulatory proceedings scheduled during 2009, the Digital Working Group has found it difficult to determine (1) which conventional television stations will be operating in 2011, and (2) where analogue transmitters will not be replaced by digital transmitters."[8] The ambiguity surrounding the future of digital OTA in Canada was endemic, and stretched from the everyday viewer to the highest levels of industry and policy. Between 2009 and 2010, there was a complete volte-face by powerful players within the Canadian private broadcasting industry; in fact, a drastic change seems to have occurred over the summer months of 2010. In 2009, CTVglobemedia, then Canada's largest private network, wrote in a submission to the CRTC: "Even if we were to invest the financial resources to convert our major market stations at this time, for practical, technical and regulatory reasons, it is unlikely CTVgm would be able to meet the current deadline set by the Commission."[9] However, in a July 2010 letter to the CRTC, CTV vice president Kevin Goldstein wrote: "At this time, we have budgeted to convert all transmitters in mandatory markets for both our CTV and 'A' stations."[10]

Canada's other major private English broadcaster, Canwest Global, had a similar change of plans. In 2009, Canwest told the CRTC, "conversion of all mandated markets by August 2011 is unachievable."[11] However, in a letter dated 23 June 2010, Canwest vice president Charlotte Bell advised the CRTC's Chris Seigl that "we plan to transition to DTV in the mandatory markets by the 31 August 2011 deadline."[12]

This drastic change in position on OTA television is not accounted for. Did the CRTC call the broadcaster's bluff when it refused to extend the deadline in the spring of 2010? Was the CRTC's 2010 change of position on FFC enough to encourage the broadcasters, even though the final decision still rested with the Federal Court of Appeal? Like so much of this crucial area of the Canadian digital transition, very little is certain. There will undoubtedly be more questions surrounding the validity of many statements made during the lengthy transition process as Canada bids a prolonged good bye to analogue broadcasting.

It is ironic that of all television delivery systems, Canada's beleaguered OTA sector potentially stands to benefit most from the transition to digital in terms of quality of product. Using the ATSC technical standard, digital terrestrial broadcasting can offer striking HD signals at a quality that is superior to cable and satellite because the signal does not undergo the same compression. Digital OTA offers a better viewing experience, with none of the "snow" or fading in and out common to analogue and with superb sound quality. One of the key reasons the United States pursued the ATSC platform with such vigour in the early 1990s was because it was a good fit for the country's robust OTA sector. Since its complete switch in June 2009, the United States has enjoyed a wide range of free OTA channels, many broadcast in HD. The smaller frequency requirements of digital OTA also allow for multiplexing, in which different channels can share the same transmitter, thus reducing costs. As discussed in the previous chapter, OTA signals can also be configured to be received by mobile computing devices. What should be a significant next step in the evolution of OTA broadcasting has been held back in Canada by a powerful mix of industry resistance and political inertia.

The OTA transition is the key that unlocks the door to the primary dividend of moving to digital in the first place: creating space in the electromagnetic spectrum. The spectrum previously held by channels 52 to 69 in Canada will be sold via the 700 MHz auction set for 2013 after a one-year delay. Thus, a deferred OTA transition postpones not just new television services to Canadians and increases the dominance of BDUS within the system, but stalls the development and implementation of new spectrum-based technologies. For the Canadian government and taxpayers) this also meant prolonged uncertainties regarding the auction of the valuable 700 MHz region of the spectrum. To help facilitate the change to digital, on 21 May 2005, Industry Canada published the *DTV Transition Allotment Plan*, which provided an additional allotment of spectrum for purposes of launching digital TV for all Canadian analogue OTA broadcasters.[13] This allowed broadcasters to transmit simultaneously in digital and analogue during the transition period. Broadcasters are required to return the extra spectrum when the transition is complete.

The debate over OTA television brings forth essential political questions not found to the same degree in cable or satellite services. At the centre of the OTA debate is the publicly owned radio spectrum. Public representatives, in this case Industry Canada, oversee the use of this limited resource. Unlike the more commercially focused concerns of the digital television switch, such as video on demand or the wide array of specialty options provided by cable and satellite companies, the central question of universality is at stake in the OTA sector of Canadian broadcasting. Freely accessible, advertising-supported television ensures that no Canadian citizen with a television is excluded from the system.[14] This concept has been a central pillar of the Canadian digital transition since the beginning. *Canadian Television in the Digital Era*, the report that initiated Canada's digital roll-out in 1997, states: "Over-the-air broadcasters are at the heart of the successful transition to digital television."[15]

It took a full decade from the first major study on digital television in Canada to establish a firm analogue shut-off date. Though in 2009 the CRTC restricted the transition to major Canadian markets, the broadcasting industry struggled to make the ASO deadline or declared it unachievable. Many of the same Canadian companies that operate OTA stations are also BDUS that hold numerous profitable specialty channels and, as such, have a conflict of interest in promoting a robust digital OTA sector.[16] The real money lies in specialty's dual revenue streams of advertising and cable subscription. Canada's increasingly vertically integrated broadcasting sector has little reason to pursue the limited audiences of conventional broadcasting. The major consolidations of 2010, when Bell purchased CTV and Shaw purchased Canwest, were about access to the content held by these conventional broadcasters and delivering them across a range of integrated platforms and properties; it was not about selling to the few Canadians who relied on the OTA sector.

The downward trajectory of the OTA sector has continued for more than a decade, and OTA broadcasters have attempted to spin their financial difficulties to great advantage. In 2007, several broadcasters sought to retain the policies designed to support local OTAS (priority carriage, simultaneous substitution) without investing in transmitters. According to the 2007 CRTC report *Determinations Regarding Certain Aspects of the Regulatory Framework for over-the-Air Television*:

> A number of broadcasters submitted that it is no longer economical to build transmitters, given the declining number of viewers who receive television signals off-air rather than through the facilities of BDUS. Accordingly, they proposed that digital/HD programming be delivered by cable and DTH BDUS. However, they also submitted that their programming services should continue to receive priority carriage status, and that they should be able to request simultaneous substitution, even in the absence of providing local OTA services.[17]

This was clearly an effort on behalf of broadcasters to have their digital cake and eat it too. The CRTC rightly rejected the proposition and emphasized the continued importance of OTA in the greater system.

In 2008, the CRTC tried to strengthen the OTA sector when it introduced the Local Programming Improvement Fund (LPIF) to support the production of local programming provided by private and public conventional television stations operating in non-metropolitan markets. The fund was to be financed by a levy of 1 per cent of the gross revenues of licensed BDUS (later raised to 1.5 per cent). The objectives of the LPIF were:

> to ensure that viewers in smaller Canadian markets continue to receive a diversity of local programming – particularly local news programming;
>
> to improve the quality and diversity of local programming broadcast in these markets; and
>
> to ensure that viewers in French-language markets are not disadvantaged by the smaller size of those markets.[18]

The CRTC reviewed the LPIF at a public hearing in April 2012 and plans to phase it out by August 2014.[19]

Despite this effort at a regulatory patch, OTA television in Canada is undergoing digitalization, the greatest technical leap in its history, at a time when economic forces are decidedly stacked against it. Is the cornerstone of the system an increasingly redundant method of transmission? To dismiss OTA as inconsequential misses the point:

- OTA ensures no Canadians are excluded from broadcasts over public airwaves due to financial constraints.
- OTA can act as competition for BDU services.

- Many cable and satellite subscribers have additional TV sets that still rely on OTA signals.
- The number of OTA viewers varies greatly by region in Canada.

The supposed heart of the Canadian digital television transition has been badly neglected. In this chapter, I will discuss two key elements of the OTA transition in more detail: the analogue shut-off date and the uncertainty surrounding the size of the Canadian OTA market. I will then examine the possible growth of the sector, including a case study of a Canadian broadcaster who is bucking the dominant trend and investing in the OTA market. Lastly, I will look at the unique and significant place of the national public broadcaster, the CBC.

THE ANALOGUE SHUT-OFF DATE: 31 AUGUST 2011

The CRTC has been forced to backtrack on some of the initial plans for OTA broadcasting in the digital era. Like much of the digital transition, the original schedule for over-the-air broadcasting called for no fixed date at all. In the 2002 *Licensing Policy to Oversee the Transition from Analogue to Digital over-the-Air Television Broadcasting*, the CRTC was resolute: "A voluntary, market-driven transition model, without mandated deadlines, is the most appropriate approach for Canada."[20] This approach contradicted the original position recommended by the digital task force in 1997, which called for all analogue transmissions in Canada to cease by the end of 2007.[21]

In the following years, the market charged with leading the transition failed to deliver tangible results, and the government provided no guidance along the way. In 2007, after years of relative inactivity, the CRTC had to take regulatory action. Michel Arpin describes the process of setting the ASO date:

> Sometime in 2006–2007 I did get a letter [from Industry Canada] asking the commission to set a date for the digital transition. The department [Industry Canada] was looking at what was going on in the US where they had set the cut-off date for February 2009. We had a review in 2007 where fee for carriage was discussed more than any other topic. What we heard from numerous applications was, "at least a year after the US, maybe a year and a half, we'll be fine."

> During our deliberation, I remember well how it happened, the chairman [Konrad von Finckenstein] turned to me and said, "Well Mr Vice Chair, what's your date?" The broadcasting year ends on 31 August of each year. Industry wanted at least a year and a half, we decided to give them a bit more, so I recommend 31 August 2011. And that's what finally appeared in the decision.[22]

In the 2007 *Determinations Regarding Certain Aspects of the Regulatory Framework for over-the-Air Television*, the CRTC mandated a date of 31 August 2011 as the shut-off point for analogue OTA transmissions in Canada.[23] The CRTC's reluctant flexing of regulatory muscle arrived only in light of mounting pressure from various sources:

- The imminent US ASO of February 2009 risked drawing Canadian viewers to American digital stations;
- Industry Canada supported a firm ASO so that part of the spectrum would be clear, as per agreements with the United States over shared air space;
- Hardware developers saw growing sales of new digital televisions.

The confused state of this key part of the transition also caused numerous problems. By 2007, the CRTC finally admitted, "the pace of transition in Canada has been slow," and introduced the OTA deadline.[24]

Most, but not all, broadcasters agreed that a firm date needed to be set. This regulatory intervention was a clear admission of the inadequacy of the laissez-faire policy structure up to that point in the Canadian digital conversion. This market-based process was later criticized by Michael Geist, who wrote in a July 2010 *Toronto Star* column: "The Canadian government seems content to leave the switch to the private sector, implausibly claiming 'industry-led solutions will ensure a smooth transition for consumers.'"[25] The continually confused state of the Canadian ASO date is a clear example of the limitations of the market-led approach. As Michael McEwen, Hernan Galperin, and others have noted, governments and regulators have an essential role to play in successful national transitions.[26]

The march toward the ASO for OTA television in Canada has been the scene of great struggles. After nearly a decade of market-led inaction, the federal regulator felt compelled to act and establish a deadline.[27] The CRTC has been forced into a delicate balancing act of seizing regulatory control to give some semblance of order while recognizing the legitimate challenges broadcasters face. Some broadcasters still called foul and argued the change was quickly thrust on them. In a 2009 submission, CTV, the country's largest private broadcaster, wrote: "The Commission first outlined the framework for over-the-air television's transition to digital in Broadcasting Public Notice CRTC 2003-61. However, it was not until Broadcasting Public Notice 2007-53 that the current switchover date of 31 August 2011 was established."[28] The essential facts of this statement are true, though it was inaction on the part of broadcasters such as CTV that necessitated such a call. Despite this protest, industry can hardly claim it was blindsided by the decision to establish a deadline. CTV was prominently represented by former president and CEO John Cassaday on the original 1997 digital task force – he even chaired the task force's Working Group on Economics and Consumer Services and Product Implementation. The task force's final report called for digital television to be available in Montreal as of 1999 – something CTV failed to do until 2010 – and recommended a full Canadian ASO by 2007.[29] Nevertheless, in its 2009 CRTC submission, CTV saw fit to complain about "the tight time frame."[30]

The commission has demonstrated flexibility and, after establishing the 2011 ASO, has incrementally scaled back the scope of this fixed date. The original 2007 deadline was designed for the end of *all* analogue television broadcasting transmissions in 2011, only allowing concessions for northern and remote communities. Even in those cases, the CRTC only went so far as to say it was "willing to consider" exceptions for northern and remote communities, only in exceptional circumstances and following a public hearing.[31]

In Broadcasting Regulatory Policy 2009-406, after recognizing that the costs associated with the digital transition may make it financially impractical for some stations located in smaller markets to convert, the CRTC eased its all-encompassing ASO and established a baseline group of mandatory markets for transition to digital. These markets included the National Capital Region and all provincial and territorial capital cities, as well as centres with populations greater than 300,000. With this significant change, OTA broadcasters gained a substantial concession, and Canada would not complete a full digital television transition by the planned ASO of August 2011. After contentious public hearings in the fall of 2009, the CRTC formalized this new plan in March 2010. Several new cities joined the list of markets with populations over 300,000 and capital cities that were expected to comply by 31 August 2011.[32] There is no formal deadline for analogue broadcasting in communities outside the mandatory zones, which consist of:

BRITISH COLUMBIA: Vancouver, Victoria
ALBERTA: Calgary, Edmonton, Lethbridge, Lloydminster
SASKATCHEWAN: Regina, Saskatoon
MANITOBA: Winnipeg
ONTARIO: Toronto (includes Barrie and Hamilton since their stations compete in the Toronto market), London, Windsor, Kitchener, Thunder Bay
QUEBEC: Montreal, Quebec, Trois-Rivières, Sherbrooke, Rivière-du-Loup, Saguenay, Rouyn-Noranda/Val d'Or
NEW BRUNSWICK: Saint John, Moncton, Fredericton
NOVA SCOTIA: Halifax
PRINCE EDWARD ISLAND: Charlottetown
NEWFOUNDLAND AND LABRADOR: St John's
YUKON: Whitehorse
NORTHWEST TERRITORIES: Yellowknife
NUNAVUT: Iqaluit
NATIONAL CAPITAL REGION (Ottawa-Gatineau).[33]

Needless to say, this list leaves wide areas of the country out of the digital transition. With this announcement, the CRTC conceded that the OTA transition in Canada will not be complete, as was the case in the successful United States national switch, but leaves a patchwork of transitions where some regions will benefit from OTA, often in HD, and others will have inferior analogue signals for a limited time and/or rely more on BDUS for television access.

This list does not mean that all television stations outside the mandatory markets may continue broadcasting in their allotted frequencies. Early in the Canadian transition, Industry Canada worked out a detailed agreement with its counterparts at the FCC in the United States on regulating common border frequencies as both countries moved toward digital broadcasting. According to Industry Canada: "To facilitate analogue-to-digital conversions, administrations of Canada and United States signed an Exchange of Letters in 2008. The Exchange of Letters outlines the provisions for television allotments and assignments within 360 km of the common border until both countries have completed their transition to digital."[34] These letters formalized the clearing of the channels between 52 and 69 after 31 August 2011 on both sides of the border. That region of the spectrum was reassigned for use in the United States and even broadcasters outside the mandatory centres that traditionally used one of these channels migrated to one between 2 and 51.[35] Vacating these frequencies was not optional. According to the CRTC, approximately 550,000 Canadian households in non-mandatory markets were served by transmitters that operated on channels 52 to 69.[36]

Of course, as with every bureaucratic procedure, there is paperwork. In 2010, the CRTC readied a plan to expedite the licensing process for new transmitters and told broadcasters they had to file for a license by 31 August 2010 in Vancouver, Calgary, Edmonton, Winnipeg, Toronto, Ottawa-Gatineau, Montreal, Quebec, and Halifax; and 31 December 2010 in all other mandatory markets.

Even given the apparent concessions of the revised mandatory market list and accelerated licensing procedure in 2010, many in industry and some within the CRTC itself believed this revised schedule was simply unobtainable. Since it was established, many major broadcasters, public and private, were steadfast that they did not see the 2011 deadline as feasible. Rogers was a notable exception, and in a 2009 CRTC submission, it stated that its recently expanded television properties, including CityTV and Omni, would "complete the transition for its transmitters by 31 August 2011, but acknowledge that it is difficult and expensive to meet the deadline."[37]

In series of CRTC hearings that followed the commission's call for comments on OTA broadcasting in November 2009, CTV president Ivan Fecan stated: "We are already operating digital transmitters in transitional mode for CTV Toronto, Calgary, and Vancouver, and we will have CTV Ottawa, Montreal, and Edmonton completed by 31 August 2011 ... We think that 2013 is an aggressive but achievable deadline and it's one that, provided we can work out some economic stability for the organization, we can commit to."[38] CTV did not only say 2011 was not viable; it would not even commit to 2013. At the same hearings, the other major private OTA broadcaster, Global TV, stated similar intent:

> For Canwest, this would mean that aiming towards the 31 August 2011 deadline we would complete 11 transmitters; this would include Toronto, Vancouver, Edmonton and Calgary where we

> already have HD signals on the air, we would move to their final location, Winnipeg, Ottawa, Windsor, and Barrie. Montreal, Sherbrooke, and Quebec would follow immediately after the 31 August 2011 deadline, because we are already running into some resource constraints in those markets. And the final nine would be completed by 31 August 2012.[39]

This timeline was a long way from the schedule established by the regulator. The CBC, while further ahead at the time than many of its private sector colleagues, also made it clear it would have trouble meeting the deadline without a substantial infusion of money from the government – a move that was not on the government's list of priorities. In 2009, the broadcasting industry and the CRTC no longer played by the same book.

In her dissenting opinion to the March 2010 CRTC decision, commissioner Suzanne Lamarre distanced herself from the schedule set out by her colleagues and declared the OTA transition out of reach:

> No one can be expected to achieve the impossible. Based on the evidence on the public record, my intimate conviction is that it is unrealistic to think that all transmitters in all mandatory markets can be converted by 31 August 2011.
>
> In the mandatory markets, there are a total of 174 transmitters to be converted.
>
> In light of the above, and given that the evidence on the Commission's record combined with plain logic shows that not all broadcasters in mandatory markets can meet the deadline, on the morning of 1 September 2011, several television services that are part of the daily lives of many Canadians will disappear from the air.
>
> In short, we need to protect a tool that is essential to democratic life. To achieve this goal, it is not enough to state that 31 August 2011 be the mandatory deadline.[40]

Despite the rhetoric that surrounded the OTA transition, in the summer of 2010, CTV and Global said they would achieve what only a year previously they had called "impossible." This change of plans followed an announcement by the CRTC in March 2010 that the ASO deadline would not be extended – a position that Industry Minister Tony Clement supported a month later.[41] Later that summer, in an abrupt change of position, CTV and Global announced they might indeed complete the digital transition in the required markets. In an interview conducted in August 2010, CTV's Kevin Goldstein credited the CRTC's expedited licensing procedure and cited ongoing negotiations of value-for-signal and programming requirements (neither of which were resolved at the time) with changing the transition picture; however, he emphasized the still-precarious nature of the transition and noted: "Any hiccup could still delay it."

THE OTA TELEVISION MARKET

It is legitimate to ask whether OTA television is still a necessary broadcasting medium for Canada or whether it has become an antiquated means of distribution. Finding clear information on this matter requires sifting through sometimes-contradictory data and considering the economic interests of the information source. Given the devotion to market statistics across a wide swath of modern industries, it seems inconceivable that the primary empirical question of, "How many Canadians use OTA?" should still be unclear. But it is.

One thing is certain: the audience for OTA signals in Canada has been dwindling for more than a decade. The perks for OTA broadcasters (prime dial location, local advertising, simultaneous substitution of their ads on American programming, and recently added unlimited advertising minutes) have become less and less valuable. Conventional broadcasters receive a substantial boost in viewership from mandatory carriage on BDUs; however, the largest profits in the current Canadian broadcasting system are found in the distribution industry and specialty channels. Digital or analogue, OTA broadcasters were eventually going to want a piece of the financial windfall happening with specialty channels on BDUs that receive a portion of subscription revenue. Pay and specialty channels have thrived and their future looks even more promising in the digital environment as they do not have to bear the substantial costs faced by OTA broadcasters of constructing transmitters and, in most cases, studio equipment to provide their upgraded services.

According to Goldstein, the financial viability of OTA broadcasting in Canada is "past the tipping point."[42] He cites the cost of running local news programs, the debates with DTH satellite over distant signals, and the value for signal conflict as evidence that the OTA sector is no longer financially viable. In 2009, an event seemed to support

Goldstein's "tipping point" thesis. CHCN, a local OTA broadcaster in Red Deer, Alberta, first licensed in 1957, went off the air after owner Canwest Global could not find a buyer.[43] The loss of the established station sent a chill through Canadian broadcasting as a key CRTC hearing into the future of OTA and the fee-for-carriage issue was set to begin.

The essential questions remain: who still watches OTA television, and why should the roughly 90 per cent of Canadians with cable and satellite services care? Is television's "cornerstone" industry truly past the economic tipping point and on the way to becoming a redundant technology?

The 90 per cent figure (sometimes the number is as high as 93 per cent) is regularly singled out at CRTC hearings as irrefutable evidence of a weak OTA sector.[44] While there is little doubt that the vast majority of Canadians rely on a broadcasting distributor for their television signals, the 90 per cent figure is somewhat misleading. OTA remains a significant element of the broadcasting system, especially for Canadian programmers. The Canadian Association of Broadcasters certainly painted a more positive picture for the CRTC in 2002: "According to the CAB, across the regions of Canada, over-the-air reception accounts for amounts varying from 18 per cent to 44 per cent of all viewing of programming broadcast by conventional television networks (Canadian and non-Canadian). Overall, 25 per cent of viewing of Canadian stations is by over-the-air reception."[45] Could there really be such a drastic shift in less than ten years?

In the rapidly evolving world of Canadian television, these numbers are dated, but they do demonstrate that the overwhelming dominance of BDUs in Canada does not have a long history and there is a clear connection between OTA and Canadian broadcasting. At this juncture for the Canadian broadcasting system, the debate over Canadians who rely on OTA signals has been contentious. The number has enormous implications for the overall strategy behind the digital transition.

In July 2010, the CRTC observed: "As noted by parties, there is uncertainty with regard to changes in the number of Canadian households relying solely on over-the-air reception as the transition date nears."[46] Thus, just over one year before the scheduled ASO, the federal broadcasting regulator sought further information about the number of Canadians who risked losing service due to the transition.[47] The CRTC examined the available data and estimated that approximately 826,000 to 857,500 households required over-the-air digital converter boxes to ensure viewers with older television sets retained access to OTA services.[48] There is by no means uniformity over this issue in the regions and cities across Canada and other factors may skewer the OTA figures.

Like much in the transition, the American experience remains a strong point of comparison. In a 2010 article on the American transition, Greg O'Brien of Cartt.ca observes:

> It may well be that less than 10% of Canadians rely strictly on OTA TV [the Commission's estimates say nearly a million people, but no one really knows for sure]. But, as the Americans found out, the surveys didn't account for people who have one or two TVs tied into their cable or satellite subscription and only realized as the deadline approached and the consumer awareness campaigns did their job that their old TV at the cottage, in the garage, the kitchen or bedroom that uses rabbit ears won't work after the transition. Then there was a run on coupons for decoders.
>
> According to reports I've read during and after the American transition, initial estimates were that about 20 million DTV conversion coupons would be requested. Instead, 34 million coupons were redeemed, with 64 million having been requested.
>
> The FCC, too, said that just 10% of Americans relied solely on OTA TV. But it found that 35% to 50% of homes had at least one OTA set somewhere to supplement their cable or satellite hook-ups.[49]

Many Canadians have more than one television in the house, and often that second or third television is not equipped with a cable or satellite connection. As a result, even Canadians with cable or satellite at home may still have found themselves with no signal on their secondary television after August 2011.[50] The CRTC projected that post-transition, over 44,000 households outside the mandatory markets may require digital receiving equipment, such as satellite receivers and dishes.[51] This was assuming all mandatory markets make the digital transition – a very uncertain prospect in 2010.

It is misleading to think of television habits in Canada as monolithic, particularly when it comes to OTA reception. So where are the OTA users? Table 5.1 comes from a CRTC report published in 2009 and provides a detailed summary of Canadian cable, satellite (DTH), and OTA usage.[52]

Table 5.1
OTA households by region and market type

Region	*Households*	*Estimated Cable Households*	*Estimated DTH Households*	*Estimated OTA Households*
Western Canada Mandated	2,277,815	1,626,733	502,797	148,285
Western Canada Non-mandated	1,457,018	940,488	321,617	194,912
Ontario Mandated	2,944,291	2,039,669	649,913	254,709
Ontario Non-mandated	1,609,960	1,081,190	355,377	173,393
Quebec Mandated	2,247,496	1,505,827	496,105	245,564
Quebec Non-mandated	941,217	560,026	207,761	173,430
Atlantic Canada Mandated Conversion Markets	384,761	254,145	84,931	45,685
Atlantic Canada Non-mandated	538,268	315,170	118,816	104,282
Territories Mandated	18,022	8,798	3,978	5,246
Territories Non-mandated	16,672	6,889	3,680	6,103
Canada Mandated	7,872,385	5,435,171	1,737,725	699,489
Canada Non-mandated	4,563,135	2,903,764	1,007,251	652,120

Source: CRTC, *Digital Transition Models*, 2009, appendix C.

This study estimates that approximately 1.24 million Canadian households rely on OTA television as their primary or only means of TV reception, of which approximately 650,000 households are situated outside the proposed mandatory markets and about 700,000 within. These estimates are equal to 14 per cent of the households in the non-mandated markets, and approximately 8 per cent per cent in the proposed mandated markets.

The 90 per cent figure is also problematic because the penetration of cable and satellite services in the rest of Canada varies greatly by city and by region. A 2007 study prepared for Canadian Association of Broadcasters by Wayne Stacey, an Ottawa-based engineer who has been involved in the digital television for more than two decades, concluded OTA numbers for several key Canadian cities (see table 5.1).

However, a detailed Canwest submission of OTA figures that appear in the appendix to a CRTC policy announcement in July 2010 paints a slightly different picture of the OTA viewership in the same centres (see table 5.3).

Table 5.2
OTA as a percentage of total viewing

City	Percentage
Windsor	18.8
Montreal	10.0
Quebec	8.1
Ottawa	5.4
Halifax	4.1
Toronto	1.9
Vancouver	1.4

Source: Wayne A. Stacey, "CAB Engineering Report," 19 September 2008.

Table 5.3
Canwest submission to CRTC Broadcasting Notice of Consultation CRTC 2010-169, *Call for Comments on Issues Related to the Digital Television Transition*

City	Percentage
Windsor	24.8
Montreal (anglophone)	9.0
Montreal (francophone)	5.1
Quebec	7.7
Ottawa-Gatineau	7.9
Halifax	6.0
Toronto (including Hamilton)	5.9
Vancouver (including Victoria)	2.8

Source: CRTC 2010-485, appendix – original includes other Canadian markets.

On a provincial level, a 2006 report prepared for the CRTC, entitled *How Many Canadians Subscribe to Cable TV or Satellite TV?*, found that 9.7 per cent of Canadians relied on OTA reception in spring 2006. There was a low of 3.2 per cent in Newfoundland and a high of 14.3 per cent in Quebec. The report observed that "a significant percentage of Quebec residents have opted not to access cable TV or DTH. The French-language TV industry, as is the case in much of Europe, is still dominated by traditional over-the-air broadcasters."[53] This does not coïncide with the Canwest numbers from 2009. There is evident uncertainty surrounding this important figure at the highest levels of transition planning. There are approximates for the OTA numbers; not clear and unequivocal data. Unlike the United States, Canada still does not have a much clearer picture of national OTA viewership after the digital transition since analogue transmissions continue in many regions of the country.

There are clearly thousands of Canadians who remain steadfastly against the grain of BDU dominance of Canada's television system. In 2009, the Strategic Council conducted a study to look at the households that do not subscribe to cable, satellite, or microwave TV service (a wireless short-range distribution service with a maximum of fifteen channels) in the communities of Kamloops, British Columbia; Red Deer, Alberta; Timmins, Ontario; Rouyn-Noranda, Quebec; and Sydney, Nova Scotia. When told that OTA broadcasts might not be accessible after 31 August 2011, the sample group responded with a range of intentions:

- More than one-quarter (26 per cent) reported that they will "do nothing and just live without television channels";
- 21 per cent would consider subscribing to cable or satellite service;
- 7 per cent reported they would consider the options available at the time;
- 20 per cent reported they "have not thought about it yet";
- 18 per cent will do "something else" (not clarified in the report);
- 9 per cent said they do not know what they would do.[54]

It is noteworthy that the largest group in this sample chose to opt out of television altogether rather than be pressured into paying for a distribution service.

Of the communities surveyed, only Rouyn-Noranda appeared on the CRTC's 2010 list of mandated markets. From the results of this study, it is clear that the percentage of the population that did not opt for cable or satellite services contained a core group who resisted the pressure to pay for television. If this trend held post-2011, those Canadians found themselves cut off from the television broadcasting system.

The CRTC considered two plans to make certain Canadians in the transition markets that used the OTA sector were not left with a blank screen in September 2011. The first plan was used in the United States and would have required the government to issue coupons to assist citizens who need to purchase a converter set-top box to translate digital signals for older analogue sets. The United States set aside more than $1.5 billion generated from spectrum auctions to support a coupon program (it should be noted the US transition involved a full national switch, rather than one in just targeted markets). According to CRTC figures, based on one digital converter box costing up to $75 per affected household, the aggregated cost to consumers affected by the transition for the boxes would be up to $64 million.[55] The Canadian government has repeatedly resisted calls for such a program in Canada.[56]

The second plan, based on the successful Freesat model in the United Kingdom, would call on the distribution industry to provide a free package of local signals to households in the targeted areas. In 2010, the CRTC authorized "the provision by BDUs of a free package consisting of all local and regional conventional television signals currently available over the air in a given market (local package)."[57] The "free" in this statement is debatable. The installation of such a system would cost approximately $300 and there is no guarantee that the BDUs will see the viability in offering it. In February 2010, a new distributor named Free HD Canada received a license to provide this service and originally planned to be running in 2011.[58] The company has since changed its name to BluSky HDTV and has delayed its launch until 2013.

The CRTC was increasingly concerned about the OTA sector as the 2011 ASO drew near. In 2010, in the public benefits package following Shaw's purchase of Canwest Global for just over $2 billion, the CRTC required that Shaw direct $15 million "towards providing a satellite receiver and dish, and associated installation, to households that had relied solely on OTA reception to access at least one local and/or regional television station that was operating on channels 52 to 69 outside mandatory markets, and that had ceased OTA transmission due to the transition."[59] Though Shaw offered the service, it poorly promoted it and received a weak response (see chapter 6). For any BDU offering this type of service, the economic rationale is in getting subscribers to upgrade to more costly services after they have received the free limited channel package.

It remains to be seen if these services will function as a distribution band-aid or if they will work as an effective component of the overall transition strategy. When I asked Michel Arpin in late summer of 2010 if the Freesat solution was a viable alternative for Canada, he answered without hesitation: "No."[60] Like so much of the transition strategy, the future of these BDU packages depends on the number of Canadians who wish to maintain the option of a free service of local channels.

SIGNS OF LIFE

There is far more volatility in the Canadian OTA market than the approximately 10 per cent figure suggests. Given Canada's enormous geography, location is a key factor. Windsor, Ontario, remains a hot spot for OTA reception, but not for Canadian digital signals; as of 2009, none were broadcast in the region, though in 2011, five channels were available in digital OTA.[61] In comparison, there are forty-one digital OTA channels for the Detroit area across the river.[62] Loss of Canadian viewers to American broadcasters has been a reason cited for the necessity of an efficient Canadian transition.[63]

The interest in OTA has sparked some spin-off industries. Save and Replay, a west Toronto retailer that specializes in high-end OTA antennas, has enjoyed enormous sales growth since 2008. According to owner Karim Sunderani, after a very slow start to the business in 2006 and 2007, business grew ten-fold between 2008 and 2009, including sales of roughly 2,000 antennas a month in the peak 2009 summer season.[64] The growth was directly related to the rise in digital OTA in Southern Ontario and the completion of the US transition. He is enthusiastic about his business prospects and the future of digital OTA in Canada. Sunderani is among the minority of business operators who remain convinced there could be a future for OTA television if given a regulatory environment in which it could be allowed to flourish.

Local OTA resurgence is not simply the stuff of analogue nostalgia; there have been some signs of OTA life south of the border. In 2009, the *Los Angeles Times* reported a strong local growth in OTA reception as people discovered the quality of digital OTA post-digital transition.[65] The article claims OTA reception increased three-fold in the metropolitan Los Angeles region in 2009. In 2012, there were over ninety OTA channels in metropolitan Los Angeles, and many broadcasters have opted to multiplex their signals and only use sporadic HD broadcasts.[66] Any Google search of an American urban centre and "over-the-air television" reveals a far more active American OTA sector. In Canada, while writing this book in 2009, I was able to access approximately nine OTA channels in both downtown Montreal and Toronto (though the geographic obstacle Mount Royal can prove problematic in Montreal). Similar size markets in the United States have far more OTA channels: Chicago has fifty-six and Houston has twenty-six.[67]

This clear difference is largely due to the wider political economies of the two broadcasting systems. As Peter Miller noted in 2009: "It is noteworthy that this transformation of OTA TV in Canada is by no means identical to that which occurred in the US. US networks continue to have vibrant independent affiliates ... Moreover the relative market power and degree of vertical integration of US TV distributors is far less than that of Canadian equivalents."[68] The multiplexing of OTA signals, popular in many American markets, has not gained traction in Canada. There is little incentive to expand the OTA market in an increasingly vertically integrated industry in which OTA broadcasters are owned by companies whose primary revenue is generated in the BDU sector. One of the only broadcasters to make use of the multiplexing option afforded by the ATSC standard is Global Television, purchased by Shaw in 2011. Since 2011, Global has multiplexed its OTA signal in both high and standard definition. The second transmission usually appears as a .2 following the main HD channel. Dan Gold, the senior director of media technology strategy and standards at Shaw, explains that the purpose of multiplexing the identical signal is to give BDUS the option to pick up the conventional Global signal in either standard or high definition.[69] Not all BDUS have the carrying capacity to accept all signals in HD, though Gold expects that to change shortly and believes that Global will discontinue the multiplex signal accordingly.

Thus, even what appears to be an expansion of services in the OTA market is still about access to BDU distribution. Multiplexing, which has gained a strong base in the United States, is allowed in Canada, but the economics of the current system are stacked against it. The contemporary industrial regime of Canadian broadcasting is at odds with exploiting a key technological benefit of digital television.

There is a unique example during the Canadian digital television transition of a Canadian business that made a bid to become a new OTA national network. In 2007, the CRTC issued a call for applications from parties that wished to obtain OTA digital/HD broadcasting licenses in markets across Canada.[70] HDTV Networks, led by digital radio owner John Bitove, proposed an over-the-air, fully HD network based out of Vancouver to compete with established national networks CBC, CTV, and Canwest/Global. In its application, HDTV Networks stated it had no plans to broadcast local programming and would not solicit local advertising. This triggered an outcry from broadcasters that believed it would constitute an unfair advantage over those mandated to provide local programming.[71]

The HDTV network never launched in Canada. In 2008, the CRTC rejected HDTV Networks' application, and noted:

> The Commission has not accepted a model of national distribution without significant local programming content as being appropriate for Canada as it is inconsistent with the Commission's overall OTA policy. It would be untenable and fundamentally unfair to allow HDTV Networks to be relieved of the local content obligation (or accept a minimum of two hours per broadcast week per region) while insisting that others provide an average of 22 hours of local content per broadcast week.[72]

In a dissenting opinion, Len Katz, then-vice chairman of telecommunications, argued the benefits of the proposed network far surpassed the local programming problems: "I do not believe it is contrary to the Broadcasting Act or its accompanying regulations to allow new entrants some period of time to establish themselves prior to holding them to the same conditions as well-established industry participants ... To force everyone into the same box is to deny entrepreneurs the ability to innovate."[73] Katz's objection had regulatory precedent at the CRTC. Broadcasting upstarts such as PPV, video on demand, mobile television, and the online community have enjoyed relaxed regulatory oversight, if not outright exemption, in an effort to encourage their development. However, in this case the CRTC insisted on consistent levels of local programming for all broadcasters. There were no further submissions to develop a national digital OTA network.

Despite this setback, there are voices that disagree with Kevin Goldstein's assessment that Canadian OTA is "past the tipping point." A report prepared for the CRTC in 2009 advised that the future of OTA television in Canada need not be so dreary:

> The real issue going forward is whether OTA DTV transmission is a merely cost centre or is a potential incremental revenue opportunity. In broad terms, if one accepts a capital upgrade cost for a DTV transmitter of $250,000 to $500,000, a reasonable estimate of associated annualized interest, depreciation and operating costs might be in the $50,000 range. For a station earning $10 million annually, this would represent as little as 0.5 per cent of revenues – not requiring a big increment in advertising sales to be justifiable. Given the quality, price (free), interest in and ease of OTA DTV reception it is not hard to imagine a slight resurgence in OTA reception.[74]

The same report concluded the CRTC's emphasis on national initiatives has often worked to the detriment of local OTA stations, however, in 2009 the authors saw some hope for the sector: "The pendulum appears to have swung away from purely national TV issues and concerns to local ones ... there is no particular reason why a national OTA TV business cannot be scaled down by an order of magnitude and still, as in smaller analogue and digital specialty services, make money."[75] Many of the report's suggestions for the OTA sector echoed Katz's call for a more flexible policy approach. The report's author, Peter H. Miller, encouraged the CRTC to adopt an OTA policy in which a station's programming obligations are scaled to its profitability.

Late in the decade, an unexpected development gave credence to Millar's theory. In July 2009, a little-known company named Channel Zero applied to purchase CHCH television in Hamilton and CJNT in Montreal from Canwest Global. The price reflects the attitude of most private industry toward the Canadian OTA sector. As the CRTC stated in the notice of approval the following month: "The purchase price for the whole transaction (including the undertaking CJNT-TV Montreal), as set out in the purchase agreement, is $12."[76] One of the longest-serving OTA broadcasters in Southern Ontario, with a multicultural broadcaster in Montreal thrown in, was purchased for lunch money. The CRTC determined CHCH's value was negative, but although the purchasers took on a money-losing venture (Canwest had planned to close the station), they managed to complete the acquisition without making lay offs. In accordance with Millar's report, the CRTC gave some policy relief to Channel Zero and suspended its priority programming obligations until the it gained some profitability, with a re-evaluation planned for 2012. As a condition of its license, CHCH had to be fully digital by 31 August 2011. In 2010, CHCH broadcasted in HD from its main Hamilton transmitter and upgraded its transmitters to digital in London, Ottawa, and Muskoka by 31 August 2011.[77]

Until 2010, Channel Zero had acted as a category two broadcaster and had established itself with the brands Movieola and Silver Screen classics. Romen Podzyhun, Channel Zero chairman and chief executive officer, remains enthusiastic about the future of CHCH and the greater Canadian OTA industry a year after the CHCH purchase. The following exchange is from an August 2010 interview:

ROMEN PODZYHUN: In the case of Hamilton [CHCH] we planned to lose three million in the first year. I'm happy to report we lost less

than that. We expect by 2011 it will be profitable. CJNT is a similar time frame, maybe a little longer.
GREGORY TAYLOR: Is the digital transition a burden or opportunity?
RP: It's a big investment but I think the whole process has been telegraphed ahead of time. I think it's been a fair process. We were able to go behind the US and watch and learn what worked and what didn't work.
GT: What didn't work in your view?
RP: I think they underestimated how many people still use rabbit ears. The US did a good job explaining what it meant to the consumer.
GT: Could more be done to encourage growth in the OTA sector?
RP: I'm surprised the lack of entrepreneurs who've jumped in. From a regulatory point of view they could make sure the BDUS don't become the gatekeepers. It is still the Broadcast Act that is the gatekeeper as opposed to private enterprise telling you what should go on the air and what shouldn't ... I believe over the air is not dead. We have to just readjust how we do business. That's what the big players haven't done ... Nobody learned from the record industry.[78]

It is noteworthy that despite the protests by some of the largest private broadcasters in Canada, most independent broadcasters, such as Channel Zero, were ready for the ASO. In an August 2010 article, the *Wire Report* noted Channel Zero's progress, as well as that of independents such as CHEK TV in Victoria, BC, which claimed it would probably broadcast in digital well before the deadline.[79] CHEK TV also claimed to complete the transition substantially under budget. I brought up this fact with Michel Arpin, former CRTC vice chair of broadcasting, and his response was brief and telling:

GREGORY TAYLOR: Most independent channels are reporting that they will be ready for August 2011, yet many of the major networks are struggling. I don't understand that.
MICHEL ARPIN: Neither do I.

It is of course premature to call these few independents a resurgence in Canadian OTA broadcasting, but after years of bleak news in the sector, they are recognizable shoots of growth.

THE CBC

As Canada's public broadcaster, the CBC's position in the digital transition is unique and difficult. The CBC faces the same expenses as national private broadcasters in equipping transmitters and studios for digital broadcasting; a limited annual budget, of which it controls approximately one third through advertising; the need to maintain national television and radio networks in both official languages; a sitting government (the Conservative Party) that has a history of opposing it; and a public who justifiably sees it as a public service that must be available to all Canadians.[80] In comparison to other national broadcasters, the CBC faces greater demands with fewer financial resources at its disposal. According to a 2011 Nordicity study commissioned by the CBC, among eighteen major Western countries in 2009, Canada had the third-lowest level of public funding on a per-capita basis for its public broadcaster.[81] At $34 per citizen, Canada's level of funding was only ahead of New Zealand and the United States, and was 60 per cent less than the $87 average across the other countries in the study. Its level of funding was also about one-fifth of Norway, the level of the leading country in terms of public funding, where public broadcaster NRK received the equivalent of $164 per capita in 2009.[82]

The data from the Nordicity study came before the Conservative party imposed a 10 per cent budget cut on the CBC in 2012. Whereas in 2010 CTV and Global managed to complete the transition despite saying it was not possible one year earlier, there was no last minute change in store for the CBC. The only possible scenario for the CBC to complete the required transmitters for August 2011 was a substantial one-time infusion of money from the federal government, instead they received no extra funding and shortly after received a 10 per cent cut. Transition funds were not forthcoming from a government that in April 2010 brought forward a private members bill that sought to have the CBC investigated for Liberal bias at a Commons heritage committee.[83] Relations between the government and the CBC hit one of their lowest points as the summer of 2010, the key period for the final push for the transition, approached. That particular 2010 conflict notwithstanding, there was no indication from the government at any point during the transition that extra funding for the CBC would be forthcoming.

Table 5.4
CBC digital over-the-air transition plan (August 2010)

BY 31 AUGUST 2011	
CBC (6)	RADIO CANADA (9)
Toronto*	Toronto*
Montreal*	Montreal*
Ottawa*	Ottawa*
Vancouver*	Quebec City*
Calgary	Rimouski
Edmonton	Trois-Rivières
	Sherbrooke
	Chicoutimi
	Moncton
BY 31 AUGUST 2012	
CBC (8)	RADIO CANADA (4)
Yellowknife	Vancouver
Regina	Edmonton
Winnipeg	Regina
Windsor	Winnipeg
St John/Fredericton	
Charlottetown	
Halifax	
St John's	

(*) Already in operation in 2010

In August 2010, the CBC officially announced it would not have its OTA operations ready for the August 2011 deadline in the required markets and asked the CRTC for an extension on its analogue transmitters (see table 5.4).[84] This did not come as a great surprise to people who have followed the progression of the Canadian digital television transition. As early as 2002, a CRTC public notice referenced the CBC's presentation on the transition to digital OTA: "[The CBC] added that it will be obliged to seek additional funding for this activity because its 'current programming priorities and limited resources do not permit the Corporation to pursue digital television programming activities in any substantive manner at this time.'"[85]

In 2002, the CBC proposed that a "realistic approach" to ensuring its television network services remained available in small and remote communities would be to use OTA digital transmission to serve residents of the ten largest markets, representing 70 per cent of Canada's population. It would serve the remaining 30 per cent by satellite.[86]

This plan would put rural Canadians at a distinct disadvantage by restricting free OTA to the cities. The CBC abandoned this proposal, but it demonstrates that the CBC saw the digital transition as a financial challenge early in the process.

As the decade progressed and the spectre of a mandated national ASO loomed ever larger, the CBC's proposals on the issue became increasingly bold and further removed from its obligations as a public broadcaster. In the 2007 CRTC hearings that preceded the establishment of the ASO, the CBC proposed an OTA television subscriber fee to ensure it would be able to continue to fulfill its regulatory obligations.[87] This suggestion defeats the purpose of a freely accessible OTA system and was an effort for the public broadcaster to access another revenue stream. In its denial of this early effort at fee-for-carriage, the CRTC ruled "the Commission is not convinced that the case has been made for the making of such a fundamental change to the revenue structure of the broadcasting system at this time."[88] In 2009, the CBC employed free market rhetoric in its submission to the CRTC to such an extent that it was difficult to distinguish between the public broadcaster and its privately funded colleagues. There was much said about markets and consumer choice and little mention of the obligations of a public broadcaster.[89] For this hearing, the CBC pursued the same potential fee-for-carriage dollars as other OTA broadcasters and wasted little time on the inherent responsibilities of a public service broadcaster. On the matter of funding set-top boxes to ensure no Canadians with older sets were left behind, the CBC commented: "The question as to how people with analogue sets will receive digital signals is a simple commercial issue which should be left to the market and individual choice."[90] The same CRTC submission made the CBC's position clear: "While the Corporation acknowledges that the loss of an over-the-air signal may represent an inconvenience for some Canadians, it is important to recognize that there is no public policy which requires that Canadians have access to free television."[91] While that might be legally true, it seems far removed from any sense of public service. Loss of access to the public broadcaster by Canadian citizens is more than an "inconvenience." The 1991 Broadcasting Act mandates that the programming the CBC provides should "be made available throughout Canada by the most appropriate and efficient means and as resources become available for the purpose."[92] The act allows for a great deal of wriggle room. However, the act also requires the CBC to "reflect Canada and its regions to national and regional audiences, while serving the special needs of those regions" and "contribute to shared national consciousness and identity."[93] National OTA coverage is an appropriate vehicle for meeting these obligations.

While the CRTC granted other broadcasters the right to negotiate FFC with BDUS in 2010 (pending ruling at the Federal Court of Appeal), it did not do the same for the CBC. Despite the CBC's free-market rhetoric, the CRTC did not view its position as similar to that of private broadcasters:

> The regime foreseen by the Commission would allow broadcasters to require program deletion when negotiating for a fair value for the distribution of their programming services. In light of the objective above, the Commission considers that it would be inconsistent to permit the CBC to require deletion of its programming from a BDU and hence prevent the public from receiving its programming ... Accordingly, the Commission has determined that the market-based regime ... will apply only to private local television stations.[94]

Shortly after this announcement, Global and CTV found the funding to complete the OTA transition, while the CBC asked the CRTC to extend its analogue licenses.

Despite these difficulties, there has been some public support for the CBC's digital dilemma. In 2010, the CBC found a sympathetic ear to its cause in an unexpected source. That January, the conservative C.D. Howe Institute published a study that found severe flaws in Canadian content policy in the digital media environment and, surprisingly, supported an increased role for the CBC: "Public broadcasting, including the CBC, should be bolstered with sufficient funding to ensure significant outlets for Canadian content."[95] The authors of the study believe a robust public broadcaster was the only way to ensure the continued vitality of Canadian content in a digital environment.

In March 2010, the CBC did not receive the FFC revenue it had sought from the CRTC; however, the regulator did take up the CBC's cause in a report submitted to the government in tandem with the policy announcement. The report encouraged a much more engaged government role in the final year of the transition, and called for increased funding for the CBC. The CRTC notes that this infusion of capital has precedent: the Accelerated Coverage Plan of 1974 to extend CBC radio and TV to small communities. The report states:

> The digital transition date of 31 August 2011 is fast approaching and the Government needs to take additional measures to ensure that Canadians maintain access to over-the-air television stations. Therefore, the Commission recommends that:
>
> The Government set out a clear policy and coordinate an implementation plan for Canada's digital transition, including support for the CBC's digital transition plans. In this regard, the Commission notes that the Government provided capital funding to increase coverage of the CBC's services beginning in the 1970s with its Accelerated Coverage Plan.[96]

In the 1970s, Canada's overall political economy was a far different environment than anything deemed remotely acceptable by Stephen Harper's Conservative Party. The Accelerated Coverage Plan of 1974 brought CBC TV and radio to all Canadian communities of more than 500 people (99 per cent of the population) and cost the Trudeau Liberal government $50 million.[97] The Conservative government obviously did not agree that a freely accessible CBC was a priority and did not officially respond to this CRTC report.

In August 2011, less than one month before the scheduled transition, the CBC received permission from the CRTC to keep broadcasting in analogue in twenty-two markets. The mandated markets of Saskatoon, London, St John, and Lethbridge remained analogue. The CBC sought a further extension almost immediately. Then, faced with 10 per cent budget cuts in 2012, CBC president Hubert T. Lacroix announced the CBC would not upgrade the 600 transmitters in these remaining regions, saving $10 million.[98] In Ontario, provincial educational broadcaster TV Ontario followed suit in July 2012 and announced it would not complete the switch and that OTA signals would not longer be available in Bancroft, Hawkesbury, Huntsville, Kenora, Kingston, North Bay, Owen Sound, Parry Sound, Pembroke, Penetanguishene, Peterborough, Sault Ste Marie, Sudbury, and Timmins.[99]

The failure of these two key broadcasters to duplicate the analogue OTA footprint finalized the incomplete over-the-air television transition in large areas of the country.

CONCLUSION

The over-the-air sector has been the site of the most contentious debates during the Canadian digital television transition. From an economic perspective, the issue revolves around the large capital investment required to maintain analogue levels of coverage in an OTA industry that has not seen the same levels of profit as specialty channels. As a matter of public policy, the transition involves the key normative debate of OTA television as a service that uses a public resource – the spectrum – that should be freely available to all citizens. For years, the transitional process was delayed while OTA broadcasters fought over fee-for-carriage. Ironically, given the Global and CTV purchases by BDUS Shaw and Bell respectively, the entire FFC debate may be moot.

In a real sense, the 31 August 2011 ASO encapsulates the whole Canadian digital television transition process. The CRTC only established the date after it was clear the industry-led transition would not progress at an acceptable pace. The deadline was modeled after the national shut off that had been planned for the United States. At no time did the government show any leadership in this vital development. After 2007, cracks started to appear in the stone edifice of the ASO, and by 2009, the plan had been reduced to major markets. Perhaps sensing a complete policy capitulation, major broadcasters were adamant that 2011 was neither financially nor technologically feasible, and pushed the CRTC to extend the analogue era. In the spring of 2010, the CRTC held fast to its now "ASO-lite," and the national private networks had a change of mind and found the date possible.

This is the stuff of farce, not of sound policy on a central element of the nation's communications system.

The odd broadcaster out in this last-minute OTA revival is the CBC. Recent history dictates there is a slim-to-none chance that the Harper Conservatives will give the public broadcaster fiscal relief in the foreseeable future. For too many years during the transition, the CBC seemed far more interested in finding new streams of revenue than in creating a cohesive strategy to address its formidable problem. Steven Guiton, CBC vice-president and chief regulatory officer, seemed to say as much in an interview with the *Wire Report* in the summer of 2010: "Perhaps you'd say we should have started earlier, and perhaps we should have in some sense. But we have been planning for this over a number of years, trying to figure out what would be the best way to go at this. We knew we couldn't replicate all 650 of our transmitters, so there has been a period of time to actually plan the thing out."[100] The inference that it did not have enough time is weak – the CBC has been involved with the Canadian transition since day one, and more than ten years should be plenty of time for planning and implementation. Still, one cannot help but feel a tinge of sympathy for the CBC's predicament. As I noted in 2009: "There is a familiarity to CBC presentations at CRTC hearings: the main issue will inevitably come around to funding and the CRTC Chair will eventually remind the CBC that such matters are beyond the regulator's jurisdiction."[101]

Yes, the CBC receives public financial support; however, it is the only one of the three national broadcasters to go through the digital transition with an almost completely Canadian prime-time line up. The playing field is hardly level when the other networks can offer viewers a steady stream of *American Idol* and *House*. Canadian policy makers offered little support to the CBC at this key juncture. Galperin wrote of the place of the public broadcaster in the UK transition: "From the outset policy makers sought to ensure that the new legislative framework did not impair the corporation [BBC]."[102] The same certainly cannot be said of Canada.

I do not contest the fact that cable and satellite currently rule the distribution game in Canada. What remains uncertain is the potential reactions of Canadians to digital OTA. Will viewers in major centres walk away from BDU specialty channels in favour of a limited, but free, selection of OTA stations? Will Canadians actually cut the cord? More likely, it will remain much as it is now: varying by cities and regions.

Despite all the posturing and statistics that support the belief that the OTA industry is on its last legs, there have been very few broadcasters willing to simply walk away and forfeit their OTA licenses. CHCN in Red Deer, Alberta, has proven an exceptional case, not the canary in the broadcasting coalmine as some had feared.

In a world of growing niche broadcasting, the OTA sector remains defiantly "mass." Perhaps more importantly, OTA stations maintain a local appeal that the specialty sector cannot match. Bob Reaume explains some of OTA's continued relevance: "Amazon notwithstanding, the old fashioned geographical trading area is still the way it works. In other words, where you live pretty much still determines mostly where you will buy goods and services, and therefore how advertisers will attempt to reach you ... The truth is that very few advertisers have the budget and product category to want or need to target the whole country. Most times 'top 10' or 'top 20' markets are the rule, and so that is where the budget is spent."[103]

Conventional broadcasters may not yet receive fee-for-carriage from cable and satellite providers, but they remain an attractive conduit to the local market. The digital transition challenges, but in no way defeats, the classic Canadian abundance of geography.

6

Other Voices

Digital television in Canada has overwhelmingly been the story of a powerful industry, a reluctant regulator, and a disengaged federal government. Broadcasting has also historically been the site of political activism: from the pioneering work of the Canadian Radio League in the late 1920s and 1930s to some of the individuals and organizations who are engaged in contemporary debates over the public right to communicate, whether the medium in question is defined as new or old.[1] In this brief chapter, I seek to shine a light on the efforts of individuals and organizations that offer a vision for Canadian digital television that does not merely reinforce the analogue status quo. All of the featured activists and community representatives featured in this chapter have had to operate with relatively limited resources. Major commercial broadcasters assemble teams of experts and lawyers to draft CRTC submissions and speak in Ottawa before the commissioners; most of the voices below consist of very few people with small or negligible budgets. Just because the efforts of a particular group may not have been fully realized does not mean the effort was a failure. As anyone who has ever engaged in political activism can attest, established interests are not always receptive to original ideas. Some of these groups and individuals saw a degree of success in their campaigns, some were rejected, and others have plans that are still unfolding. This range of perspectives demonstrates a vision for digital television in Canada that addresses public interest issues at the local and national level.

CACTUS – CANADIAN ASSOCIATION OF COMMUNITY TELEVISION USERS AND STATIONS

Cable packages from larger BDUs often include community channels in Canada. Though community channels are not technically required by regulation, the CRTC's stance is clear: "Licensed BDUs must contribute 5% of their gross broadcasting revenues to support Canadian programming. Licensees are authorized to allocate up to 2% of those revenues to local expression."[2] Though community broadcasters are "local expression," they have had to fight for recognition in recent years, and CACTUS has been a regular presence in Ottawa as it lobbies on behalf of community broadcasting. Currently, not all community channels are available strictly through BDUs – there are nine OTA broadcasters that are not-for-profit, are run by and for a community as a whole, and have a community access and outreach mandate.[3] These broadcasters receive no government funding of any kind.

Cathy Edwards, the national coordinator for CACTUS, has been a passionate advocate for Canadian community programming during the digital television transition. CACTUS formed in 2007 to intervene at the CRTC's Diversity of Voices hearing and incorporated as a non-profit in 2010. Despite a limited budget, CACTUS has been a constant presence at CRTC hearings and industry gatherings and often advances ideas that run contrary to the prevailing commercial orthodoxy. At a time when community broadcasting is a diminishing force in the Canadian television, CACTUS consistently reminds the power structure of Canadian media that the key preamble to policies outlined in the 1991 Broadcasting Act explicitly states: "It is hereby declared as the broadcasting policy for Canada that (*b*) the Canadian broadcasting system, operating primarily in the English and French languages and comprising public, private *and community elements* [italics added]" and that Canadian programming will "include educational and community programs."[4] Given the industrial orientation of the Canadian digital transition, CACTUS has faced a difficult challenge but it has still managed to form proposals that challenge the widespread adherence to market forces and the overall dominance of BDUs within the system.

As the ASO approached in 2011, CACTUS announced that communities that were going to lose their OTA signal should create a rebroadcasting system offering not only television but also potentially radio, wireless Internet, and cell phone service from the local television towers for a fraction of the price they would cost separately.[5] Rebroadcasting is not a new development in Canada and, in the past, has connected smaller communities to the greater broadcasting system.[6] It involves building or using an existing a tower in the community to receive distant signals, often via satellite dish, and distribute them by either local cable infrastructure or wireless local transmission. According to CACTUS, "More than 100 communities in Canada already act as their own rebroadcasters and approximately 70 are part of cable co-operatives (non-profit, and owned by the community). Many of these communities have only a few hundred residents."[7] Small communities do not require a BDU license to provide these services.

CACTUS' rebroadcasting plan for the digital transition sought to harness the common digital language of various media to offer a range of local services. The group encouraged the development of more community radio and television channels via community rebroadcasting and offered to help community groups obtain a community broadcasting license. The overall goal of CACTUS' digital transition plan was to ensure universal access to OTA signals in Canada and strengthen the community sector of Canadian broadcasting.

CACTUS has also strongly opposed the CBC's plan to shut down its transmitters in areas of Canada outside the mandated markets. In June 2012, CACTUS filed a submission to the CRTC outlining a plan urging town and band councils, community colleges, community media groups, and concerned citizens to ask the CRTC to make the CBC transmission equipment available for local use (a position the Friends of Canadian Broadcasting, the Public Interest Advocacy Centre, and the Canadian Media Guild supported).[8] The scope of the submission was broad and bold: it also called on the CRTC to urge OTA broadcasters that switched to digital to carry the CBC signal as a standard definition multiplex in places it would otherwise no longer be available, and asked the CBC to offer decommissioned towers to local communities free of charge so that communities could experiment with rebroadcasting and local wireless transmissions.

The CBC responded to CACTUS in a press release that stated: "CBC/Radio-Canada is decommissioning only a small proportion of its towers." It also claimed: "The Corporation has every intention of reaching out to communities interested in purchasing the site to pursue their own community broadcasting interests."[9] Whether or not the CBC reaches out to the smaller communities that have been badly neglected in the transition, it is clear that CACTUS' efforts attracted the attention of major Canadian broadcasters.

KAMLOOPS, BRITISH COLUMBIA

The town of Kamloops, British Columbia, has been one of the few sites of lively citizen participation in the digital television transition. A group called Save Our CBC Kamloops (SOCK) has been active in recent years, trying to restore the local CBC OTA television broadcasts that were cut in 2006. Notably, SOCK is taking advantage of the opportunities offered by digital television technology to further its cause. The group has appealed to broadcasters and the CRTC to establish a digital television multiplex broadcast in the region that would support multiple OTA channels, not just the CBC.

The Canadian Media Guild (CMG), which represents media workers and has actively promoted a continuing role for a vibrant OTA sector, supported SOCK's position. In a 2009 submission to the CRTC that discusses OTA in smaller communities, the CMG argues:

> The real solution is the multiplexing of digital OTA signals. And not only is multiplexing a solution to the transition, it is also a way to breathe new life into local and independent TV in smaller communities, where there is currently limited choice for OTA viewing. We look at this as an opportunity to de-fragment TV viewing by providing an appropriate and affordable service to the significant proportion of Canadians interested in a modest selection of local and Canadian TV. It's also an effective way to maintain the necessary infrastructure to broadcast localized emergency information.[10]

At a hearing before the CRTC in 2009, Pam Astbury presented on behalf of SOCK. She spoke of the promise of OTA digital television for her community, and in particular the multiplexing option: "We believe that the future of television will be constructed upon a digital foundation and that digital technology is the answer to both large and small market areas across Canada."[11] The group also claimed the transition would be affordable for industry, citing an independent engineering study that revealed the conversion costs from the analogue transmitter to digital would be less than $90,000. Divided between six multiplexed broadcasters, that is, less than $15,000 per channel. Astbury stated that the multiplexing option was "quite simply a cost-effective option for small market areas."

In response, CRTC Chair Konrad von Finckenstein argued: "And what is stopping the local broadcaster from multiplexing right now? As far as I know there is no regulatory impediment." Later in the series of hearings, CTV president Ivan Fecan indirectly answered: "It is important to understand that a multiplexed channel while digital, is not HD." In other words, CTV was only interested if investing enabled HD broadcasts. There is little private sector will to explore the possibilities of multiplexing several channels in standard definition.[12] Mid-size towns, such as Kamloops, that were not part of the mandated markets – and they are numerous in Canada – lose out.

The March 2010 CRTC policy announcement that followed the 2009 hearings offered only tepid support of multiplexing: "Broadcasters should continue to explore opportunities such as multiplexing to ensure that Canadians continue to have access to free [over-the-air] conventional television services."[13] There are no regulatory teeth behind this statement – broadcasters are free to do as they wish. Industry resistance to multiplexing possibilities means a key element of the promise of digital television remains underdeveloped and a segment of the population loses its OTA signal.

HAMILTON, ONTARIO

As anyone in Southern Ontario will tell you, Hamilton is not Toronto. Nevertheless, Hamiltonians have long lived in the broadcasting shadow of Canada's largest city. Digital communications have allowed for a new local media centre in Hamilton, although one that falls under the more vaguely defined category of "new media" rather than traditional broadcasting.

Historically, it made sense for private broadcasters to broadcast from Toronto and sell the larger audience to advertisers without having to invest in local Hamilton content. The Hamilton region has the geographical disadvantage of being right between the major centres of Toronto and Buffalo, which meant there were few available radio frequencies for local media. Since there was little market incentive to provide programming in Hamilton, a local community group began to target the CBC to establish local content. A 2005 report by the Centre for Community Study, a local group committed to Hamilton civic renewal, noted that Hamilton, "with a population of over 700,000, is the largest urban area in the country with no local presence from the CBC."[14] The city had not enjoyed a local CBC radio station since 1992. The Centre for Community Study noted in a 2006 submission to the CRTC: "Hamilton is included as part of the Toronto extended market despite the fact that there is a very low level of integration between the two cities and the fact that Hamilton is not part of the Greater Toronto Area."[15] The local media landscape in Hamilton looked grim as the 2011 ASO approached. In 2009, when Channel Zero purchased CHCH, a local private broadcaster with fifty years of service, it kept the station alive but limited funds to invest in local programming.

The arrival of CBC president Hubert Lacroix in 2008 was accompanied by a renewed interest in local services at the CBC. In November of 2011, the CBC announced that Hamilton would be the first city in Canada to receive a flagship new digital CBC service. The launch of that service in May 2012 was a welcome development, though the actual product was an underwhelming web page that details local news, weather, and traffic. Though the site is still in beta, rather than acting as a multimedia centre for the region, it offers no audio or video streaming. Podcasts, radio, and television programs streamed from CBC.ca have become a digital extension of the national public broadcaster but these services were not part of the Hamilton launch.

Nevertheless, according to Sonja Macdonald of the Centre for Community Study, the arrival of the CBC on the local Hamilton news scene in 2012 has improved the overall coverage of community news and has made other Hamilton media more responsive to local matters.[16] Macdonald believes being part of the CBC's overall news network may help Hamilton shake the industrial, steel-town image that has been inaccurate for two decades.

LEAMINGTON, ONTARIO

Over-the-air community television stations are few and far between in Canada, and yet one is home to some of the more innovative usage of digital broadcasting in the country. In the Southwest Ontario town of Leamington, approximately half an hour from Windsor, Ontario, community television CFTV34 went to air on 9 March 2005. CFTV34 is a low-power television station that broadcasts OTA in the region on UHF 34 and digital cable 100, and serves Leamington, Tilbury, Wheatley, Essex, Kingsville, Windsor, and Tecumseh. The station decided to avoid constant struggles with BDUs over funding; instead, it is financed through donations, partnerships, and local sources such as the Leamington town council and the Essex County Federation of Agriculture. Like many community broadcasters, it focuses on local issues such as town council meetings, festivals, fairs, and other area events. One program is called *The Real Dirt on Agriculture* – a thirteen-part series about regional farming issues. The funding for the project largely came from a grant from the Ontario Ministry of Agriculture Food and Rural Affairs.

CFTV34 is especially noteworthy for the Canadian digital television transition because of the way it has embraced and used the possibilities of new digital technologies. CFTV34 has developed a live video streaming system that incorporates a small digital transmission device connected to a satellite relay (CFTV34 rents space on an American satellite on a stand-by basis for $300 per month) that is small and affordable. The system, which has the angelic nickname Gabriel, allows the community broadcaster to transmit live mobile coverage. It gets the community broadcaster out of the studio and into the community it serves.

Another initiative that separates CFTV34 from the broadcasting mainstream in Canada is its ambitious plan to make use of the opportunities allowed by digital multiplexing of its OTA signal. In 2012, CFTV34 submitted a proposal to the CRTC to offer four multiplex signals on its allotted frequency.[17] The first channel would be the main broadcast; the second would have Spanish language programming for the substantial Spanish-speaking community who often work on local farms in the region, as well as French programs for the small French population that has been part of the region since the early settlers; the third channel would cover municipal politics, including all town council meetings in the viewing region; and the fourth channel was undecided but the station wanted it available for future use.[18] The CRTC officially approved this application in August 2012.[19] CFTV34 also plans to explore mobile broadcasting of its OTA signal.[20]

Thus, a community broadcaster in rural Ontario who has rejected the local-funding-via-BDU model is exploring ways to improve its OTA signal in ways that have eluded, or been avoided by, the most deep-pocketed of Canadian conventional broadcasters. This creative initiative clearly demonstrates the limited vision of the market-led Canadian digital television transition.

DUDE, WHERE'S MY TV?

Not all civil society efforts surrounding Canada's digital television transition were community based. In May 2010, Ryerson University graduate student Steven James May began Dude, Where's My TV?, a website whose mission was to "provide Canadian citizens with a platform to voice their thoughts, findings, concerns and solutions related to Canada's ongoing digital over-the-air (OTA) television transition."[21] Despite the irreverent name, May offers insightful critique of the Canadian digital television transition. His use of social media and creative submissions to the CRTC provide a unique approach to Canadian broadcasting activism. At a 2011 hearing concerning Bell's purchase of CTVglobemedia, May's testimony before the CRTC commissioners consisted of a short film he had made about OTA reception in Eastern Ontario. Dude, Where's My TV? is filled with May's frequent letters posted to Heritage Minister James Moore, yet May acknowledges, "I've yet to hear back from him. To be fair, it is possible that he doesn't know this blog exists."[22]

Whether or not Moore is a frequent visitor to the site, May illuminates issues absent from most mainstream media. His blog is perhaps the only media source in the country to advance a critical analysis of Shaw's Local Television Satellite Solution (LTSS) program (see chapter 4). Information on the scope of the implementation of this program has been difficult to access. In a discussion with May, I discovered we had each phoned Shaw to inquire about the service and found that representatives had little idea what we were talking about. A November 2011 letter from the CRTC's secretary general to Shaw noted "the modest uptake of the LTSS" and that "public awareness of the program has been limited."[23] The letter also indicates that Shaw requested permission to redirect $10 million of the $15 million required in the benefit package of the Canwest purchase to convert its transmitters to MPEG-4 compression technology. Though the CRTC decided the conversion did not qualify as a public benefit and denied the request, it serves as an example of the gamesmanship that is part of the Canadian broadcasting process.

May's website ran a three-part post that chronicles his parents' efforts to receive the LTSS service in Denbigh, Ontario.[24] They eventually succeeded, but the procedure was not a smooth one. Commenters noted their own frustrations with this program designed to assist OTA viewers in rural Canada.

This social media site fills a void in the coverage of the digital transition from mainstream Canadian media. May's post-transition work on Dude, Where's My TV? explores the limitations of mobile television access, an area of the technological potential of digital television that remains underdeveloped in Canada.

CONCLUSION

Voices from outside the traditional power structure of broadcasting offer a range of visions for the future of Canadian television at this key technological juncture. They serve as a clear example of how the wider political economy of Canadian broadcasting has limited the potential of digital television. As is often the case when new communications technologies are introduced in Canada, the rural regions are left behind.

While in this chapter, I seek to demonstrate that there was civil society activism in the digital television transition, Canada is also home to organizations whose foci include the digital television transition but are committed to a wider range of media issues. This includes Friends of Canadian Broadcasting, which formed in 1985 to "defend and enhance the quality and quantity of Canadian programming in the Canadian audio-visual system" and claims the support of 66,000 Canadian households.[25] Friends of Canadian Broadcasting speaks regularly on a range of broadcasting issues at the CRTC. In recent years, OpenMedia.ca, a grassroots organization dedicated to "informed & participatory digital policy," has successfully rallied public support around Internet-based issues such as copyright and data limits and had some involvement in the digital television transition.[26] DigitalHome.ca was not politically engaged but served as a useful forum for Canadians to discuss technical issues related to the digital television transition, in particular the reception of OTA signals.

The public interest goals expressed by these civil society actors deal with the fundamental questions of universal access to television and the place of local broadcasting within the greater Canadian system.

CONCLUSION

Paying Dividends

Though the arrival of digital should have signalled a bold new era in Canadian television, it instead indicates many wider issues facing contemporary structures of media governance. Canada limped past a weakened analogue shut-off date that excluded many Canadians outside of major urban centres and cut over-the-air access to the CBC in many parts of the country. City viewers can enjoy a limited number of HD signals with a simple antenna, while rural viewers must subscribe to a BDU to access even public television. Several countries have experienced setbacks along the way to digital broadcasting, but few have had Canada's advantage of a lengthy period of involvement with advanced television technology and a history of successfully absorbing technological upheavals (cable and satellite) into the greater system. Canada was at the vanguard of advanced television technologies in the 1980s, but for ten years (1997 to 2007) was unable to mount a coherent national transition program. There have been serious failures in the Canadian transition.

Television has particular implications for a country as vast and diverse as Canada. In *Empire and Communications*, Harold Innis develops his theory of the relationship between time-binding and space-binding media and determined that space-binding media play a fundamental role in the political organization of large territories and "are suited to wide areas in administration and trade."[1] In his chapter on Innis in *Canadian Communication Thought*, Robert Babe views television as the most space-binding of all media.[2] Digitalization may have enabled the growth of an array of delivery platforms, but television's power and political impact has not diminished. The lessons from this transition are not a simple matter of finger pointing, though some degree of blame is certainly warranted; more importantly, the failures of the digital television transition speak to the development of Canadian communications policy in the twenty-first century. Governments and regulation clearly have a role to play.

The poorly executed move to digital has placed Canadian communications at a competitive disadvantage for budding new technologies beyond television that require access to spectrum frequencies occupied by broadcasters. It has also cost the Canadian government and taxpayers substantial potential income, as the billions in revenue generated by selling the spectrum freed by the digital transition has been delayed. The auction for frequencies in the 700 MHz region of the spectrum remained uncertain until 2012 and is now scheduled for the summer of 2013. The United States ran its auction in 2008, one year before its scheduled national analogue shut off.

In Canada, the first public hint of progress in this file came from Industry Minister Tony Clement's Twitter feed on 10 September 2010: "Finished a meeting with telecom provider Huawei. They are set to hire more Cdns. I've concluded we must get the 700 mHz auction going soon."[3] The spectrum auction, a fundamental building block of Canada's emerging digital infrastructure and the key event for the digital television dividend, was announced to Canada in 140 characters or less. The message was clear that, with one year to go before the analogue shut-off date, the government had yet to prepare for this essential next step. The auction did not even merit its own tweet.

It seems fitting that the Canadian government appears disengaged despite the fact that billions of dollars are at stake. The Canadian digital television transition has been hindered by the government's steadfast faith in the dominant ideology of the last two decades. The foundational neoliberal principles of smaller government and utilizing economic incentives instead of regulatory intervention came to full fruition in this period and manifested in the Canadian plan to introduce digital television.

Canada did indeed strike a distinctive path at this key communications juncture: one that placed Canada as a leader in market-led digital television transitions. Governments in the United States, United Kingdom, France, Australia, and other countries have all been far more active in their national transitions. When many countries developed initial transition plans in the 1990s, even new-left advocates such as Tony Blair and Bill Clinton advocated unwavering faith in the wisdom of markets. Canada was not alone in pursuing a relaxation of the traditional broadcasting policy paradigm; however, in the case of digital television, it has taken a more industrially driven path than either its UK or US counterparts, with decidedly poorer results. The uncertain Canadian spectrum auction is merely the culmination of over a decade of government detachment from the digital transition process. Early in the transition, the government and the CRTC turned the central responsibilities of the digital television strategy over to the broadcasting industry. For almost ten years, the broadcasting industry set the schedule and the rules of the game for all involved. To employ the nautical metaphor common to discussions of government, industry did not merely help chart the course – it steered the ship.

Early groups charged with key roles in the Canadian transition were uniformly comprised of an industrial membership with little or no representation from the government or civil society organizations. These groups included the Task Force on the Implementation of Digital Television, which published the key 1997 study *Canadian Television in the Digital Era*; the Digital Migration Working Group and Digital Code Working Group, which both formed in 2001 did not fully completed their mandates largely due to internal divisions; and Canadian DTV Inc (CDTV), which assembled in 1999 following the recommendation of the 1997 report to offer advice on a range of technical issues and monitor progress and ceased operations in 2006. Task forces and working groups are not a novel approach in the early stages of broadcasting policy development; however, what is noteworthy is the lack of input from public officials or indeed anyone outside the broadcasting industry throughout the process.[4] Having received more policy leeway than at any critical juncture in Canadian broadcasting history, the industry subsequently failed to provide the kind of foresight and compromise required to guide the system. The very commercial interests charged with this responsibility have instead created problems for the overall system, including the private sector.

Since 2007, the CRTC has created order by mandating the analogue shut-off date, and then, recognizing its involvement may have come too late, modifying the ASO through the use of mandatory markets for the digital conversion. The Canadian transition, particularly the OTA sector, has fallen short of the recommendations of the original 1997 report. In 2010, reflecting on the early years of the transition, Michel Arpin acknowledged the weak start: "Between 2002 and 2007 there was nothing ... that's why we came with a clear date. Even with a firm date we know where we are today."[5] In the post-transition period,

Canada is a mix of digital and analogue, with a public broadcaster unable to complete the switch to digital over-the-air transmission in many markets and regions of the country without OTA reception altogether since the analogue system shut down.

CO-REGULATION AND THE DIGITAL TRANSITION

The Canadian digital transition is a case study of the inherent possibilities and limitations of co-regulatory policies and practice. In a May 2007 speech, CRTC chair Konrad von Finckenstein said of such policies: "We at the CRTC are strong believers in the usefulness of self-regulation in the industry ... Over the next five years I will be encouraging the industry to improve our broadcasting system through self-designed initiatives and self-made rules."[6] Self- and co-regulation have been fashionable methods of governance since the 1990s, though there has been a large degree of regulatory re-evaluation since the 2008 and 2009 financial collapse.[7] While debates over co- and self-regulatory semantics can prove tiresome, there are important differences. Distinct from self-regulation, which is industry initiated and administered (as in the medical profession), co-regulation is typically a government initiative that allows for considerable industry autonomy under clearly defined parameters set out in a statutory framework, such as the Broadcasting Act. In a co-regulatory structure, the government has little direct involvement but remains in a position of authority through legislation and the threat of punitive action should regulation not be followed. Co-regulation is not a free ride for industry, but a way of making industry assume responsibility for some of the regulatory burden. Though the term "self-regulation" is often used interchangeably with "co-regulation," the latter is a more appropriate description for Canadian broadcasting. The government must always remain in the picture.

The birth of digital television coincided with a high degree of international acceptance of the virtues of a co-regulatory system. In a 1999 speech in Montreal, former Australian Broadcasting Authority Vice Chair Gareth Grainger stated categorically: "Co-regulation is a sound approach to take with a mature industry such as broadcasting."[8] Indeed, several Canadian co-regulatory policy applications have become integral parts of the greater broadcasting system. The Canadian Broadcast Standards Council, launched in 1990, allows the broadcasting industry to deal with viewer concerns over content issues. The CBSC involves a governing body composed of industry representatives as well as experts and local representatives from across Canada. It operates under the auspices of private sector broadcasters and, in co-regulatory fashion, complements, not replaces, the traditional work of the CRTC. The CBSC is clearly co-regulatory as the CRTC still maintains final authority and can overrule its decisions.

In theory, the inherent benefit of co-regulation is that it is far more efficient than traditional top-down regulation. In *Communication Technology*, Darin Barney observes the common critique that legitimate democratic decision making can be "slow, ponderous, risk averse, prone to reversals, lacking in clarity, easily seduced by superficial imaginings, and often irrational: qualities inimical to technological enterprise."[9] Co-regulation therefore seemed to fit digital television: it promised a quicker, more flexible approach that would not get bogged down in the cumbersome process of government activity. But there were clear caveats as well.

Studies of co-regulation have unambiguously stated that there are limitations to its effectiveness – guideposts that the Canadian digital television transition has sorely missed. In a report entitled *Principles and Guidelines for the Community's Audiovisual Policy in the Digital Age*, the European Commission, which has supported co- and self-regulatory broadcasting initiatives, outlines key parameters for their use: "Self-regulation must not be allowed to be used by major incumbent operations to define 'rules of the game' that are best suited to their own interest to the detriment of smaller competitors and/or new market entrants."[10] In Canada, the 2007 Dunbar-Leblanc study was largely positive in its analysis of co-regulation; however, echoing European concerns, the authors noted the inherent dangers in this approach: "Industry self-regulation, when properly implemented and administered, can "result in achievement of policy objectives with less regulatory burden for both the regulator and the regulated undertakings. However, it can result in the substitution of private interests for public interests if it is not properly structured."[11]

Who has represented the public interest in the Canadian digital television transition? The central democratic institutions in Canadian broadcasting, the government and CRTC, stood aside for most of the key formative years of the transition. The various groups and task forces that guided much of the initial transition had so much leeway that some were clearly examples of self-, not co-regulation.[12] This position runs contrary to the more successful transitions in the United

Kingdom, France, the United States, Brazil, and Australia, where governments have been more directly involved. Canada's hands-off position was established by the Liberal Party under Jean Chretien and Paul Martin and has been reinforced by Stephen Harper's Conservative Party. A distinct lack of government involvement (Galperin's conscious inaction, discussed in the introduction), and instructions that the CRTC should follow suit, is a consistent theme in the Canadian digital conversion.

Early in their mandate, the Conservative Party made it clear that the government's position was for the CRTC to intervene in industrial matters as little as possible. A rare policy direction issued to the CRTC in 2007 from then-Industry Minister Maxime Bernier formalized this position. The direction was specific to telecommunications but clearly outlined how the government viewed the role of the CRTC: "In creating the Policy Direction, the Government is signaling its vision for the future of telecommunications policy in advance of more substantial regulatory change by providing policy guidance on how the Commission should exercise its regulatory mandate and direct it to take a more market-based approach to implementing the Act."[13] The basis for this intervention was the 2006 *Telecommunications Policy Review Panel Final Report*, which called for regulation and government to "interfere with the operation of competitive market forces to the minimum extent necessary to meet the objectives [of the Telecommunications Act]."[14] Thus, the federal government ordered the market-based approach, but by 2006 this philosophy was well-entrenched in the transition. Industry set the pace and rules, while the CRTC remained largely on the periphery.[15] This was supposed to result in a more efficient, profitable, and consumer-friendly transition.

Market forces by definition seek out the cheapest, most profitable path and have little concern for public interest elements such as universal accessibility or clear transition schedules. The areas that fall outside the theories of a classic market paradigm are "externalities," which may be both positive (social cohesion, education) and negative (monopoly formation, financial exclusion, similarity of product). Broadcasting is rife with externalities. A system that relies on co-regulatory codes instead of clear and enforceable regulations increases the risk of regulatory capture and weakens fundamental policy objectives. Codes, note Salter and Odartey-Wellington, "are about making broadcasting market-friendly and markets fair, as much as they are about strengthening broadcasting."[16]

Since 2007, the CRTC has been forced into a position where it had to intervene and has been less hesitant to assert its authority. According to a September 2010 story in the *Globe and Mail*, "the CRTC seems to have got its mojo back."[17] If so, then the digital television transition may eventually be viewed as the crest of the deregulatory movement in Canadian broadcasting policy. The broadcasting industry had unprecedented independence, with the formal blessing of the CRTC and the government, yet could not generate a comprehensive, progressive agenda for the country.

ONE BROADCASTING INDUSTRY?

At the root of the many hurdles encountered by the Canadian digital transition is the persistent expectation that a cohesive broadcasting industry would work together to forge a national strategy that would simultaneously be profitable and serve the public interest. This was doomed from the outset.

As the Canadian transition has ably demonstrated, there is no singular "broadcasting industry"; there are, however, a number of complementing and competing industries that jockey for positions of power and influence, both in relation to the government and regulator, and amid each other. During the first ten years of the digital television transition, with the government and regulator largely out of the picture, the industries quickly reduced to squabbling amongst themselves. This was most apparent in the interminable fee-for-carriage debates.

As Salter and Odartey-Wellington observe: "'The broadcasting industry' is not a very useful term – various facets have developed their own 'industry' with their own interests."[18] Notwithstanding recent purchases by Shaw (Canwest) and Bell (CTV) which marry distributors and broadcasters, the co-regulatory structure of the transition laid bare the divisions between BDUs and broadcasters, small and large companies, public and private broadcasters, and new and old media. There was little common purpose.

The divorce within the broadcasting industry became official with the 2010 demise of the Canadian Association of Broadcasters, a long-established private broadcasting advocacy group. The end of the CAB is a significant event in Canadian broadcasting governance that went largely underreported. The CAB's history in Canada runs deep, longer than the CBC. It was established in 1926 to defend the interests of private broadcasters against the encroaching movement for public broadcasting. The CAB was involved in the earliest struggles in Canadian broadcasting, running a campaign against Graham Spry, Alan Plaunt, and the Canadian Radio League in an (unsuccessful) effort to block the establishment of public broadcasting in Canada in the early 1930s.

The CAB had spoken before every major public hearing into radio and television since the 1920s, but could not survive the strong internal industry divisions of the last ten years. Greg O'Brien of Cartt.ca first reported in November 2008 that the very future of the CAB was in question after Quebecor Media-owned TVA, Canada's largest French broadcaster, pulled out of the organization.[19] Less than two years later, the organization was finished. This irreparable separation occurred at the very time the industry was supposed to be working together toward a common digital transition. A 2010 article in the *Wire Report* on the fall of the CAB observed: "You're getting essentially what was an homogeneous group becoming very heterogeneous, very different agendas, with very little synergy in terms of working together on issues. They all have different interests."[20]

The CAB was not the only industry organization to crumble amid acrimony during the years of the transition. In 2006, the Canadian Cable Television Association (CCTA) announced it was ceasing operations after fifty years of representing Canadian cable companies. Clearly, Canada's policy of a "voluntary transition model, i.e., one that would develop at a pace set by the marketplace rather than mandated" did not anticipate these growing fissures within the industry.[21] Many companies had become so individually powerful, that they no longer saw the necessity of collective negotiations. In the essential years leading to the 2011 Canadian digital television transition, neither the broadcasting nor the distribution industry were able to speak with a collective voice, thus the market-led approach was left in disarray.

CANADA'S DIGITAL DIVIDEND

European and Australian studies on the digital television transition use the term "digital dividend" often, but Canadian and US studies use it less frequently. However, it is an appropriate expression for the spoils of this massive technological upheaval. The dividend of the digital television transition is the freed spectrum space; however, "dividends" are also portions of a corporation's profits distributed to stockholders – a share of the rewards of a successful venture. Multiple stockholders are involved in the Canadian digital television transition. Broadcasters, producers, and distributors have made large infrastructure investments to facilitate the changeover and expect compensation from the new revenue streams found in digital's opportunities for video on demand, high definition, IPTV, and additional services. The other key, yet silent, partner in this project is the public, the shareholders who collectively own the spectrum allotted to OTA broadcasters. The public has been generally absent from the formulation of digital policy and there is no clear plan for how it will benefit after the transition is complete.

Former CRTC chairman Michel Arpin sees the digital dividend this way:

> That's a word you never hear in Canada – the digital dividend – you hear it overseas. To be frank, I think the government is only interested in getting money for the spectrum. It's public knowledge that the government was pretty upset by the commission suggesting that a task force should be set up to examine the digital transition in its broad sense ... I don't think there is any motivation by this government to do anything. Their vision is not to interfere with the ability of industry to do something.
>
> When you read about what other jurisdictions have done including the US, they look at health issues, information issues, and economic issues. I'm also disappointed it's never in the platform of the Liberals or the NDP. They don't put the minister of industry and heritage on the spot in the House. Maybe they're holding back their vision until they release their electoral platform.[22]

There has been no forward-thinking vision for the Canadian digital television transition for far too long. It has never been a clear part of any national platform. Robust discussion from a range of actors is necessary to think critically about potential uses for the spectrum space freed by digitalization. In June 2010, Industry Canada launched the Digital Economy Consultation website to call for public input about a range of issues concerning Canada's digital direction. This welcome initiative demonstrated that Canadians want a say in their digital future: according to Industry Canada, more than 2,000 individuals and organizations registered to voice their opinions.[23] Unfortunately, though perhaps expectedly, there has been no official government response to the range of issues expressed in the public forum.

As of 2012, despite repeated assurance from the government that it is forthcoming, Canada does not have a digital economy strategy. In the 2011 budget, the government went so far as to announce: "Budget 2011 sets the stage for the release of Canada's Digital Economy Strategy later this spring."[24] Though the budget was tabled in March, no such strategy was ever introduced and no reason was ever given for the delay. Unlike other countries against which Canada often compares itself, such as the United States, the United Kingdom, Australia, and Germany, the government has offered no overarching framework for how Canada will harness the opportunities of digital communications.[25]

There are opportunities in the freed spectrum beyond selling licences to mobile operators; however, such thinking requires planning and research that has evaded the Canadian government. The United Kingdom and Australia have already tabled lengthy studies to analyze the possibilities of the digital dividend.[26] In the United States, work has begun on new smart-automated information systems that use unlicenced spectrum (white space) and can support long-range communications.[27] This progressive approach follows other developments: in 2009 in the rural town of Claudville, Virginia, Spectrum Bridge, with help from Dell and Microsoft, became the first company in the world to offer wireless access over television white space.[28] In 2010, the US National Broadband Plan encouraged expediting the development of further white space technologies.[29] In Canada, the discussion of white space usage has yet to happen as a direct result of the poor transition, a point lamented in a 2010 article in the *Wire Report* that stated: "White space does not yet seem to be on Canada's radar. 'We still haven't done the digital transition,' [Duncan] Stewart [Deloitte Canada director of research for technology] said. 'You can't talk about white spaces until you've moved people [off the spectrum].'"[30]

Ironically, Canada's market-led approach is now cited as a hindrance to investment and technological development. Financial investors took notice of Canada's weak efforts at facilitating an orderly shift from analogue to digital broadcasting. Malcolm White, a vice president at Signature Global advisors, believes the problems of the Canadian transition have placed new telecom companies at a considerable disadvantage. In his opinion, Canada's disorganized transition led new mobile phone operators to over bid for lesser quality spectrum in the 2008 auction: "By sitting on that high quality spectrum and not pushing digital TV ahead ... the unintended consequence is that you put new wireless entrants at a major competitive disadvantage."[31] White believes if the 700 MHz spectrum had been available earlier, new entrants such as Wind, Public Mobile, and Mobilicity would be a stronger market force in Canadian mobile. Thus, the poor digital television transition has a communications ripple effect: it has already created problems for wireless and mobile applications.

There is far more at stake in the Canadian digital television transition than the ability to watch hockey in HD. The Canadian market-led approach has failed to deliver a coherent strategy to optimize the potential of this fundamental shift in technology. The ATSC digital standard was designed to offer quality terrestrial broadcasting service; economics and weak political leadership have led to the current malaise of the OTA sector. The switch from analogue to digital broadcasting in no way changes the obligation of the Canadian system to provide programming for all Canadians, whether or not they choose to purchase the services broadcasting distribution undertakings provide. The traditional normative elements of broadcasting have not altered with digitalization; in fact, the digital transition has increased the rationale for the public to expect compensation for the use of the increasingly valuable electromagnetic spectrum.

Since industry was in control of much of the early transition, it should come as little surprise that digital television in Canada has been about protecting incumbent interests, rather than exploring the true potentials of this fundamental shift in communications technology. Legacy industries protect their financial interests, not welcome new competition. The ATSC standard was designed to enhance OTA broadcasting and does so in the United States, yet this sector has been the weakest part of Canada's digital switch.

The transition to digital television involves a range of Canadian industries and offers an early view into the politics of digital communications in the twenty-first century. This bridge between analogue and digital exemplifies the power dynamics in Canada's increasingly market-led communications sector. The result of this approach has been a loss in universal accessibility and a poor adoption of technological potential. Digital television provides a sharper picture of the necessary place of regulation in Canadian broadcasting.

Notes

INTRODUCTION

1 Krasnow and Longley, *The Politics of Broadcast Regulation*, 19.
2 Thomas McPhail, "Interactive Cable Communication Services: The Duplex Society Problem," 3.
3 Nash, *The Microphone Wars*, 87.
4 There are many examples that emphasize the public service element of television in Canada. One strong voice is *Our Cultural Sovereignty: The Second Century of Canadian Broadcasting* (the Lincoln Report), a 2003 report prepared for the Department of Canadian Heritage.
5 As this book is an effort to instigate public debate and awareness concerning the central role of mass media, a debt of recognition must be paid to Graham Spry and the Canadian Radio League, whose lobbying efforts to convince a sitting Conservative government to fund public broadcasting in the early years of the Great Depression still seem Herculean decades later.
6 Collins, *Culture, Communication, and National Identity: The Case of Canadian Television*; see also Marc Raboy, "The Role of the Public in Broadcasting Policy-Making and Regulation: Lessons for Europe from Canada"; Herman and McChesney, *The Global Media: The New Missionaries of Corporate Capitalism*; Canada, "Task Force on Broadcasting Policy. Report," 1986.
7 Raboy, *Missed Opportunities: The Story of Canada's Broadcasting Policy*, 17; Stewart and Hull, *Canadian Television Policy and the Board of Broadcast Governors, 1958–1968*, 5; Charland, "Technological Nationalism," 197.
8 Williams, *Television: Technology and Cultural Form*, 13.
9 Stefaan Verhulst, interview with the author, 29 June 2007.
10 A 2010 report published by the C.D. Howe Institute entitled *Scrambled Signals: Canadian Content Policies in a World of Technological Abundance* calls for

a removal of Canadian content policies that the authors Hunter, Iacobucci, and Trebilcock see as unenforceable in a digital mediascape.

11 Flavelle, "Newspapers Still among the Most Trusted Media," *Toronto Star*, 15 May 2010.

12 *Economist*, "The Shock of the Old," *Economist*, 22 April 2010, http://www.economist.com/node/15964393.

13 *Economist*, "The Great Survivor; In Praise of Television," *Economist*, 1 May 2010, 12.

14 *Economist*, "Changing the Channel," *Economist*, 1 May 2010, 3.

15 Kate Taylor, "Next Year's Big Issue: Digital TV," *Globe and Mail*, 1 January 2006.

16 *Globe and Mail*, "Editorial: Tories Take Step in Right Direction in Liberalizing Telecom Industry," 16 March 2012.

17 All data from the CRTC *Communications Monitoring Report 2011*.

18 BDU numbers from the 2010 and 2011 *Communications Monitoring Report*.

19 Lemée and Gauthier, "Cost Estimate of Digital Television (DTV) Conversion for Canada," 7.

20 Konrad von Finckenstein, "Speech to the 2008 Broadcasting Invitational Summit."

21 Salter and Odartey-Wellington, *The CRTC and Broadcasting Regulation in Canada*, 779.

22 In Broadcasting Regulatory Policy CRTC 2010-485, the CRTC stated it "expected" broadcasters to begin public service announcements in March 2011.

23 CRTC, *Digital Transition Models*, October 2009.

24 Greg O'Brien, "Commentary: A Digital Disaster in the Making. Where's the Leadership?" Cartt.ca, 1 April 2010.

25 O'Brien, "The Cartt.ca Interview: Industry Minister Tony Clement on All Things Digital," Cartt.ca, 27 April 2010.

26 Galperin, *New Television, Old Politics*, 21.

27 Seabright and von Hagen, *The Economic Regulation of Broadcasting Markets*, 11.

28 Insight Information Inc, *The Changing Role of the CRTC (Toronto 1996)*, 46; see also Gow and Smith, *Mobile and Wireless Communications: An Introduction*.

29 Terence Corcoran, "CRTC Botches Another Decision," *National Post*, 18 January 2003; *Globe and Mail*, "Editorial: Ads and the CRTC," 4 June 2007; Standing Committee on Canadian and Clifford Lincoln, *Our Cultural Sovereignty: The Second Century of Canadian Broadcasting*.

30 Price, *Media and Sovereignty*; Habermas and Pensky, *The Postnational Constellation*.

31 Canada Royal Commission on Radio Broadcasting, *Report of the Royal Commission on Radio Broadcasting*, 6.

32 Canada, Broadcasting Act, 1991, 3.1.b.

33 Canada, External Advisory Committee on Smart Regulation, *Smart Regulation: A Regulatory Strategy for Canada. Report to the Government of Canada*, 12.

34 Feintuck, *"The Public Interest" in Regulation*, 248.

35 A rare exception is Bonin's "Canada's Transition to Digital Television: From Policy to Reality."

36 Raboy, *Missed Opportunities*, 103.

37 Smythe, *Dependency Road*; Grant, *Lament for a Nation*; Taras, *Power and Betrayal in the Canadian Media*.

38 McChesney, *Communication Revolution*, 37.

39 Galperin, *New Television, Old Politics*, 6.

40 Taras, *Power and Betrayal in the Canadian Media*, 220.

41 Freedman's statement is not entirely complete: a chapter in Hernan Galperin's *New Television, Old Politics* is entitled, "Why Digital TV"?

CHAPTER ONE

1 Shannon, "A Mathematical Theory of Communication," 1.

2 Bell, *Inventing Digital Television: The inside Story of a Technology Revolution*, 15–16.

3 Nyquist, "Certain Topics in Telegraph Transmission Theory," 283.

4 Nakamura, "HDTV – Past, Present and Future," (paper presented at the Third International Colloquium on Advanced Television Systems, Ottawa, 4–8 October 1987) 0.1.3.

5 McLuhan, *Understanding Media*, 22.

6 Powers, "Keynote Address: Getting it All Together for Compatible HDTV" (paper presented at the Third International Colloquium on Advanced Television Systems, Ottawa, 1987).

7 West-Cyr, "Closing Plenary Address" (paper presented at the Third International Colloquium on Advanced Television Systems, Ottawa, 1987).

8 Powers.

9 Committee for the North American HDTV Demonstrations to the Public, "The North American High Definition Television Demonstrations to the Public: An Overview of the Survey Results," 11.

10 Starks, *Switching to Digital Television: UK Public Policy and the Market*, 21.

11 Brinkley, *Defining Vision: The Battle for the Future of Television*, 29.

12 Packard, "The Coming US-Japan Crisis," 348.

13 Galperin, *New Television, Old Politics*, 76.
14 Ibid., 44.
15 Woo Paik became the chief technical officer and president of LG Electronics Inc in January 2008.
16 Brinkley, 266–67.
17 CRTC, *The Future Environment Facing the Canadian Broadcasting System: A Report Prepared Pursuant to Section 15 of the Broadcasting Act*, (2006) appendix B2.
18 This section was written with assistance from Canadian electrical engineer Wayne Stacey.
19 Controversy around the decision to award the standard to the ATSC group continued. In 2002, a lawsuit between MIT and Dolby was settled over the question of royalties for the ATSC sound system patent. Two main systems competed to be the standard under the ATSC model. MIT professor of electrical engineering Jae Lim voted for Dolby laboratories over Philips Electronics "Musicam system" (later known as MPEG), a decision that benefited both MIT and Lim himself. In an 8 November 2002 article in *Tech*, the MIT newspaper, Keith Winstein revealed MIT won a settlement of $30 million from Dolby Laboratories, $8 million of which was to go to Lim as the inventor of the technology. Dolby had promised money to MIT as part of a royalty-sharing agreement for Lim's support but never paid, citing a termination provision of their contract. MIT and Dolby reached a settlement out of court.
20 CRTC, *Communications Monitoring Report 2010*, 56.
21 Dunbar and Leblanc, "Review of the Regulatory Framework for Broadcasting Services in Canada," 2007.
22 Smythe, *Dependency Road*, 176.
23 Astor, "Common Digital TV Standard Urged for Western Hemisphere: US Industry Hopes to Benefit," *Export America. US Department of Commerce's International Trade Administration* (February 2004).
24 Google, "Google Intends to Bid in Spectrum Auction if FCC Adopts Consumer Choice and Competition Requirements," 20 July 2007, http://www.google.com/intl/en/press/pressrel/20070720_wireless.html.
25 Galperin, *New Television, Old Politics*, 23.
26 Cave and Nakamura, *Digital Broadcasting*, 12.
27 Wood, "Technical Standards," *International Journal of Digital Television*, 2, no. 1 (2011): 109.
28 McKnight and Neil, "The HDTV War: The Politics of HDTV Standardization" (paper presented at the Third International Colloquium on Advanced Television Systems, Ottawa, 1987), 5.6.8.

29 Ibid., 5.6.15.
30 Ibid., 5.6.7.
31 Negroponte, *Being Digital*, 43.
32 Wood, "Technical Standards," 114.
33 Digital Video Broadcasting, "Introduction to the DVB Project: Creating Global Standards for Digital Television," http://www.dvb.org/technology/fact_sheets/DVB-Project_Factsheet.pdf.
34 Digital Video Broadcasting, "The Global Standard for Digital Television," http://www.dvb.org/index.xml.
35 Francois Gauthier (Spectrum Experts), interview with the author, 13 September 2010.
36 María García Leiva and Starks, "Digital Switchover across the Globe: The Emergence of Complex Regional Patterns," 794.
37 Hiroshi Asami, "Digital Broadcasting in Japan: HDTV and Mobile Reception as Key Application," *Broadcast Asia*, 12 May 2005.
38 Leiva and Starks, 794.
39 O'Neill, "Digital Audio Broadcasting in Canada: Technology and Policy in the Transition to Digital Radio," 74.
40 Ibid., 77
41 Ibid.
42 Ibid., 87.
43 Industry Canada, *Consultation on the Spectrum Allocations and Spectrum Utilization Policies for the Frequency Range 1435–1525 MHz (L-Band)*, (2009) 15.

CHAPTER TWO

1 Trudel in Raboy et al., eds, *The Role of the State in Broadcasting Governance*, 136.
2 Siegel, *Communication Law in America*, 495.
3 Huff, *Regulating the Future: Broadcasting Technology and Governmental Control*, Contributions to the Study of Mass Media and Communications, no. 61.
4 United States, Telecommunications Act of 1996, 1996.
5 Barendt, *Broadcasting Law*, 6.
6 Salter and Odartey-Wellington, *The CRTC and Broadcasting Regulation in Canada*, 112.
7 Raboy, *Missed Opportunities*, 45.
8 Canada, Broadcasting Act 1991.
9 United States, "Advisory Committee on Public Interest Obligations of Digital Television Broadcasters," National Telecommunications and Information Administration, *Charting the Digital Broadcasting Future*, 1.

10 Galperin, *New Television, Old Politics*, 242.
11 United States, Telecommunications Act of 1996, 336.c.
12 United States, *Charting the Digital Broadcasting Future*, 1.
13 Ibid., 134.
14 Ibid., 26.
15 Ibid., 56.
16 Napoli, "The Public Interest Obligations Initiative: Lost in the Digital Television Shuffle," 154.
17 Federal Communications Commission, "Notice of Inquiry. Public Interest Obligations of TV Broadcast Licencees," in *MM Docket No. 99–360*, 20 December 1999.
18 For a detailed account of the history of this issue, see Benton Foundation, "Public Interest Obligations of Digital Television Broadcasters Timeline 1995–2007," http://benton.org/node/4754.
19 Napoli, "The Public Interest Obligations Initiative: Lost in the Digital Television Shuffle," 154. It should be noted that, as an FCC commissioner, Powell wrote that he agreed with the 1999 Notice of Inquiry (see FCC 1999, Concurring Statement of Commissioner Michael K. Powell).
20 Federal Communications Commission, *Children's Television Obligations of Digital Television Broadcasters*, 23 November 2004.
21 See Minow, "Television and the Public Interest," 399. After this 1961 speech, program producers subtly protested Minow's request for quality by naming the ship on *Gilligan's Island* after him.
22 Benton Foundation, "Citizen's Guide to the Public Interest Obligations of Digital Television Broadcasters," 2005, 19, http://benton.org/public_interest_obligations_of_dtv_broadcasters_guide.
23 Federal Communications Commission, *Recommendation Regarding Consumer Interest Obligations of Digital Television Broadcasters. Consumer Advisory Committee. Shirley L. Rooker, Chair,* 18 November 2005.
24 Fraser, *Free-for-All*, 155.
25 John McCain, "Statement Regarding Free TV Air Time from Broadcasters," http://mccain.senate.gov/public/index.cfm?FuseAction=PressOffice.Speeches&ContentRecord_id=d14fd0eb-6ecc-4c8e-9aaa-85a7c1ff9f5c&Region_id=&Issue_id=6f4c5955-818b-4157-bc80-3b4bef26f7ab.
26 National Commission on Terrorist Attacks upon the United States, *The 9/11 Commission Report: Final Report of the National Commission on Terrorist Attacks upon the United States*, 397.
27 Obama, "Statement by the President on the Transition to All-Digital Programming," Office of the Press Secretary, 4 June 2009.

28 Adelstein, "Questions for Federal Communications Commission Members from the Hon. John D. Dingell, Chairman, House Committee on Energy and Commerce and the Hon. Edward J. Markey, Chairman, Subcommittee on Telecommunications and the Internet," 7 February 2007.

29 United States, Deficit Reduction Act of 2005, 8 February 2006, s. 3,005.

30 United States, National Digital Television Consumer Education Act, 8 January 2009, s. 4.

31 McEwen, *A Report to the CRTC on Digital Transition Strategies in a Number of Different Countries*, 46.

32 CRTC, *Public Notice CRTC 1994-118. Exemption Order Respecting Experimental Video-on-Demand Programming Undertakings.*

33 Canada, Task Force on the Implementation of Digital Television, *Canadian Television in the Digital Era: The Report of the Task Force on the Implementation of Digital Television*, 12.

34 Ibid., 3.

35 Industry Canada, *Consultation on Issues Related to Spectrum Auctioning*, 1 August 1997.

36 McEwen, "The Digital Transition: In Search of the Holy Grail," in *Broadcast Dialogue – The Voice of Broadcasting in Canada*, 8.

37 Robert Scarth (CBC director of regulatory affairs), interview with the author, 13 April 2010.

38 CRTC, *Broadcasting Public Notice CRTC 2000-113. Establishment of an Industry Working Group to Examine the Digital Distribution of Existing Pay and Specialty Services.*

39 CRTC, *Public Notice CRTC 2001-58. Digital Migration Issues – Reconvening of Working Group Regarding Large Cable Systems, and Call for Comments Regarding Small Cable Systems.*

40 CRTC, *The Distribution of Existing Analogue Pay and Specialty Services on a Digital Basis. The Report of the Digital Migration Working Group*, 2001, 62.

41 Perry Hoffman, "Programmers and Distributors at Odds on How to Roll out Digital TV across Canada," *Wire Report*, 14 March 2001.

42 CRTC, *Public Notice CRTC 2001-62. A Call for Comments on a Proposed Policy to Oversee the Transition from Analogue to Digital over-the-Air Television Broadcasting.*

43 CRTC, Broadcasting Public Notice CRTC 2006-23. Digital Migration Framework.

44 CRTC, "CRTC 2001-62."

45 McEwen, *A Report to the CRTC on Digital Transition Strategies in a Number of Different Countries*, 2006, 220.

46 Ibid., 39.

47 CRTC, *Broadcasting Public Notice CRTC 2006-160. Digital Radio Policy.*

48 CRTC, *Broadcasting Public Notice CRTC 2004-58. Call for Comments on a Proposed Framework for the Licensing and Distribution of High Definition Pay and Specialty Services.*

49 CRTC, *Public Notice 2008-100. Regulatory Frameworks for Broadcasting Distribution Undertakings and Discretionary Programming Services.*

50 To encourage HD in digital television, the CRTC made licensing easier for broadcasters that reached a certain percentage of HD programming, as established in public notices 2002-31 and 2003-61. In order to receive guaranteed distribution rights under transitional DTV licences, incumbent broadcasters are allowed to broadcast a maximum of fourteen hours per week of HD programming that was not duplicated on the analogue version of the service. A minimum of 50 per cent of this unduplicated HD programming must be Canadian and all of the unduplicated programming must be in HD.

51 Lemée and Gauthier, "Cost Estimate of Digital Television (DTV) Conversion for Canada," 8.

52 Raboy, "The Role of Public Consultation in Shaping the Canadian Broadcasting System," *Canadian Journal of Political Science*, 455.

53 CRTC, *Broadcasting Regulatory Policy CRTC 2012-181: Broadcasting Participation Fund.*

54 Barney, *Communication Technology*, 64.

55 While the CBC was present at the meetings, its role was to look after its own interests and it did not act in a broader public interest capacity. Interviews with Task Force Chair Michael McEwen and Robert Scarth in Regulatory Affairs at the CBC (13 April 2010) confirmed this point.

56 Priya Ganapati, "FCC White Spaces Decision Kicks off the Next Wireless Revolution," *Wired*, 5 November 2008.

57 *Economist*, "Wireless at Warp Speed: White Space Promises to Put Wifi on Steroids," *Economist*, 7 November 2008, http://www.economist.com/node/12581204.

58 Pooley, "From Psychological Warfare to Social Justice: Shifts in Foundation Support for Communication Research," 1.

59 Groups that enjoy funding in Canada tend to be more conservative, such as the Fraser Institute or C.D. Howe. See Abelson, *Do Think Tanks Matter? Assessing the Impact of Public Policy Institutes.*

CHAPTER THREE

1 Starks, *Switching to Digital Television*, 198.

2 Given, *Turning off the Television*, 191.

3 Germany is a notable exception to this rule, as individual states (Länders) have their own regulatory authority. Though I do not offer Germany as a case study in this chapter, it is noteworthy that the city of Berlin was the first jurisdiction in the world to switch to exclusively digital television broadcasting in 2003.

4 European Commission, "Council Directive 89/552/EEC on the Coordination of Certain Provisions Laid Down by Law, Regulation or Administrative Action in Member States Concerning the Pursuit of Television Broadcasting Activities. (Television without Frontiers Directive)," 1989.

5 Ó Siochrú, Girard, and Mahan, *Global Media Governance*, 76. For another example of the efforts at global regulation, see the International Commission for the Study of Communication Problems report *Many Voices, One World*, presented to UNESCO in 1980.

6 McEwen, *A Report to the CRTC on Digital Transition Strategies in a Number of Different Countries*, 35.

7 Smith, *The Politics of Television Policy*, 78.

8 Gary Smith (former director of subscriber services at BSkyB, 2000 to 2004, and President Bell ExpressVu, 2005 to 2009), interview with the author, 20 July 2010.

9 Starks, *Switching to Digital Television*, 26.

10 Richard Wray, "Freeview Conquers New Heights: More than 3.8m Devices Sold in Last Quarter of 2007, Exceeding Expectations," *Guardian*, 11 March 2008.

11 Ibid.

12 Freeview, http://www.freeview.co.uk, accessed 2 May 2012.

13 Galperin, 231, 235.

14 Digital UK, "About Digital UK," http://www.digitaluk.co.uk/about_digital_uk.

15 Digital UK, "Image Gallery," http://www.digitaluk.co.uk/press_office/image_gallery.

16 Great Britain. Dept. for Culture Media, and Sport and Great Britain, and Dept. for Business Enterprise and Regulatory Reform, *Digital Britain: The Interim Report*, 84.

17 BBC News, "London Analogue TV Signal Switched Off," 18 April 2012, http://www.bbc.co.uk/news/uk-england-london-17752322.

18 Ibid., 86.

19 BBC, "Switchover Help Scheme," http://www.helpscheme.co.uk/en/home.

20 McEwen, *A Report to the CRTC on Digital Transition Strategies in a Number of Different Countries*, 28.

21 Ritter and Grengaroli, "Digital Television in Australia: The Story so Far," in *Broadcasting Asia 2000 Conference*.

22 McEwen, *A Report to the CRTC on Digital Transition Strategies in a Number of Different Countries*, 6.
23 Given, *Turning off the Television*, 164.
24 García Leiva and Starks, "Digital Switchover across the Globe," 797.
25 Australian Government. Digital Switchover Taskforce, *Digital Tracker Report on Quarter 4: October–December 2011*, 2012.
26 Australian Government. Digital Switchover Taskforce, "Are You Ready for Digital TV?" http://www.digitalready.gov.au/Households/media-centre/media-gallery.aspx.
27 Ibid.
28 Grimme, *Digital Television Standardization and Strategies*, 81.
29 Julien Mailland, interview with the author, 22 August 2010.
The high level of Internet penetration in France is also explained by the fact that with a virtual penetration rate of a hundred percent by the late 1980s, the French pre-Internet information network, *Minitel*, made France the world's most wired country for computer networks, which gave the population an early level of digital literacy and Internet readiness.
30 Benoit, *Digital Television*, 185.
31 Autorité de régulation des communications électroniques et des postes, *Annual Report 2011*, 159.
32 European Commission and European Audiovisual Observatory, "TV Market in France," http://mavise.obs.coe.int/country?id=1.
33 France Télé Numérique, "Tous Au Numérique," http://www.tousaunumerique.fr (my translation).
34 François Fillon, "Communiqué: Comité Stratégique Pour Le Numérique," 22 July 2009, http://www.gouvernement.fr/presse/comite-strategique-pour-le-numerique (translation by the author and Clémentine Sallée).
35 Ibid.
36 Raj Karamchedu, "Does China Have the Best Digital Television Standard on the Planet?"
37 Starks, "China's Digital Switchover: International Context," 90.
38 Karamchedu.
39 Starks, 92.
40 Karamchedu,
41 Ibid.
42 Shenzhen Huada Video Technology Co Ltd, "China's Terrestrial Digital TV Gb Achieve its First Overseas Applications," accessed May 2011 (unavailable May 2012), http://www.hdtv168.cn/en/NewsView.asp?ID=78.
43 de Souza, Taynah Lopes, and Rodolfo Saboia Lima de Souza, "Building the Digital TV Standard: The Brazilian Experience," 7.

44 Farias, Carvalho, and Alencar, "Digital Television Broadcasting in Brazil," *Multimedia, IEEE* 15, no 2 (2008): 64.

45 Mario Osava, "Brazil to Join Digital TV World," Inter Press Service News Agency, 3 January 2007, http://ipsnews.net/news.asp?idnews=36055.

46 *Tech Law Journal*, "TLJ News from April 6–10, 2006: State Department Official Addresses IPR and Trade in Brazil," 2006.

47 Samuel Possebon (editor of *TELA VIVA News*, an online news service devoted to the television and telecom industry in Brazil), personal correspondence with the author, September 2010.

48 Larry Claasen, "Digital Television: Still No Clear Picture," *Financial Mail*, 29 April 2010.

49 International Telecommunications Union, "Digital Broadcasting Set to Transform Communication Landscape by 2015," 16 June 2006, http://www.itu.int/newsroom/press_releases/2006/11.html.

50 Duncan McLeod, "Digital TV Distress," *Financial Mail*, 6 May 2010.

51 Ibid.

52 Digital Video Broadcasting, "South African Industry Favours DVB-T," http://www.dvb.org/about_dvb/dvb_worldwide/south_africa/index.xml.

53 García Leiva and Starks, "Digital Switchover across the Globe."

54 Galperin, 247.

55 Patrick Nixon, "ATSC Forum to Close at Month's End," *Business News Americas* (English), 14 September 2009.

56 García Leiva and Starks, "Digital Switchover across the Globe," 801–03.

57 Karen Wirsig (Canadian Media Guild), interview with the author, 25 October 2010.

58 Crane, *The Politics of International Standards*, 6.

CHAPTER FOUR

1 CRTC, *Communications Monitoring Report 2011*, 29.

2 CRTC, *CRTC Public Notice 2008-100*.

3 "Regulations" and "policy" are not interchangeable terms. CRTC policy statements have a decidedly different purpose than regulations and the impact of regulations has distinct legal implications. The regulations of the CRTC are legally binding; however, under the 1991 Broadcasting Act, 6, the CRTC is legally mandated to "issue guidelines and statements with respect to any matter within its jurisdiction under this Act, but no such guidelines or statements issued by the Commission are binding on the Commission."

Since the policy statements are not obligatory, this allows the CRTC the leeway to grant exemptions from certain policies and later change the policy as it sees fit. The fact these policy statements are not legally binding should not diminish their significance. In many ways, these statements set the agenda that the entire industry follows. As Salter and Odartey-Wellington observe, these policy statements "outline the rules of the game for everyone." Just as policy announcements are not legally binding on the commission, neither can they be appealed to, or overturned by, the Cabinet. They alert the industry to how the regulator sees the system evolving.

4 Bird, *Documents of Canadian Broadcasting*, 423.

5 CRTC, CRTC Public Notice 2008-100. *Regulatory Policy – Regulatory Frameworks for Broadcasting Distribution Undertakings (BDUS) and Discretionary Programming Services.*

6 A recent amendment to the Broadcasting Distribution Regulations, the broadcasting regulatory policy CRTC 2009-543, allowed new forms of targeted advertising (a feature of digital distribution) and changes to the programming funding model. See Grant and Buchanan, *Canadian Broadcasting Regulatory Handbook*, 147.

7 CRTC, Broadcasting Public Notice CRTC 2003-48. *A Regional Approach to Licensing Cable Distribution Undertakings – Adoption of Related Amendments to the* Broadcasting Distribution Regulations.

8 In September 2009, a legal feud erupted when Shaw purchased a small cable company in Hamilton, Ontario, territory that Rogers claimed as its own. Rogers and Shaw agreed Shaw would not own cable operations east of Manitoba and Rogers would not move west of Ontario, dividing English speaking Canada between them. The courts refused to recognize the agreement and allowed the sale to Shaw. See Theresa Tedesco and Jamie Sturgeon, "Cable Rivals Drop Gloves," *Financial Post*, 24 October 2009.

9 For further reading on BDUS in Canada, see Salter and Odartey-Wellington, *The CRTC and Broadcasting Regulation in Canada*; Grant and Buchanan, *Canadian Broadcasting Regulatory Handbook*; Buchanan, Abramson, and Grant, *Regulatory Guide to Canadian Television*; and Robert Armstrong, *Broadcasting Policy in Canada*.

10 Taras and Raboy, "Canada," 364.

11 *Review of the Regulatory Framework for Broadcasting Services in Canada*, A report prepared for the CRTC in 2007 by Dunbar and Leblanc, found the policy results in Canadian programming being pushed off prime time so that Canadian broadcasters can reap extra revenue when broadcasting American programming.

12 Michel Arpin (former CRTC vice chair of broadcasting, 2005–2010), interview with the author, 2 September 2010.

13 Mercer, Rick, Irwin Barker, Greg Eckler, Chris Finn, Tim Steeves, and

George Westerholm, *The Rick Mercer Report*, season 7, episode 9, aired 1 December 2009.

14 CRTC, *Broadcasting Order CRTC 2010-168. Reference to the Federal Court of Appeal – Commission's Jurisdiction under the Broadcasting Act to Implement a Negotiated Solution for the Compensation for the Fair Value of Private Local Conventional Television Signals.*

15 CRTC, *Communications Monitoring Report 2011*, 33.

16 CRTC, BPN 2008-100.

17 CRTC, *Communications Monitoring Report 2011*, 30.

18 Ibid, 29.

19 The CRTC imposed some restrictions on BDU and media ownership in Broadcasting Public Notice CRTC 2008-4. *Regulatory Policy: Diversity of Voices*, 105: "The Commission, as a general rule, will not approve applications for a change in the effective control of broadcasting distribution undertakings (BDUS) in a market that would result in one person being in a position to effectively control the delivery of programming services in that market. The Commission is not prepared to allow one person to control all BDUS in any given market."

20 CRTC, Public Notice CRTC 2001-66-1. *Ownership of Analogue Discretionary Services by Cable Undertakings – Amendment to the Commission's Policy.*

21 Abramson, "Open and Closed: Looking Ahead to the CRTC's New Media Broadcast Hearings," McCarthy Tétrault LLP, accessed 16 July 2012, http://www.mccarthy.ca/article_detail.aspx?id=4428.

22 Canada, Broadcasting Act, 1991, 3(1)(t).

23 CRTC, BPN CRTC 2006-23. Digital Migration Framework.

24 CRTC, Broadcasting Notice of Public Hearing CRTC 2006-5. *Review of Certain Aspects of the Regulatory Framework for over-the-Air Television.*

25 CRTC, BPN CRTC 2006-74. *Regulatory Framework for the Licensing and Distribution of High Definition Pay and Specialty Services.*

26 CRTC, Broadcasting Decision CRTC 2008-234. *Various Cable Broadcasting Distribution Undertakings in Western Canada – Short-Term Licence Renewals and Licence Amendments.*

27 Spot beam technology, which can target local markets, exists for satellite broadcasting, is used in the United States, and has been proposed in Canada by Free HD Canada.

28 CRTC, CRTC Public Notice 2008-100.

29 CRTC, Public Notice CRTC 1997-150. Broadcasting Distribution Regulations, 17.

30 CRTC, CRTC Public Notice 2008-100.

31 CRTC, Broadcasting Notice of Public Hearing CRTC 2007-10. *Review of the*

Regulatory Frameworks for Broadcasting Distribution Undertakings and Discretionary Programming Services.

32 CRTC, "BPN CRTC 2006-23."

33 Ibid.

34 CRTC, CRTC Public Notice 2008-100.

35 Canada, Broadcasting Act, 3(t)(i).

36 Parts of this section are taken from Taylor, "Grey to Black: Satellite Piracy in Canada."

37 Schultz, "Still Standing," 30.

38 Lessig, *Free Culture*, 53.

39 CRTC, *Communications Monitoring Report 2010*, table 4.4.3. This data is not included in the 2011 CMR.

40 CRTC, Broadcasting Public Notice 2003-61. *The Regulatory Framework for the Distribution of Digital Television Signals.*

41 CRTC, BPN CRTC 2006-23.

42 For this section I would like to acknowledge the importance of Grant's *Regulatory Guide to Canadian Television*.

43 CRTC, *Communications Monitoring Report 2011*, 56.

44 CRTC, *Individual Pay Television, Pay-per-View, Video-on-Demand and Specialty Services: Statistical and Financial Summaries 2007–2011*.

45 Salter and Odartey-Wellington, *The CRTC and Broadcasting Regulation in Canada*, 468.

46 Andre Bureau (Astral Media), interview with the author, 18 August 2008, Montreal.

47 CRTC, Broadcasting Notice of Consultation CRTC 2009-732. *Call for Comments on Proposed Revisions to the Criteria Used to Assess Applications for Mandatory Distribution Pursuant to an Order under Section 9(1)(H) of the Broadcasting Act*.

48 CRTC, Broadcasting Information Bulletin CRTC 2010-198. *Amendment to the Timeframe for Consideration of New Category A Services.*

49 Greg O'Brien, "CRTC Tells Quebecor a Category 1 Licence for Sun TV News Is a Non-starter until Fall 2011," Cartt.ca, 16 July 2010.

50 Armstrong, *Broadcasting Policy in Canada*, 183.

51 CRTC, *Communications Monitoring Report 2010*, table 4.3.13.

52 CRTC, Pay Television Regulations, 1990, section 2.

53 CRTC, *Communications Monitoring Report 2011*, 103.

54 CRTC, *Communications Monitoring Report 2010*. The CRTC stopped providing the overall number for this sector in 2011.

55 CRTC, Public Notice CRTC 2000-172. *Introductory Statement to Decisions CRTC 2000-733 to 2000-738: Licensing of New Video-on-Demand and Pay-per-View Services.*

56 CRTC, Broadcasting Regulatory Policy CRTC 2010-190. *Regulatory Framework for Video-on-Demand Undertakings*, 110.
57 Ibid., 31.
58 CRTC, Broadcasting Distribution Regulations, 47(2).
59 T. Fennell, "Is Canada's Broadcast Policy Lost in Space?" *Maclean's*, 27 May 1996, 38–39.
60 Schultz, "Still Standing," 36.
61 Ibid., 37.
62 Seven government directions have been issued to the CRTC since 1991.
63 CRTC, Broadcasting Decision CRTC 2004-130. *Star Choice – Licence Renewal.*
64 Ibid.
65 CRTC, Broadcasting Decision CRTC 2008-234. *Various Cable Broadcasting Distribution Undertakings in Western Canada – Short-Term Licence Renewals and Licence Amendments.*
66 In CRTC, Broadcasting Public Notice CRTC 2001-130. *Small Cable Systems – Digital Migration Policy*, the CRTC defined a "small cable system" as "one that is not owned or operated, directly or indirectly, by Rogers, Shaw, Vidéotron, or Cogeco, without regard to the number of subscribers." In CRTC, Broadcasting Order CRTC 2009-544. *Exemption Order for Terrestrial Broadcasting Distribution Undertakings Serving Fewer than 20,000 Subscribers*. The CRTC changed this regulation to allow exemption for systems owned by one of the big four but serving fewer than 20,000 customers.
67 The final two points come from CRTC, BPN CRTC 2001-130. *Small Cable Systems – Digital Migration Policy.*
68 Ibid.
69 CRTC, Broadcasting Order CRTC 2009-544. *Exemption Order for Terrestrial Broadcasting Distribution Undertakings Serving Fewer than 20,000 Subscribers.*
70 CRTC, "BPN CRTC 2001-130."
71 Chris Edwards (vice president of corporate and regulatory, Canadian Cable Systems Alliance Inc), interview with the author, 21 July 2010.
72 According to Chris Edwards, "Some small BDUS will choose to migrate tier by tier to avoid one enormous digital switch."
73 Greg O'Brien, "The Cartt.ca Interview: CCSA Chief Alyson Townsend Talks AGM, Member Challenges, Wireless Potential," 30 July 2010.
74 CRTC, *Communications Monitoring Report 2011*, 102.
75 Ibid., 108.
76 Noam, *TV or Not TV: Three Screens, One Regulation*? Canadian Radio-television and Telecommunications Commission, 11 July 2008.
77 Armstrong, *Broadcasting Policy in Canada*, 199.
78 CRTC, Public Notice CRTC 1999-197. *Exemption Order for New Media Broadcasting Undertakings.*

79 Hudson Janisch, "ICraveTV: Pirate or Pathfinder?" *Globe and Mail*, 1 February 2000.
80 Ziegler, United States District Judge, "Civil Action No. 00-121 Consolidated with Civil Action No. 00-120," United States District Court for the Western District of Pennsylvania, 8 February 2000.
81 CRTC, *Results of the Fact-Finding Exercise on the over-the-Top Programming Services*, 2011, 2.
82 Armstrong, 173.
83 *Leader-Post* (Regina), "Internet HDTV Unveiled: The Signal from Customers was Crystal Clear and Sasktel has Finally Delivered," 17 October 2006, http://www.canada.com/reginaleaderpost/news/business_agriculture/story.html?id=ebc83348-ad20-4c37-817d-308a6df69cce.
84 CRTC, *Communications Monitoring Report 2010*, table 4.4.3.
85 CRTC, *Communications Monitoring Report* 2009.
86 CRTC, *Communications Monitoring Report 2011*, 144.
87 Especially since the rare use of an Order in Council in 2006 directing the CRTC to rely on market forces for telecom as outlined in the 2006 *Telecommunications Policy Review Panel Final Report*. See Order Issuing a Direction to the CRTC on Implementing the Canadian Telecommunications Policy Objectives. P.C. 2006-1534, 14 December 2006.
88 CRTC, *Communications Monitoring Report* 2009, 160.
89 CRTC, *Communications Monitoring Report 2011*, figure 4.4.1.
90 Cartt.ca, "Spurred by IPTV, Digital TV Subscriptions top 10m, Says New Report," 30 April 2012, http://t.co/52gzakl8.
91 Manitoba Telecom Services Inc, *Annual Report*, 2011, 16.
92 Cartt.ca, "Bell's IPTV Coming in 2010; Fibre-to-the-Home across Quebec City," 4 February 2010, http://www.cartt.ca/news/9359/Cable-Telecom/Bell-s-IPTV-coming-in-2010-fibre-to-the-home-across-Quebec-City.html.
93 Iain Marlow, "BCE Takes Aim at Canada's TV Market," *Globe and Mail*, 18 May 2010.
94 Greg O'Brien, "Cartt.ca Investigates Looks at Cord-Cutting. Real, or Baloney?" Cartt.ca, 31 May 2011, http://www.cartt.ca/news/11935/Cable-Telecom/Cartt-ca-INVESTIGATES-looks-at-cord-cutting-real-or-baloney-.html.
95 CRTC, "Results of the Fact-Finding Exercise on the over-the-top Programming Services," October 2011.
96 Ibid.
97 Alexei Oreskovich, "Google Unveils Web-Ready TVs," *Globe and Mail*, 21 May 2010.
98 Abramson, "Open and Closed: Looking ahead to the CRTC's New Media Broadcast Hearings."

99 Jason Snell, "Apple TV 'Hobby' Nets 1.4m Quarterly Sales," *Macworld*, 24 January 2012, http://www.macworld.com/article/1164978/apple_tv_hobby_nets_1_4m_quarterly_sales.html.

100 Randall Stross, "Digital Domain: YouTube Wants You to Sit and Stay Awhile," *New York Times*, 28 May 2010.

101 Nicolas Kyonka, "Google Plays down Imminent Expansion of Google TV to Canada," *Wire Report*, 11 August 2011.

102 CRTC, *Communications Monitoring Report 2011*, 103.

103 CRTC, Broadcasting Public Notice CRTC 2007-13. *Exemption Order for Mobile Television Broadcasting Undertakings*.

104 Bell, "Bell Mobile TV Overview," accessed 16 July 2012, http://www.mobiletv.bell.ca.

105 Ibid.

106 Negroponte, *Being Digital*.

107 Abramson, "Open and Closed."

108 CRTC, Broadcasting Order CRTC 2009-660. *Amendments to the Exemption Order for New Media Broadcasting Undertakings (Appendix A to Public Notice CRTC 1999-197); Revocation of the Exemption Order for Mobile Television Broadcasting Undertakings*.

109 Ibid.

110 Kevin J. O'Brien, "Mobile TV's Last Frontier: US and Europe," *New York Times*, 20 May 2010.

111 Perry Hoffman, "Rogers Possibly Migrating Mobile TV to DVB-H Network," *Wire Report*, 26 February 2007.

112 Stefan Dubowski, "Government Sets up Ottawa Testbed to Showcase Mobile DTV to Broadcast Industry," *Wire Report*, 15 November 2009.

113 Noam, "TV or Not TV: Three Screens, One Regulation?"

114 Greg O'Brien, "Why Are New Media Opportunities Taking so Long?" Cartt.ca, 15 April 2008, http://www.cartt.ca/news/PrinterFriendly.cfm?NewsNo=6016.

115 Ibid.

116 Industry Canada, "Broadband Canada: Connecting Rural Canadians," accessed 16 July 2012, http://www.ic.gc.ca/eic/site/719.nsf/eng/home.

CHAPTER FIVE

1 All found in CRTC, "Public Notice 2008-100."

2 CRTC, "News Release: CRTC Releases Financial Results of Conventional Television Stations," 18 March 2010.

3 Winseck, "Financialization and the 'Crisis of the Media,'" 366.

4 CRTC, *Communications Monitoring Report 2011*, i.
5 Miller, "The Business of Canadian OTA Television," 2009.
6 Ibid.
7 CRTC, *Navigating Convergence: Charting Canadian Communications Change and Regulatory Implications*, 2010, 6.
8 DTV Working Group, *DTV Working Group Report: Issues Raised by Going Digital*, CRTC, April 2009.
9 CTV Submission to CRTC, "Broadcasting Notice of Consultation CRTC 2009-411. Policy Proceeding on a Group-Based Approach to the Licensing of Television Services and on Certain Issues Relating to Conventional Television," 6.
10 Goldstein (CTV), "Letter Re: CTVglobemedia Inc's Digital Television Transition Plans," (CRTC, 14 July 2010). This change was apparently attributed to confidence in the value-for-signal case at the Federal Court of Appeal and relaxed regulations for A stations.
11 Canwest Global, "Final Submission CRTC 2009-411," CRTC, 2009.
12 Bell (Canwest Global), "Re. CRTC Letter Dated June 23, 2010 Re. Digital Television (DTV) Transition Plans." This change may be attributed to the influx of new capital from the 2010 Shaw takeover bid.
13 Industry Canada, "DTV (Digital Television) Transition Allotment Plan, Issue 3," April 2005.
14 Approximately 11.2 million, or 82.8 per cent, of all Canadian households had access to analogue over-the-air television in the mandatory transition markets based on 2006 Census data, according to the CRTC's Broadcasting Notice of Consultation CRTC 2010-169. *Call for Comments on Issues Related to the Digital Television Transition*.
15 Canada. Task Force on the Implementation of Digital Television, *Canadian Television in the Digital Era: The Report of the Task Force on the Implementation of Digital Television*, 14.
16 CTV is owned by Bell Media, which also owns specialty channels like TSN, MuchMusic, and Bravo; Global is owned by Shaw Media, which owns specialty channels like Showcase and the Food Network.
17 CRTC, Broadcasting Public Notice CRTC 2007-53. *Determinations Regarding Certain Aspects of the Regulatory Framework for over-the-Air Television*.
18 CRTC, Broadcasting Public Notice 2008-100, *Regulatory Frameworks for Broadcasting Distribution Undertakings and Discretionary Programming Services*, 359.
19 http://www.crtc.gc.ca/eng/info_sht/tv13.htm
20 CRTC, Broadcasting Public Notice CRTC 2002-31. *A Licensing Policy to Oversee the Transition from Analogue to Digital, over-the-Air Television Broadcasting*.
21 Canada. Task Force on the Implementation of Digital Television, *Canadian Television in the Digital Era*," 15.

22 Michel Arpin (former CRTC vice chair of broadcasting), interview with the author, 2 September 2010.

23 CRTC, BPN CRTC 2007-53.

24 Ibid.

25 Michael Geist, "Digital TV Transition Could Lead to New Divide," *Toronto Star*, 26 July 2010.

26 McEwen, "The Digital Transition: In Search of the Holy Grail"; Galperin, *New Television, Old Politics*.

27 In a 30 March 2010 interview with the author, Chris Seidl, then-CRTC director general of convergence policy, stated: "The market-led approach has changed."

28 CTV submission, CRTC, "Broadcasting Notice of Consultation CRTC 2009-411. Policy Proceeding on a Group-Based Approach to the Licensing of Television Services and on Certain Issues Relating to Conventional Television," 38.

29 Canada. Task Force on the Implementation of Digital Television, *Canadian Television in the Digital Era*," 14. The same deadline was recommended for Toronto and Vancouver.

30 CTV submission, CRTC, *Broadcasting Notice of Consultation* CRTC *2009-411*, 38.

31 CRTC, BPN CRTC 2007-53.

32 CRTC, Broadcasting Regulatory Policy CRTC 2010-167. *A Group-Based Approach to the Licensing of Private Television Services.*

33 CRTC, Broadcasting Notice of Consultation CRTC 2010-169. *Call for Comments on Issues Related to the Digital Television Transition.*

34 Industry Canada, http://www.ic.gc.ca/eic/site/smt-gst.nsf/eng/sf09576.html. (accessed June 2010, not available 25 August 2010). See also Industry Canada, "Letter of Understanding between the Federal Communications Commission of the United States of America and Industry Canada Related to the Use of the 54–72 MHz, 76–88 MHz, 174–216 MHz and 470–806 MHz Bands for the Digital Television Broadcasting Service along the Common Border," January 2001.

35 According to CRTC decision 2010-167, the CRTC may allow some exceptions to this rule but only in consultation with Industry Canada.

36 CRTC, Broadcasting Regulatory Policy CRTC 2010-485. *Issues Related to the Digital Television Transition.*

37 Rogers Communications Inc, Submission to Canadian Radio-television and Telecommunications Commission, Broadcasting Notice of Consultation CRTC 2009-411, *Policy Proceeding on a Group-Based Approach to the Licensing of Television Services and on Certain Issues Relating to Conventional Television*, 14 September 2009.

38 CRTC 2009-411. *Policy Proceeding on a Group-Based Approach to the Licensing of Television Services and on Certain Issues Relating to Conventional Television.*
39 Ibid.
40 Dissenting opinion of Commissioner Suzanne Lamarre, CRTC, Broadcasting Regulatory Policy CRTC 2010-167. *A Group-Based Approach to the Licensing of Private Television Services.*
41 Canadian Press, "Clement Says He won't Delay Digital TV Transition," 7 April 2010.
42 Kevin Goldstein (vice president of regulatory affairs at CTV), interview with the author, 18 August 2010.
43 Grant Robertson, Nathan VanderKlippe, and Susan Krashinsky, "The Battle over Local TV," *Globe and Mail*, 13 November 2009.
44 Scott Hutton and Namir Anani, "Speech to the Standing Committee on Canadian Heritage," 2011.
45 CRTC, BPN CRTC 2002-31. *A Licensing Policy to Oversee the Transition from Analog to Digital, over-the-Air (OTA) Television Broadcasting.*
46 CRTC, Broadcasting Regulatory Policy CRTC 2010-485. *Issues Related to the Digital Television Transition.*
47 CRTC, Broadcasting Regulatory Policy CRTC 2010-167. *A Group-Based Approach to the Licensing of Private Television Services.*
48 CRTC, Broadcasting Regulatory Policy CRTC 2010-485. *Issues Related to the Digital Television Transition.*
49 Greg O'Brien, "Commentary: A Digital Disaster in the Making. Where's the Leadership?" Cartt.ca, 1 April 2010.
50 Broadcasting engineer Wayne Stacy and Channel Zero's Romen Podzyhun also expressed skepticism of the 90 per cent figure in interviews with the author.
51 CRTC, Broadcasting Regulatory Policy CRTC 2010-485. *Issues Related to the Digital Television Transition.*
52 CRTC, *Digital Transition Models*, 2009, appendix C.
53 Canadian Media Research Inc, *How Many Canadians Subscribe to Cable TV or Satellite TV? Cable TV/DTH Subscriber Estimates, Profile of Non-subscribers and Special Survey Results*, September 2006.
54 The Strategic Council, *Research Findings among OTA Viewers: Expected Action among TV Viewers When Digitization Takes Effect*, 2009.
55 CRTC, Broadcasting Regulatory Policy CRTC 2010-485.
56 Canadian Press, "Clement Says He won't Delay Digital TV Transition," 7 April 2010.
57 CRTC, Broadcasting Notice of Consultation CRTC 2010-169. *Call for Comments on Issues Related to the Digital Television Transition.*

58 CRTC, Broadcasting Decision CRTC 2010-61. *Direct-to-Home Satellite Distribution Undertaking and Satellite Relay Distribution Undertaking.*
59 CRTC, Broadcasting Decision CRTC 2010-782. *Change in the Effective Control of Canwest Global Communications Corp's Licensed Broadcasting Subsidiaries.*
60 Michel Arpin, interview with the author, 2 September 2010.
61 "Canada's Transition to Digital Television (DTV)," accessed 16 July 2012, http://www.digitaltv.gc.ca.
62 "Detroit TV Listing," accessed 16 July 2012, http://tvlistings.aol.com/listings/mi/detroit/over-the-air/48234.
63 CRTC, Broadcasting Public Notice CRTC 2007-53.
64 Karim Sunderani (Save and Replay), interview with the author, 6 April 2010, Mississauga.
65 David Sarno, "Rabbit Ears Make Comeback in Digital TV Era," *Los Angeles Times*, 25 December 2009.
66 "Los Angeles TV Listings," accessed 16 July 2012, http://tvlistings.aol.com/listings/ca/los-angeles/over-the-air/90008.
67 "Chicago and Houston TV Listings," accessed 16 July 2012, http://tvlistings.aol.com/listings/il/chicago/over-the-air/60661 and http://tvlistings.aol.com/listings/tx/houston/over-the-air/77278#evt-55345_2012-07-11_00X00.
68 Miller, *The Business of Canadian OTA Television.*
69 Dan Gold (senior director of media technology strategy and standards at Shaw), interview with the author, 28 June 2012.
70 CRTC, Broadcasting Public Notice CRTC 2007-62. *Call for Applications for a Broadcasting Licence to Carry on an over-the-Air Digital/High Definition (HD) Television Programming Undertaking to Serve Locations across Canada.*
71 CRTC, Broadcasting Decision CRTC 2008-75. *National High Definition over-the-Air Digital Television Service.*
72 Ibid., 10.
73 Ibid. Dissenting opinion.
74 Miller, *The Business of Canadian OTA Television.*
75 Ibid.
76 CRTC, Broadcasting Decision CRTC 2009-537. *CHCH-TV Hamilton and Its Transmitters and CHCH-DT Hamilton – Acquisition of Assets.*
77 Millar, Channel Zero. 6 May 2010. Letter Re: Broadcasting Notice of Consultation CRTC 2010-169.
78 Romen Podzyhun (Channel Zero), interview with the author, 10 August 2010, Toronto.
79 Simon Doyle, "Independent Broadcasters Say They Can Meet the Digital Transition Deadline," *Wire Report*, 18 August 2010.

80 According to the CBC 2010–2011 *Annual Report*, 71, the CBC's annual income included $1.03 billion from Parliamentary appropriation and $367.7 million from advertising revenues.

81 Nordicity, *Analysis of Government Support for Public Broadcasting and Other Culture in Canada*, 4.

82 Ibid., 18.

83 Jane Taber, "Undaunted Conservatives Vent More Spleen at CBC," *Globe and Mail*, 30 April 2010.

84 CBC/Radio Canada, "2011-2012 Digital Transition Plan," 6 August 2010.

85 CRTC, "BPN CRTC 2002-31."

86 Ibid.

87 CRTC, "BPN CRTC 2007-53," 18.

88 Ibid., 31.

89 CBC/Radio Canada, "Submission of CBC/Radio-Canada. Policy Proceeding on a Group-Based Approach to the Licensing of Television Services and on Certain Issues Relating to Conventional Television. Broadcasting Notice of Consultation 2009-411," 14 September 2009,

90 Ibid., 145.

91 Ibid., 142.

92 1991 Broadcasting Act 3(m)(vii).

93 Ibid., 3(m)(ii), 3(m)(vi).

94 CRTC, Broadcasting Regulatory Policy CRTC 2010-167. *A Group-Based Approach to the Licensing of Private Television Services*.

95 Lawson Hunter, Edward Iacobucci, and Michael Trebilcock, *Scrambled Signals: Canadian Content Policies in a World of Technological Abundance*, 29.

96 CRTC, *The Implications and Advisability of Implementing a Compensation Regime for the Value of Local Television Signals: A Report Prepared Pursuant to Section 15 of the Broadcasting Act*, 23 March 2010.

97 Nash, 417.

98 Lacroix, "Speaking Notes for Hubert T. Lacroix Regarding Measures Announced in the Context of the Deficit Reduction Action Plan," CBC/Radio-Canada's employee town hall, 4 April 2012.

99 "TV Ontario," accessed 16 July 2012, http://about.tvo.org/who-we-are/digital-over-air-transition.

100 Karen Fournier, "Even if CBC Had the Money, it Couldn't Meet Digital Deadline," *Wire Report*, 10 August 2010.

101 Gregory Taylor, "CBC 2.0 at the CRTC Hearings on New Media," Media@McGill, 26 February 2009, http://media.mcgill.ca/en/node/1377.

102 Galperin, 238.

103 Bob Reaume (vice president, policy and research, Association of Canadian Advertisers), interview with the author, 3 March 2010.

CHAPTER SIX

1 Raboy and Shtern, *Media Divides: Communication Rights and the Right to Communicate in Canada*.

2 For further information on Canadian Community Television, see Canadian Radio-television and Telecommunications Commission, Broadcasting Regulatory Policy CRTC 2010-622, *Community Television Policy*, 34.

3 The nine not-for-profit community channels are located in Hay River, NWT; Leamington, ON; Dawson Creek and Chetwynd, BC (one channel serves two communities); Ashcroft and Cache Creek, BC (one channel serves two communities); Valemount, BC; Arichat, NS; St Andrews, NB; Northern Cape Breton, NS (francophone channel); Neepawa, MB.

4 Canada, Broadcasting Act, 1991. 3.1.a; 3.1.i(iii).

5 Canadian Association of Community Television Users and Stations (CACTUS), "The Transition to Digital over-the-Air Television: New Opportunities," June 2011.

6 CRTC, Broadcasting Public Notice CRTC 2002-61, *Policy Framework for Community-Based Media*.

7 CACTUS, "The Transition to Digital over-the-Air."

8 CACTUS, "Comment on CBC Application #2012-0509-7," 18 June 2012.

9 CBC/Radio-Canada, "Suggestions by Cactus that CBC/Radio-Canada Should Offer its Analogue Infrastructure to Communities," 25 May 2012.

10 Canadian Media Guild Karen Wirsig Communications Co-ordinator, "Letter to Mr Robert Morin, Secretary General, CRTC Re: Reply on CRTC 2009-411," 14 December 2009.

11 All of the included Kamloops and multiplex comments are available in the transcripts to 16 November 2009, *Policy Proceeding on a Group-Based Approach to the Licensing of Television Services and on Certain Issues Relating to Conventional Television*. Notice of Consultation CRTC 2009-411.

12 In an email exchange with the author on 26 August 2010, Pam Astbury from SOCK writes: "In the spring I met with Rick Arnish, president of the Jim Pattison broadcasting corporation. His company is the largest small market broadcaster in western Canada. He saw the potential for the conversion to multiplexing. He noted additional costs as the challenge. Costs such as digital cameras, routing digital signal to his current transmitter. He said that the $90,000 figure could be accurate for conversion of the transmitter, however, there were numerous other costs that the local station would have to bear."

13 CRTC, Broadcasting Regulatory Policy CRTC 2010-167. *A Group-Based Approach to the Licensing of Private Television Services*.

14 Centre for Community Study, "It's Time: CBC Investment in Hamilton," 2005, 4.

15 Centre for Community Study, *Higher Definition: Local Television as Public Service. Intervention for Broadcast Notice of Public Hearing* CRTC 2006-5, 2006, 6.
16 Sonja Macdonald, interview with the author, 26 June 2012.
17 Tony Vidal (president and CEO of CFTV34), interview with the author, 29 June 2012.
18 Ibid.
19 CRTC, Broadcasting Decision CRTC 2012-446.
20 Tony Vidal (president and CEO of CFTV34), interview with the author, 29 June 2012.
21 Steven May, "About," Dude, Where's My TV?, http://dudewhereismytv.wordpress.com/about.
22 Ibid.
23 John Traversy, CRTC, "Commission Letter: Mr Jean Brazeau, Senior Vice President, Regulatory Affairs, Shaw Communications Inc," 29 November 2011.
24 Steven May, "Shaw Direct: The Saviour of Free TV in Rural and Remote Canada?," Dude, Where's My TV?, 7 May 2012, http://dudewhereismytv.wordpress.com/2012/05.
25 Friends of Canadian Broadcasting, http://www.friends.ca.
26 OpenMedia.ca, http://www.openmedia.ca.

CONCLUSION

1 Harold Innis, *Empire and Communications*, 26.
2 Babe, *Canadian Communication Thought*, 75 (the Internet, a powerful space-based medium, does not appear on the chart).
3 Tony Clement, Twitter post, 10 September 2010, http://twitter.com/Tony Clement_MP/status/24087735101.
4 As a point of comparison, various key government and CRTC task forces since the 1980s include the Task Force on Broadcasting Policy, or Caplan-Sauvageau Task Force (1986), chaired by academic Florian Sauvageau and politician Gerald Caplan; the Task Force on the Economic Status of Canadian Television (1990), co-chaired by Jacques Girard of Société de radio-télévision du Québec and former deputy minister of the Ministry of Education of Quebec and J.R. Peters, a prominent member of the British Columbia broadcasting industry; the Task Force for Cultural Diversity on Television (2002), comprised of five industry representatives and four non-industry representatives. In each case, of the leaders and general membership of each group represented a clear balance between public and industrial viewpoints.

5 Michel Arpin, interview with the author, 2 September 2010.

6 Konrad von Finckenstein, "CRTC Chair Speech to the Annual Conference of the British Columbia Association of Broadcasters," Penticton, BC, 10 May 2007.

7 In a 18 September 2008 *Globe and Mail* article, "The Return of Regulation, and What a Difference a Decade Makes," concerning the greater applications of self-regulation in the financial marketplace, Eric Helleiner, chair in international governance at the University of Waterloo, writes: "The same private institutions that were assigned important self-regulatory roles over the past decade are now suddenly being severely criticized."

8 Grainger, "Broadcasting Coregulation and the Public Good," Montreal, 1999.

9 Barney, *Communication Technology*, 11.

10 European Commission, "Communication from the Commission to the Council, the European Parliament, the Economic and Social Committee, and the Committee of the Regions. Principles and Guidelines for the Community's Audiovisual Policy in the Digital Age," Brussels, 12 January 1999, 13.

11 Dunbar and Leblanc, 19.

12 In a 23 April 2009 interview with the author, former CDTV chair Michael McEwen describes the independence of CDTV:

GT: You point out this (digital television) transition cuts to the heart of the Broadcasting Act. Where's the public in this? Shouldn't they have a seat at that table?

MM: Everybody else paid for it. Maybe the government should have paid for that. We needed government to say, "Guys, we need a plan you can all agree to or we're going to give you one." No one ever said that.

GT: In co-regulation, the government always has a stick in the background. Was there a stick?

MM: No.

GT: So this was self-regulation?

MM: In that sense it was. The CRTC made its views known of what its expectations were [*sic*] that we had any kind of direction.

13 Industry Canada, "Canada's New Government Issues Policy Direction to CRTC that Calls for Greater Reliance on Market Forces," http://www.ic.gc.ca/eic/site/ic1.nsf/eng/02149.html.

14 Canada. Telecommunications Policy Review Panel, *Telecommunications Policy Review Panel Final Report*, 2006, recommendation 2–3.

15 See also Canada. External Advisory Committee on Smart Regulation, *Smart Regulation: A Regulatory Strategy for Canada. Report to the Government of Canada*, 2004.

16 Salter and Odartey-Wellington, *The CRTC and Broadcasting Regulation in Canada*, 778.
17 Iain Marlow, "Recent CRTC Decisions Highlight Independent Streak," *Globe and Mail*, 2 September 2010.
18 Salter and Odartey-Wellington, 20.
19 Greg O'Brien, "Opinion: Broadcasters Association Faces Uncertain Future," Cartt.ca, 6 November 2008.
20 Karen Fournier, "Following CAB Closure, Conventional Broadcasters to Fend for Themselves, Say Insiders," *Wire Report*, 15 March 2010.
21 CRTC 2001-62. *Call for Comments on a Proposed Policy to Oversee the Transition from Analog to Digital over-the-Air (OTA) Television Broadcasting.*
22 Michel Arpin, interview with the author, 2 September 2010.
23 Industry Canada, "Digital Economy Consultation," http://de-en.gc.ca/en/home.
24 Canada, Budget 2011: The Next Phase of Canada's Economic Action Plan – A Low-Tax Plan for Jobs and Growth.
25 See Federal Communications Commission, *Connecting America: The National Broadband Plan*; Great Britain, *Digital Britain: The Interim Report*; Government of Australia, *National Digital Economy Strategy*; Germany, *ICT Strategy of the German Federal Government.*
26 Communications and the Digital Economy Australian Government. Department of Broadband, *Digital Dividend Green Paper*, September 2010; Ofcom, *Digital Dividend Review: 550–630 MHz and 790–854 MHz*, 6 June 2008.
27 Chapin and Lehr, "Scada for the Rest of Us: Unlicenced Bands Supporting Long-Range Communications," in *38th Research Conference on Communication, Information and Internet Policy (TPRC)* (Alexandria, VA, 1–3 October 2010.
28 Spectrum Bridge, "Improving Access to High Speed Broadband," accessed May 2011 (unavailable May 2012), http://www.spectrumbridge.com/products-services/whitespaces/success-stories/claudville.aspx.
29 Federal Communications Commission, *Connecting America: The National Broadband Plan*, March 2010, recommendation 5.12.
30 Jonathan Migneault, "Google Says Government Should Follow US Lead on Unlicenced, 'White Space' Spectrum," *Wire Report*, 14 July 2010.
31 Malcolm White (vice president of portfolio management and a portfolio manager at Signature Global advisors who specializes in technology, media, and telecommunications industries), interview with the author, 30 September 2010, Toronto.

Bibliography

Abelson, Donald E. *Do Think Tanks Matter? Assessing the Impact of Public Policy Institutes*. Montreal: McGill-Queen's University Press, 2009.

Abramson, Bram D. "Open and Closed: Looking Ahead to the CRTC's New Media Broadcast Hearings." McCarthy Tétrault LLP, 13 February 2009, http://www.mccarthy.ca/article_detail.aspx?id=4428.

Adelstein, Jonathan S. "Questions for Federal Communications Commission Members from the Hon. John D. Dingell, Chairman, House Committee on Energy and Commerce and the Hon. Edward J. Markey, Chairman, Subcommittee on Telecommunications and the Internet." 7 February 2007.

Armstrong, Robert. *Broadcasting Policy in Canada*. Toronto: University of Toronto Press, 2010.

Asami, Hiroshi. "Digital Broadcasting in Japan: HDTV and Mobile Reception as Key Application." *Broadcast Asia*, 12 May 2005.

Astor, Linda Gossack. "Common Digital TV Standard Urged for Western Hemisphere." *Export America*. February 2004, 12–13.

Australian Government. Department of Broadband, Communications and the Digital Economy. *Digital Dividend Green Paper*. September 2010.

– *National Digital Economy Strategy: Leveraging the National Broadband Network to Drive Australia's Digital Productivity*. 2011.

– *Digital Tracker Report on Quarter 4: October–December 2011*. 2012.

Autorité de régulation des communications électroniques et des postes. "Annual Report 2011." 2011.

Babe, Robert E. *Telecommunications in Canada: Technology, Industry, and Government*. Toronto: University of Toronto Press, 1990.

– *Canadian Communication Thought: Ten Foundational Writers*. Toronto: University of Toronto Press, 2000.

– *Cultural Studies and Political Economy: Toward a New Integration*. Lanham: Lexington Books, 2009.

– *Communication and the Transformation of Economics: Essays in Information, Public Policy, and Political Economy*. Boulder, CO: Westview Press, 1995.

Barendt, E.M. *Broadcasting Law: A Comparative Study*. New York: Clarendon Press, 1993.

Barney, Darin David. *Communication Technology*. Vancouver: UBC Press, 2005.

Bell, Charlotte (Canwest Global). "Re. CRTC Letter Dated June 23, 2010 Re. Digital Television (DTV) Transition Plans." 2010.

Bell, Martin L. *Inventing Digital Television: The Inside Story of a Technology Revolution*. Great Britain: The London Press, 2007.

Benoit, Hervé. *Digital Television: Satellite, Cable, Terrestrial, IPTV, Mobile TV in the DVB Framework*. 3rd ed. Burlington, MA: Focal Press, 2008.

Bird, Roger. *Documents of Canadian Broadcasting*. Ottawa: Carleton University Press, 1988.

Bonin, Genevive A. "Canada's Transition to Digital Television: From Policy to Reality." *International Journal of Digital Television* 1, no. 2 (2010): 135–54.

Brinkley, Joel. *Defining Vision: The Battle for the Future of Television*. New York: Harcourt Brace, 1997.

Canada. Broadcasting Act. 1991.

– Broadcasting Distribution Regulations. 1997. Current to 10 June 2012.

– *Budget 2011: The Next Phase of Canada's Economic Action Plan – A Low-Tax Plan for Jobs and Growth*. 2011.

– *Task Force on Broadcasting Policy. Report*. 1986.

– External Advisory Committee on Smart Regulation. *Smart Regulation: A Regulatory Strategy for Canada. Report to the Government of Canada*. September 2004.

– Lincoln, Clifford and the Standing Committee on Canadian Heritage. *Our Cultural Sovereignty: The Second Century of Canadian Broadcasting*. Ottawa: Standing Committee on Canadian Heritage, 2003.

– Royal Commission on Radio Broadcasting, and John Aird. *Report of the Royal Commission on Radio Broadcasting*. Ottawa: F.A. Acland, Printer, 1929.

– Task Force on the Implementation of Digital Television. *Canadian Television in the Digital Era: The Report of the Task Force on the Implementation of Digital Television*. Ottawa, 1997.

– Telecommunications Policy Review Panel. *Telecommunications Policy Review Panel Final Report*, 2006.

Canadian Association of Community Television Users and Stations (CACTUS). "The Transition to Digital over-the-Air Television: New Opportunities." June 2011.

Canadian Media Research Inc. *How Many Canadians Subscribe to Cable TV or Satellite TV? Cable TV/DTH Subscriber Estimates, Profile of Non-Subscribers and Special Survey Results*. Canadian Radio-television and Telecommunications Commission, September 2006.

Canadian Radio-television and Telecommunications Commission. Broadcasting Decision CRTC 2004-130. *Star Choice – Licence Renewal*. 31 March 2004.

– Broadcasting Decision CRTC 2008-75. *National High Definition over-the-Air Digital Television Service*. 3 April 2008.

– Broadcasting Decision CRTC 2008-234. *Various Cable Broadcasting Distribution Undertakings in Western Canada – Short-Term Licence Renewals and Licence Amendments*. 28 August 2008.

– Broadcasting Decision CRTC 2009-537. *CHCH-TV Hamilton and its Transmitters and CHCH-DT Hamilton – Acquisition of Assets*. 28 August 2009.

– Broadcasting Decision CRTC 2010-61. *Direct-to-Home Satellite Distribution Undertaking and Satellite Relay Distribution Undertaking*. 8 February 2010.

– Broadcasting Decision CRTC 2010-782. *Change in the Effective Control of Canwest Global Communications Corp's Licensed Broadcasting Subsidiaries*. 22 October 2010.

– Broadcasting Information Bulletin CRTC 2010-198. *Amendment to the Timeframe for Consideration of New Category A Services*. 31 March 2010.

– Broadcasting Notice of Consultation CRTC 2009-411. *Policy Proceeding on a Group-Based Approach to the Licensing of Television Services and on Certain Issues Relating to Conventional Television*. 6 July 2009.

– Broadcasting Notice of Consultation CRTC 2009-732. *Call for Comments on Proposed Revisions to the Criteria Used to Assess Applications for Mandatory Distribution Pursuant to an Order under Section 9(1)(h) of the Broadcasting Act*. 30 November 2009.

– Broadcasting Notice of Consultation CRTC 2010-169. *Call for Comments on Issues Related to the Digital Television Transition*. 22 March 2010.

– Broadcasting Notice of Public Hearing CRTC 2006-5. *Review of Certain Aspects of the Regulatory Framework for over-the-Air Television*. 12 June 2006.

– Broadcasting Notice of Public Hearing CRTC 2007-10. *Review of the Regulatory Frameworks for Broadcasting Distribution Undertakings and Discretionary Programming Services*. 5 July 2007.

– Broadcasting Order CRTC 2009-544. *Exemption Order for Terrestrial Broadcasting Distribution Undertakings Serving Fewer than 20,000 Subscribers*. 31 August 2009.
– Broadcasting Order CRTC 2009-660. *Amendments to the Exemption Order for New Media Broadcasting Undertakings (Appendix A to Public Notice CRTC 1999-197); Revocation of the Exemption Order for Mobile Television Broadcasting Undertakings*. 22 October 2009.
– Broadcasting Order CRTC 2010-168. *Reference to the Federal Court of Appeal – Commission's Jurisdiction under the Broadcasting Act to Implement a Negotiated Solution for the Compensation for the Fair Value of Private Local Conventional Television Signals*. 22 March 2010.
– Broadcasting Public Notice CRTC 2001-130. *Small Cable Systems – Digital Migration Policy*. 21 December 2001.
– Broadcasting Public Notice CRTC 2002-31. *A Licensing Policy to Oversee the Transition from Analogue to Digital, over-the-Air Television Broadcasting*. 12 June 2002.
– Broadcasting Public Notice CRTC 2002-61. *Policy Framework for Community-Based Media*. 10 October 2002.
– Broadcasting Public Notice CRTC 2003-48. *A Regional Approach to Licensing Cable Distribution Undertakings – Adoption of Related Amendments to the Broadcasting Distribution Regulations*. 17 September 2003.
– Broadcasting Public Notice CRTC 2003-61. *The Regulatory Framework for the Distribution of Digital Television Signals*. 11 November 2003.
– Broadcasting Public Notice CRTC 2004-58. *Call for Comments on a Proposed Framework for the Licensing and Distribution of High Definition Pay and Specialty Services*. 6 August 2004.
– Broadcasting Public Notice CRTC 2006-23. Digital Migration Framework. 27 February 2006.
– Broadcasting Public Notice CRTC 2006-160. *Digital Radio Policy*. 15 December 2006.
– Broadcasting Public Notice CRTC 2007-13. *Exemption Order for Mobile Television Broadcasting Undertakings*. 7 February 2007.
– Broadcasting Public Notice CRTC 2007-53. *Determinations Regarding Certain Aspects of the Regulatory Framework for over-the-Air Television*. 17 May 2007.
– Broadcasting Public Notice CRTC 2007-62. *Call for Applications for a Broadcasting Licence to Carry on an over-the-Air Digital/High Definition (HD) Television Programming Undertaking to Serve Locations across Canada*. 11 June 2007.

– Broadcasting Public Notice CRTC 2008-4. *Regulatory Policy: Diversity of Voices*. 15 January 2008.
– Broadcasting Regulatory Policy CRTC 2012-181. *Broadcasting Participation Fund*. 26 March 2012.
– Broadcasting Regulatory Policy CRTC 2010-167. *A Group-Based Approach to the Licensing of Private Television Services*. 22 March 2010.
– Broadcasting Regulatory Policy CRTC 2010-190. *Regulatory Framework for Video-on-Demand Undertakings*. 29 March 2010.
– Broadcasting Regulatory Policy CRTC 2010-485. *Issues Related to the Digital Television Transition*. 16 July 2010.
– Broadcasting Regulatory Policy CRTC 2010-622. *Community Television Policy*. 26 August 2010.
– *Communications Monitoring Report 2011*. 2011.
– *Communications Monitoring Report 2010*. 2010.
– *Communications Monitoring Report 2009*. 2009.
– "CRTC Releases Financial Results for Canadian Broadcasting Distributors." 18 March 2010.
– "CRTC Releases Financial Results of Conventional Television Stations." 18 March 2010.
– *Digital Transition Models*. October 2009.
– DTV Working Group. *DTV Working Group Report: Issues Raised by Going Digital*. April 2009.
– *Individual Pay Television, Pay-per-View, Video-on-Demand and Specialty Services: Statistical and Financial Summaries 2007–2011*.
– Pay Television Regulations. 1990.
– Public Notice CRTC 1994-118. *Exemption Order Respecting Experimental Video-on-Demand Programming Undertakings*. 16 September 1994.
– Public Notice CRTC 2000-172. *Introductory Statement to Decisions CRTC 2000-733 to 2000-738: Licensing of New Video-on-Demand and Pay-per-View Services*. 14 December 2000.
– Public Notice CRTC 2001-58. *Digital Migration Issues – Reconvening of Working Group Regarding Large Cable Systems, and; Call for Comments Regarding Small Cable Systems*. 25 May 2001.
– Public Notice CRTC 2001-62. *A Call for Comments on a Proposed Policy to Oversee the Transition from Analogue to Digital over-the-Air Television Broadcasting*. 5 June 2001.
– Public Notice CRTC 2001-66-1. *Ownership of Analogue Discretionary Services by Cable Undertakings – Amendment to the Commission's Policy*. 24 August 2001.

– Public Notice CRTC 2008-100. *Regulatory Frameworks for Broadcasting Distribution Undertakings and Discretionary Programming Services*. 30 October 2008.
– *Results of the Fact-Finding Exercise on the over-the-top Programming Services*. October 2011.
– *The Distribution of Existing Analogue Pay and Specialty Services on a Digital Basis. The Report of the Digital Migration Working Group*. 2001.
– *The Future Environment Facing the Canadian Broadcasting System: A Report Prepared Pursuant to Section 15 of the Broadcasting Act*. 2006.
– *The Implications and Advisability of Implementing a Compensation Regime for the Value of Local Television Signals: A Report Prepared Pursuant to Section 15 of the Broadcasting Act*. 23 March 2010.

Canwest Global. "Final Submission CRTC 2009-411." Canadian Radio-television and Telecommunications Commission, 2009.

Cave, Martin, and Kiyoshi Nakamura. *Digital Broadcasting: Policy and Practice in the Americas, Europe and Japan*. Northampton, MA: Edward Elgar, 2006.

CBC/Radio Canada. *2011–2012 Digital Transition Plan*. 6 August 2010.
– *2010–2011 Annual Report*.
– "Submission of CBC/Radio-Canada. *Policy Proceeding on a Group-Based Approach to the Licensing of Television Services and on Certain Issues Relating to Conventional Television*. Broadcasting Notice of Consultation 2009-411." 14 September 2009.
– "Suggestions by CACTUS that CBC/Radio-Canada Should Offer its Analogue Infrastructure to Communities." 25 May 2012.

Centre for Community Study. "It's Time: CBC Investment in Hamilton." 2005.
– "Higher Definition: Local Television as Public Service. Intervention for Broadcast Notice of Public Hearing CRTC 2006-5." 2006.

Chapin, John M., and William H. Lehr. "Scada for the Rest of Us: Unlicenced Bands Supporting Long-Range Communications." In *38th Research Conference on Communication, Information and Internet Policy (TPRC)*. Alexandria, VA: 1–3 October 2010.

Charland, Maurice. "Technological Nationalism." *Canadian Journal of Political and Social Theory* X, no. 12 (1986): 196–220.

Collins, Richard. *Culture, Communication, and National Identity: The Case of Canadian Television*. Toronto: University of Toronto Press, 1990.

Committee for the North American HDTV Demonstrations to the Public. *The North American High Definition Television Demonstrations to the Public: An Overview of the Survey Results*. 1988.

Crane, Rhonda J. *The Politics of International Standards: France and the Color TV War*. Norwood, NJ: Ablex Publishing Corporation, 1979.

D'Haenens, L., and F. Saeys. *Western Broadcast Models: Structure, Conduct, and Performance*. New York: Mouton de Gruyter, 2007.

de Souza, Taynah Lopes, and Rodolfo Saboia Lima de Souza. "Building the Digital TV Standard: The Brazilian Experience." In *2009 GLOBELICS Conference*. Dakar, Senegal, 2009.

Department for Culture, Media and Sport, and Department for Business Enterprise and Regulatory Reform. *Digital Britain: The Interim Report*. Norwich: TSO, 2009.

Doern, G. Bruce, ed. *Changing the Rules: Canadian Regulatory Regimes and Institutions*. Toronto: University of Toronto Press, 1999.

Dubowski, Stefan. "Government Sets up Ottawa Testbed to Showcase Mobile DTV to Broadcast Industry." *Wire Report*, 15 November 2009.

Dunbar, Laurence J.E., and Christian Leblanc. *Review of the Regulatory Framework for Broadcasting Services in Canada*. Canadian Radio-television and Telecommunications Commission, 31 August 2007.

European Commission. "Communication from the Commission to the Council, the European Parliament, the Economic and Social Committee, and the Committee of the Regions. Principles and Guidelines for the Community's Audiovisual Policy in the Digital Age." Brussels, 12 January 1999.

– "Council Directive 89/552/Eec on the Coordination of Certain Provisions Laid down by Law, Regulation or Administrative Action in Member States Concerning the Pursuit of Television Broadcasting Activities. (Television without Frontiers Directive)." 1989.

European Commission and European Audiovisual Observatory. "TV Market in France." 2008. http://mavise.obs.coe.int/country?id=1 (accessed 2 May 2012).

Farias, M.C.Q., M.M. Carvalho, and M.S. Alencar, "Digital Television Broadcasting in Brazil." *Multimedia, IEEE* 15, no. 2 (2008): 64–70.

Federal Communications Commission. "Children's Television Obligations of Digital Television Broadcasters." 23 November 2004.

– *Connecting America: The National Broadband Plan*. March 2010.

– "Notice of Inquiry. Public Interest Obligations of TV Broadcast Licencees." In *MM Docket No. 99-360*, 20 December 1999.

– "Recommendation Regarding Consumer Interest Obligations of Digital Television Broadcasters. Consumer Advisory Committee. Shirley L. Rooker, Chair." 18 November 2005.

Feintuck, Mike. *"The Public Interest" in Regulation*. Oxford: Oxford University Press, 2004.

Finckenstein, Konrad von. "CRTC Chair Speech to the Annual Conference of the British Columbia Association of Broadcasters." Penticton, BC, 10 May 2007.

– "Speech to the 2008 Broadcasting Invitational Summit." Cambridge, ON, 2008.

Flavelle, Dana. "Newspapers Still among the Most Trusted Media." *Toronto Star*, 15 May 2010.

Fraser, Matthew. *Free-for-All: The Struggle for Dominance on the Digital Frontier.* Toronto: Stoddart, 1999.

Galperin, Hernan. *New Television, Old Politics: The Transition to Digital TV in the United States and Britain, Communication, Society, and Politics*. New York: Cambridge University Press, 2004.

Germany. *ICT Strategy of the German Federal Government: Digital Germany 2015*. Berlin, 2010.

Given, Jock. *Turning Off the Television: Broadcasting's Uncertain Future*. Kensington: University of New South Wales Press, 2003.

Goldstein, Kevin. "Letter Re: CTVglobemedia Inc's Digital Television Transition Plans." Canadian Radio-television and Telecommunications Commission, 14 July 2010.

Gow, Gordon, and Richard K. Smith. *Mobile and Wireless Communications: An Introduction.* Berkshire, UK: Open University Press, 2006.

Grainger, Gareth. "Broadcasting Coregulation and the Public Good." *Graham Spry Memorial Lecture.* Montreal: Université de Montréal, 1999. Fonds Graham Spry Fund. http://www.fondsgrahamspryfund.ca/en/previous-conferences/in-focusing-on-the-role-of-public-broadcasters-in-countries-such-as-canada-and-australia-i-begin-this-speech-by-examining-several-assumptions-that-underlie-broadcasting-in-general-in-order-to-reconsi/ (accessed 16 July 2012).

Grant, George. *Lament for a Nation: The Defeat of Canadian Nationalism.* 40th ed. Montreal: McGill-Queen's University Press, 2005.

Grant, Peter S., and Grant Buchanan. *Canadian Broadcasting Regulatory Handbook*. 10th ed. McCarthy Tétrault LLP, 2010.

Grant, Peter S., Grant Buchanan, and Bram D. Abramson. *Regulatory Guide to Canadian Television*. 5th ed. McCarthy Tétrault LLP, 2010.

Grimme, Katharina. *Digital Television Standardization and Strategies*. Boston: Artech House, 2002.

Habermas, Jürgen, and Max Pensky. *The Postnational Constellation: Political Essays*. Cambridge, MA: MIT Press, 2001.

Herman, Edward S., and Robert Waterman McChesney. *The Global Media: The New Missionaries of Corporate Capitalism*. London: Cassell, 1997.

Huff, W.A. Kelly. *Regulating the Future: Broadcasting Technology and Governmental Control*. Westport, CT: Greenwood Press, 2001.

Hunter, Lawson A.W., Edward Iacobucci, and Michael J. Trebilcock. *Scrambled Signals: Canadian Content Policies in a World of Technological Abundance*. C.D. Howe Institute, 2010.

Industry Canada. *Consultation on Issues Related to Spectrum Auctioning*. 1 August 1997.

– *Consultation on the Spectrum Allocations and Spectrum Utilization Policies for the Frequency Range 1435–1525 MHz (L-Band)*. 2009.

– *DTV (Digital Television) Transition Allotment Plan, Issue 3*. April 2005.

– "Letter of Understanding between the Federal Communications Commission of the United States of America and Industry Canada Related to the Use of the 54–72 MHz, 76–88 MHz, 174–216 MHz and 470–806 MHz Bands for the Digital Television Broadcasting Service Along the Common Border." January 2001.

Innis, Harold Adams. *Empire and Communications*. Lanham, MD: Rowman & Littlefield, 2007.

– *Staples, Markets, and Cultural Change: Selected Essays of Harold A. Innis*. Montreal: McGill-Queen's University Press, 1995.

Insight Information Inc. *The Changing Role of the CRTC*. Toronto, 1996.

International Commission for the Study of Communication Problems. *Many Voices, One World: Towards a New, More Just, and More Efficient World Information and Communication Order*, Critical Media Studies. Lanham, MD: Rowman & Littlefield, 2004.

Krasnow, Erwin G., and Lawrence D. Longley. *The Politics of Broadcast Regulation*. New York: St Martin's Press, 1978.

Lacroix, Hubert T. "Speaking Notes for Hubert T. Lacroix Regarding Measures Announced in the Context of the Deficit Reduction Action Plan." CBC/Radio-Canada's employee town hall. 4 April 2012.

Leiva, María García, and Michael Starks. "Digital Switchover across the Globe: The Emergence of Complex Regional Patterns." *Media, Culture and Society* 31, no. 5 (2009): 787–806.

Lemée, P. and F. Gauthier (Spectrum Expert Inc). *Cost Estimate of Digital Television (DTV) Conversion for Canada*. CRTC, March 2009.

Lessig, Lawrence. *Free Culture: How Big Media Uses Technology and the Law to Lock down Culture and Control Creativity*. New York: Penguin Press, 2004.

Manitoba Telecom Services Inc. *Annual Report*. 2011.

McEwen, Michael. "The Digital Transition: In Search of the Holy Grail."

Broadcast Dialogue – The Voice of Broadcasting in Canada (1 Feb 2009): 6–10.

– *A Report to the CRTC on Digital Transition Strategies in a Number of Different Countries*. Ottawa: Canadian Radio-television and Telecommunications Commission, 2006.

McKnight, L. and S. Neil. "The HDTV War: The Politics of HDTV Standardization." Paper presented at the *Third International Colloquium on Advanced Television Systems. From Studio to Viewer*. Colloquium Proceedings, Ottawa, 1987.

McLuhan, Marshall. *Understanding Media: The Extensions of Man*. Cambridge, MA: MIT Press, 2002.

McPhail, Thomas L. "Interactive Cable Communication Services: The Duplex Society Problem." *Canadian Journal of Communication* 4, no. 4 (1978): 1–7.

Mercer, Rick, Irwin Barker, Greg Eckler, Chris Finn, Tim Steeves, and George Westerholm. *The Rick Mercer Report,* season 7, episode 9. Directed by Henry Sarwer-Foner. Aired 1 December 2009. Toronto: CBC, 2009.

Miller, Peter H. "The Business of Canadian OTA Television." Canadian Radio-television and Telecommunications Commission, 2009.

Minow, N.N. "Television and the Public Interest." *Federal Communications Law Journal* 55 (2003): 395–406.

Mosco, Vincent. *The Political Economy of Communication: Rethinking and Renewal*. Thousand Oaks, CA: Sage Publications, 1996.

Nakamura, Yuko (NHK). "HDTV – Past, Present and Future." Paper presented at the *Third International Colloquium on Advanced Television Systems*. Colloquium Proceedings, Ottawa, 4–8 October 1987.

Napoli, Philip M. "The Public Interest Obligations Initiative: Lost in the Digital Television Shuffle." *Journal of Broadcasting & Electronic Media* 47, no. 1 (2003): 153–56.

Nash, Knowlton. *The Microphone Wars: A History of Triumph and Betrayal at the CBC*. Toronto: McClelland & Stewart, 1994.

National Commission on Terrorist Attacks upon the United States. *The 9/11 Commission Report: Final Report of the National Commission on Terrorist Attacks upon the United States*. New York: Norton, 2004.

Negroponte, Nicholas. *Being Digital*. New York: Knopf, 1995.

Noam, Eli. *TV or Not TV: Three Screens, One Regulation?* Canadian Radio-television and Telecommunications Commission. 11 July 2008.

Nordicity. *Analysis of Government Support for Public Broadcasting and Other Culture in Canada*. 2011.

Nyquist, Harry "Certain Topics in Telegraph Transmission Theory." *Proceedings of the* IEEE 90, no. 2 (2002): 280–305.

Ó Siochrú, Seán, Bruce Girard, and Amy Mahan. *Global Media Governance: A Beginner's Guide*. Lanham, MD: Rowman & Littlefield, 2002.

Obama, Barack. "Statement by the President on the Transition to All-Digital Programming." Office of the Press Secretary, 4 June 2009.

Ofcom. *Criteria for Promoting Effective Co- and Self-Regulation*. London. June 2004.

– *Digital Dividend Review: 550–630 MHz and 790–854 MHz*. 6 June 2008.

O'Neill, Brian. "Digital Audio Broadcasting in Canada: Technology and Policy in the Transition to Digital Radio." *Canadian Journal of Communication* 32, no. 1 (2007): 71–90.

Packard, George R. "The Coming US-Japan Crisis." *Foreign Affairs* 66, no. 2 (1987): 348–67.

Pooley, Jefferson. "From Psychological Warfare to Social Justice: Shifts in Foundation Support for Communication Research." In *Media & Social Justice*, eds Sue Curry Jansen, Jefferson Pooley, and Lora Taub-Pervizpour. New York: Palgrave Macmillan. 2011.

Powers, Kerns H. "Keynote Address: Getting it All Together for Compatible HDTV." Paper presented at the *Third International Colloquium on Advanced Television Systems*. Ottawa, 1987.

Fillon, François. "Communiqué: Comité Stratégique Pour Le Numérique." 22 July 2009.

Price, Monroe Edwin. *Media and Sovereignty: The Global Information Revolution and its Challenge to State Power*. Cambridge, MA: MIT Press, 2002.

Ritter, Jonquil, and Fred Grengaroli. "Digital Television in Australia: The Story so Far." In *Broadcasting Asia 2000 Conference.* Singapore, June 2000.

Raboy, Marc. *Missed Opportunities: The Story of Canada's Broadcasting Policy*. Montreal: McGill-Queen's University Press, 1990.

– "The Role of Public Consultation in Shaping the Canadian Broadcasting System." *Canadian Journal of Political Science* 28, no. 3 (1995): 455–77.

– "The Role of the Public in Broadcasting Policy-Making and Regulation: Lessons for Europe from Canada." *European Journal of Communication* 9, no. 1 (1994): 9–23.

Raboy, Marc, and Florian Sauvageau, eds. *The Role of the State in Broadcasting Governance*. Sainte-Foy, QC: Centre d'études sur les médias, 2006.

Raboy, Marc, and Jeremy Shtern. *Media Divides: Communication Rights and the Right to Communicate in Canada*. Vancouver: UBC Press, 2010.

Salter, Liora, and Felix N.L. Odartey-Wellington. *The CRTC and Broadcasting Regulation in Canada*. Toronto: Thomson-Carswell, 2008.

Seabright, Paul, and Jürgen von Hagen. *The Economic Regulation of Broadcasting Markets: Evolving Technology and the Challenges for Policy*. Cambridge: Cambridge University Press, 2007.

Shannon, C.E. "A Mathematical Theory of Communication." *Bell System Technical Journal* 27 (July and October 1948): 379–423 and 623–56.

Siegel, Paul. *Communication Law in America*. Boston: Allyn and Bacon, 2002.

Smith, Paul. *The Politics of Television Policy: The Introduction of Digital Television in Great Britain*. Lewiston, NY: The Edwin Mellen Press, 2007.

Smythe, Dallas Walker. *Dependency Road: Communications, Capitalism, Consciousness, and Canada*. Norwood, NJ: Ablex Publishing Corporation, 1981.

Stacey, Wayne A. *CAB Engineering Report*. 19 September 2008.

Starks, Michael. "China's Digital Switchover: International Context." *International Journal of Digital Television* 1, no. 1 (2009): 89–93.

– *Switching to Digital Television: UK Public Policy and the Market*. Chicago: Intellect, 2007.

Stewart, Andrew, and William H.N. Hull. *Canadian Television Policy and the Board of Broadcast Governors, 1958–1968*. Edmonton: University of Alberta Press, 1994.

Taras, David. *Power and Betrayal in the Canadian Media*. Peterborough, ON: Broadview Press, 2001.

Taras, David, Maria Bakardjieva, and Frits Pannekoek. *How Canadians Communicate*. Calgary: University of Calgary Press, 2003.

Taylor, Gregory. "Grey to Black: Satellite Piracy in Canada." *Canadian Journal of Media Studies* 4, no. 1 (2008): 89–108.

– "Shut-Off: The Digital Television Transition in the United States and Canada." *Canadian Journal of Communication* 35, no. 1 (2010): 7–26.

Tech Law Journal. "TLJ News from April 6–10 2006: State Department Official Addresses IPR and Trade in Brazil." 10 April 2006.

Traversy, John. Secretary General, CRTC. "Commission Letter: Mr Jean Brazeau, Senior Vice President, Regulatory Affairs, Shaw Communications Inc." 29 November 2011.

United States. Deficit Reduction Act of 2005. 8 February 2006.

– National Digital Television Consumer Education Act. 8 January 2009.

– Telecommunications Act of 1996. 1996.

– Advisory Committee on Public Interest Obligations of Digital Television Broadcasters and United States. National Telecommunications and Information Administration. Secretariat. *Charting the Digital Broadcasting*

Future: Final Report of the Advisory Committee on Public Interest Obligations of Digital Television Broadcasters. Washington, DC: US Dept of Commerce, 1998.

Wayne, E. Anthony. "Remarks to the Commercial Association of Sao Paulo." ACSP. Sao Paulo, Brazil, 6 April 2006.

West-Cyr, Janet A. "Closing Plenary Address." Paper presented at the *Third International Colloquium on Advanced Television Systems*. Ottawa, 1987.

Williams, Raymond. *Television: Technology and Cultural Form*. New York: Schocken Books, 1975.

Winseck, Dwayne. "Financialization and the 'Crisis of the Media': The Rise and Fall of (Some) Media Conglomerates in Canada." *Canadian Journal of Communication* 35, no. 3 (2010): 365–93.

Wirsig, Karen. Communications Co-ordinator, Canadian Media Guild. "Letter to Mr Robert Morin, Secretary General, CRTC Re: Reply on CRTC 2009-411." 14 December 2009.

Wood, David. "Technical Standards." *International Journal of Digital Television* 2, no. 1 (2011): 109–15.

Ziegler, Donald E., United States District Judge. "Civil Action No. 00-121 Consolidated with Civil Action No. 00-120." United States District Court for the Western District of Pennsylvania, 8 February 2000.

Index